"In centring Maori thought encompas
clearly demonstrates Indigenous ways (
and relational, which fundamentally counters the colonial project of homogenization, assimilation, and genocide. In having a dual conversation between philosophy and education, he clearly articulates why the dominant Western perception of an object fundamentally continues to fail Indigenous students due to the inherent contradictions between Indigenous and Western thought, philosophy, and language. And finally, in centring his Maori voice within Indigenous philosophy, Mika provides a counter-narrative to colonization. This book demonstrates the unique philosophical relationships as a Maori and the relationality and interconnectedness to other Indigenous voices and nations. It is a text that will engage, enlighten, and empower Indigenous thought and transform educational systems."

Michelle Pidgeon, *Associate Professor, Faculty of Education, Simon Fraser University, Canada*

Indigenous Education and the Metaphysics of Presence

Indigenous Education and the Metaphysics of Presence: A worlded philosophy explores a notion of education called 'worldedness' that sits at the core of indigenous philosophy. This is the idea that any one thing is constituted by all others and is, therefore, educational to the extent that it is *formational*. A suggested opposite of this indigenous philosophy is the metaphysics of presence, which describes the tendency in dominant Western philosophy to privilege presence over absence. This book compares these competing philosophies and argues that, even though the metaphysics of presence and the formational notion of education are at odds with each other, they also constitute each other from an indigenous worlded philosophical viewpoint.

Drawing on both Maori and Western philosophies, this book demonstrates how the metaphysics of presence is both related and opposed to the indigenous notion of worldedness. Mika explains that presence seeks to fragment things in the world, underpins how indigenous peoples can represent things, and prevents indigenous students, critics, and scholars from reflecting on philosophical colonisation. However, the metaphysics of presence, from an indigenous perspective, is constituted by all other things in the world, and Mika argues that the indigenous student and critic can re-emphasise worldedness and destabilise presence through creative responses, humour, and speculative thinking. This book concludes by positioning well-being within education, because education comprises acts of worldedness and presence.

This book will be of key interest to indigenous as well as non-indigenous academics, researchers and postgraduate students in the fields of philosophy of education, indigenous and Western philosophy, political strategy and post-colonial studies. It will also be relevant for those who are interested in philosophies of language, ontology, metaphysics and knowledge.

Carl Mika (Maori – Tuhourangi and Ngati Whanaunga) is a senior lecturer at the Te Whiringa School of Educational Leadership and Policy in the Faculty of Education, University of Waikato, New Zealand. He has a background in law practice, indigenous and Maori studies, and aspects of Western philosophy, including Heidegger's work and German romanticism. He publishes on indigenous colonial and counter-colonial methods, and philosophical research methods.

New Directions in the Philosophy of Education Series
Series Editors
Michael A. Peters, University of Waikato, New Zealand;
  University of Illinois, USA
Gert Biesta, Brunel University, UK

This book series is devoted to the exploration of new directions in the philosophy of education. After the linguistic turn, the cultural turn, and the historical turn, where might we go? Does the future promise a digital turn with a greater return to connectionism, biology, and biopolitics based on new understandings of system theory and knowledge ecologies? Does it foreshadow a genuinely alternative radical global turn based on a new openness and interconnectedness? Does it leave humanism behind or will it reengage with the question of the human in new and unprecedented ways? How should philosophy of education reflect new forces of globalization? How can it become less Anglo-centric and develop a greater sensitivity to other traditions, languages, and forms of thinking and writing, including those that are not rooted in the canon of Western philosophy but in other traditions that share the 'love of wisdom' that characterises the wide diversity within Western philosophy itself. Can this be done through a turn to intercultural philosophy? To indigenous forms of philosophy and philosophising? Does it need a post-Wittgensteinian philosophy of education? A postpostmodern philosophy? Or should it perhaps leave the whole construction of 'post'-positions behind?

In addition to the question of the intellectual resources for the future of philosophy of education, what are the issues and concerns that philosophers of education should engage with? How should they position themselves? What is their specific contribution? What kind of intellectual and strategic alliances should they pursue? Should philosophy of education become more global, and if so, what would the shape of that be? Should it become more cosmopolitan or perhaps more decentred? Perhaps most importantly in the digital age, the time of the global knowledge economy that reprofiles education as privatised human capital and simultaneously in terms of an historic openness, is there a philosophy of education that grows out of education itself, out of the concerns for new forms of teaching, studying, learning and speaking that can provide comment on ethical and epistemological configurations of economics and politics of knowledge? Can and should this imply a reconnection with questions of democracy and justice?

This series comprises texts that explore, identify and articulate new directions in the philosophy of education. It aims to build bridges, both geographically and temporally: bridges across different traditions and practices and bridges towards a different future for philosophy of education.

In this series:

On Study
Giorgio Agamben and educational potentiality
Tyson E. Lewis

Education, Experience and Existence
Engaging Dewey, Peirce and Heidegger
John Quay

African Philosophy of Education Reconsidered
On being human
Yusef Waghid

Buber and Education
Dialogue as conflict resolution
W. John Morgan and Alexandre Guilherme

Henri Lefebvre and Education
Space, history, theory
Sue Middleton

Thomas Jefferson's Philosophy of Education
A utopian dream
M. Andrew Holowchak

Edusemiotics
Semiotic philosophy as educational foundation
Andrew Stables and Inna Semetsky

Childhood, Education and Philosophy
New ideas for an old relationship
Walter Kohan

Between Truth and Freedom
Rousseau and out contemporary political and educational culture
Kenneth Wain

Democratic Education and the Public Sphere
Towards John Dewey's theory of aesthetic experience
Masamichi Ueno

Indigenous Education and the Metaphysics of Presence

A Worlded Philosophy

Carl Mika

Routledge
Taylor & Francis Group

LONDON AND NEW YORK

First published 2017 by Routledge

2 Park Square, Milton Park, Abingdon, Oxfordshire OX14 4RN
711 Third Avenue, New York, NY 10017

Routledge is an imprint of the Taylor & Francis Group, an informa business

First issued in paperback 2018

Copyright © 2017 Carl Mika

British Library Cataloguing-In-Publication Data
A catalogue record for this book is available from the British Library

Library of Congress Cataloging-in-Publication Data
Names: Mika, Carl.
Title: Indigenous education and the metaphysics of presence : a
  worlded philosophy / Carl Mika.
Description: New York, NY : Routledge, 2017.
Identifiers: LCCN 2016044961 | ISBN 9781138846302 (hardcover) |
  ISBN 9781315727547 (electronic)
Subjects: LCSH: Education—Philosophy. | Philosophy, Maori. |
  Maori (New Zealand people)—Education. | Ethnoscience.
Classification: LCC LA134 .M55 2017 | DDC 370.1—dc23
LC record available at https://lccn.loc.gov/2016044961

ISBN: 978-1-138-84630-2 (hbk)
ISBN: 978-1-138-35375-6 (pbk)

Typeset in Bembo
by Apex CoVantage, LLC

Contents

Preface

It can be argued that the most pressing challenge of our modern times is not what we do not imagine as an extension of a form of knowing that sees itself as universal, unlimited and liberating but, rather, what this dominant form of knowing itself prevents us from imagining and experiencing. In this sense, the first urgent task is to explore the roots, limits and overstated claims of this dominant form of knowing in order to identify its potential gifts. The fact that, within modern institutions, we cannot imagine or experience philosophy without Greece, caves, Germans, France, the alphabet, (almost exclusively) men, the city, linear time and/or (a restricted form of) reason is a case in point. But what if we conceived of philosophy not only as an exclusively human activity? What if humans and non-humans have cross-philosophised from time immemorial in multiple languages and forms of reasoning? Why does this seem inconceivable? What are the implications of opening up and/or closing down this possibility? What implications for education would this possibility entail?

Carl Mika puts these questions on the table by tracing two different philosophical orientations towards one simple event: our existence as part of a plural, undefinable and mysterious world in a constant flow of mutual co-creation. One philosophical orientation, grounded on Enlightenment principles, sees this as a liability, a problem to be solved; the other, grounded (but not exclusively) in indigenous ways of being, sees it as a gift that points to our interdependence, mutual constitution and incompleteness. The first orientation prioritises the use of knowledge to engineer something perfect that could eliminate the risks of indeterminacy, a project that justifies the use of force in the objectification and expropriation of bodies and lands for a specific idea of 'progress'. The second orientation prioritises Being, the enigmatic counterpart to knowledge, that resists the boundaries and closures of signification.

The first orientation wraps the world in a tightly woven blanket of meaning. The blanket flattens the distinction between sense-making and sensing the world. The powerful threads of narrative are tasked with seizing a stable truth: of grasping something objectively and holding it in its place, what Mika describes as a 'metaphysics of presence'. Within this blanket, the world is dissected and organised in patterned boxes neatly arranged in hierarchies of value.

The scope of relationships between things is reduced to what can be mediated by predictability-seeking knowledge, to an encounter of boxes. Mastering the world through a planned and coherent arrangement of the boxes is perceived as the only way to control the world, reducing the risks of the unforeseen, the invisible and the unexpected.

Conversely, the second philosophical orientation wraps the world in a cloak of mystery, where Being is an unknowable force within entities comprising both form and formlessness, with both visible and invisible dimensions. In Mika's words, Being amplifies the interconnectedness, obscurity and imprecision of the world, as well as our (human) embeddedness in landscape, and our inter-entity responsibilities. Sense-making, in this case, is just one of a myriad of omnidirectional, collective sensorial processes that does not take precedence over other senses. The concept of 'truth' is therefore elusive, equivocal and context (time/space) dependent encompassing both multiplicity and uncertainty.

In both orientations, education is mobilised as an event and an act. The first orientation directs education towards knowing the world; the second towards grappling with the fact of a 'worlded' existence. Mika takes this as a first step to conceptualise the limits of our ability to reflect on the nature of being formed by a world in motion. He approaches the task of delineating the two different – but mutually entangled – orientations by tracing aspects of both within and without Indigenous knowledge systems. Mika argues that the metaphysics of presence is both a colonising and constraining reality and an opening to possibility, since it is also precariously located in a mysterious world in motion.

Mika's work emphasises the gritty reality of colonisation, yet he proposes speculative thinking as an indigenous site of strength, suggesting that it resonates with the fullness of things in the world more than knowledge that seeks stability does. Thus, for Indigenous thinkers, the task of turning the metaphysics of presence on its head is both a challenge and an opportunity. Mika begins to highlight the conjoining of colonisation and tradition from the outset, moving from a broadly Indigenous perspective to the Maori concept of 'Ako', which is a term for teaching and learning (but, as Mika points out, opens onto a world of co-constitutive force).

For those who know him, it will generally be agreed that Mika is darkly optimistic; his coupling of grimness and buoyancy finds expression in his sudden turns between traditional and colonial existence, his more than brief step over into the Western tradition as he remains an indigenous thinker and his stubborn refusal to sit still in any one stated domain of thought. It is the potential yet obscurity of indigenous speculative *thinking* that Mika emphasises in his text. Those who come to this book looking for a ready dictionary or even a recounting of indigenous *knowledge* may be struck instead by how much the act of knowing is tilted back in favour of a more meditative and speculative invitation.

'Progress' in the classroom and scholarship – for both indigenous and non-indigenous alike – is conceived of through the metaphysics of presence as the drive to immediately and unquestioningly consider both self and object in unswerving ways. While its fact of existence can never be undone, we can gesture towards its other in various ways because we are also already *within* that other. Mika is aware that there is much at stake here and that indigenous learners and scholars can help themselves to the deceptions of presence and even momentarily turn it on its head. Perhaps perversely, it is not the arguments against presence that will stop us from continuing down a pathway of colonised thought and well-being; it is instead in a direct engagement with presence as itself, a worlded entity, that indigenous peoples can find a form of transformation. We may never get to that final point, but as Mika points out at when quoting Deloria at the conclusion of this book, it is the journey that is transformative, not the progress attached to an outcome.

Vanessa de Oliveira Andreotti, Canada Research Chair in Race, Inequalities and Global Change, University of British Columbia

Chapter 1

Introduction

The first hallmark of American Indian philosophy is the commitment to the belief that all things are related – and this belief is not simply an ontological claim, but rather an intellectual and ethical maxim.

(Arola, 2011, p.563)

Directed towards a specific indigenous philosophy, Arola's comment nevertheless relates to indigenous thought generally. With that preface in mind, as a Maori writer I am extending his observation and agreeing with him that all things in the world herald an ethical responsibility for the indigenous self. One version of the interrelationship that he notes expresses the eternal convergence of the world within any one thing, and so one ethical outcome is that the individual person should implicate a sense of mystery within any one object. Even more curiously, perhaps, this fundamental collapse of the All within the one also has significance for the nature of thought itself. I do not want to overemphasise thought as the sole participant with that holism, preferring instead just to begin with that focus simply because the nature of thought is often neglected in statements that argue for holism. It does strike me as a curious possibility with indigenous philosophy that, as soon as the ultimate, true ground of thought has been identified, it appears to swim out of view, to be replaced by an apparently similar idea of a ground. Another creature altogether may have moored itself. Again, we can pinpoint that fresh idea as the fundamental basis of thought, but then like its predecessor it recedes. But the idea has not necessarily separated itself off from us. This interrelationship between indigenous self and idea can be thought of as one example of the link between self and things in the world in general, and it forms the crux of this book in several ways.

To continue specifically with the *idea*: while writing, I would often intend to pick up where I left off, only to find that the basic idea had apparently moved on, to be substituted with another. The neurological decision on this might note a lapse in concentration whereas in indigenous thought it is plausible that the idea itself is taking charge. The lapse occurring is, in fact, one in the conversation between the idea and me, where the idea has simply decided to stop revealing itself to me in a way I can hear or see. It no longer sees fit to talk with me and disclose its possibilities to be reflected on. In indigenous thought, as I go on to say, the idea is a material entity (Mika, 2014a; 2015e; Mika & Tiakiwai, 2016) that is constituted by all other things in the world; it is as equal to the situation as my own neurological decision to think is. So, it should come as no surprise – to me while writing, or to anyone else – that an idea should decide of its own accord to seemingly drift away and allow another to take its place. Whether the former idea has indeed moved on or has just decided to slip into the background of the current idea can only be speculated on. And this ability to speculate is itself the convergence of both the human and non-human worlds, the latter including the world of the idea. That we can think at all, shows that the external world makes us up, or forms us. Like all other things, the idea may have moved on, or it may have simply withdrawn on its own account for a time but remain there in a hidden sense whilst still influencing us in ways we do not apprehend.

This discussion about the idea is one example of the possibility of all things forming each other. One aim of this book is to understand the oneness that sits at the core of indigenous philosophy as education itself. This oneness is not simply inert or static; it is much more *formational*. Additionally, I intend to explore a stated opposite of this indigenous philosophy – the metaphysics of presence, or, for the purposes of this book, simply 'presence' – and its impact on that indigenous suggestion of interconnection. Although the metaphysics of presence and the formational notion of education are at odds with each other, they constitute each other. This potential holds particular repercussions for presence, because presence likes to think of itself as presenting any one thing as self-sufficient and on its own. The immediate constitution of presence by its formational opposite – and the idea that they implicate each other is closer to an indigenous one – is an educational problem as well. Thinking about education and its formational nature asks me to bring my ability to speculate on the issues. To start with, emphasising an aspect of education that sits quietly at the base of indigenous literature means that I have to identify that ground of thinking that would give credit to things in general and, in doing so, allow for the current idea to drift off (shadow itself?) and have another step in for it. I do indeed seek to consider education away from its current dominant association with teaching and learning and to revive it from a theoretically indigenous and Maori perspective. However, again I consider that my speculation is not all my own. Already we see a conflict with presence, which requires the writer to represent an object as if it originates from him- or herself. The only way to achieve that more ambitious aim of incorporating the world and my thinking, as far as I can see, is to reiterate the deep indigenous philosophy that things in the world are collapsed within any one thing, not fragmented as other colonising philosophies would have it. The fact that it is reiterated attests perhaps to the sway that the fragmented view holds in both academic and everyday colonised existence. In other words, I reiterate to resist. By reasserting the idea that all things attend within one entity, and by simultaneously and continuously glancing sideways (and at some stages confrontationally) at that idea's antithesis, I discuss an education that does not let go of that holistic worldview. But the proposition needs to be repeated as it unfolds in its various contexts, not as a mere abstract mantra that threatens to divorce itself from our everyday existence by becoming overly spiritualised.

My goal of re-theorising education through some ground principles of indigenous thought is an optimistic one because it tries to account for those principles alongside colonisation. Here we have to be mindful that the very medium of the language, structure and grammar we use is likely to thwart an indigenous metaphysics, at least to some extent. We can state an absolute truth such as 'the world is interconnected', but the statement is saturated with an unseen field of truthful and rational assumptions. This field sometimes allows for something to be *said* but quietly undermines it so that it falls into line with its own expectation of truth and rationality (Mika & Southey, 2016; Mika & Stewart, 2015). This problem is due to the metaphysics of presence, which is the field and parent of that sabotaging linguistics. Both indigenous metaphysics and 'presence' propose something about things (and hence we relate to things on the basis of those propositions), and to that extent they both propose how things *form* us. They therefore *educate* us. They do so in vastly different ways, however, with an indigenous view of 'the world within an object' preferring that an idea is just as animate and interconnected with all other things as a human being. Barad notes about animacy that "neovitalist theories" (Kleinman, n.d, p.80) fail to inquire into the purpose of distinctions between animate and inanimate. She suggests that these distinctions are important because they highlight the uniqueness of some beings' natural ability to flourish. We can note here that the distinction is important now for the thriving of both colonial and precolonial thought in one entity; that is, an entity is composed of thought that distinguishes sharply between living and non-living and evolves to that extent with that demarcation as part of its makeup.

After questioning both the human/non-human and animate/inanimate divides, Barad continues that "[t]hese are important political and ethical questions that need a place in our theories if those theories are indeed thinking companions with a chance for life" (Kleinman, n.d, p.80). Presence, on the other hand, educates us as indigenous peoples by proposing and implementing that things – including those ideas that Barad talks about – are most certainly *not* all coalesced as material entities within one thing, and that we should not be thinking of ideas as living, material entities either. In both presence and interconnected metaphysics, one is not just conceptually educated; one is materially constructed by the existence of those narratives. My optimism at emphasising the worlded aspect of education is short-lived yet ongoing because presence both stalls holistic thought but opens its own self up for indigenous, holistic critique. Our reflection on that incalculable, mysterious phenomenon must similarly meet its limits. Education, as actively constitutive force and as idea, is frustrating and tantalising from an indigenous perspective as well as through the deeply implanted lens of presence.

Worldedness as education

I approach this book with a certain brand of holism in mind: that any one thing is constituted by all others. In the Maori language, there are various concepts that signal the fullness of the world within one thing. I discuss some of this naming in Chapter 3 through the Maori language and prefer the term *worldedness* to articulate this deep holism. It and its related terms, *worlded* and *worlding*, are neologistic but have been used by others to denote several phenomena. Two uses of them elsewhere are particularly well known: with specific reference to the Third World, Spivak (1985) employs worlding to describe the imperial act that glazes over the true workings of the coloniser, making what the latter does seem normal, and Heidegger (1962) discusses the worlding of the world – how the world becomes world. Worlding with Heidegger asks after the infinite myriad of relationships that are peculiarly meaningful to humanity. A third description – more directly relevant for this book – comes from Buss and Genetin-Pilawa (2014), who emphasise the interconnectedness of concepts and things in the world. This version of the active world is one preferred for this book; it "is at once rich with cohesion and contradiction . . . mutually constructed and bound to place" (p.1). Broadly I mean by *worlding* and its variations *worlded* and *worldedness* the following: one thing is never alone, and all things actively construct and compose it (Mika, 2016c). As one thing presents itself to me, others within it may appear and hide, but even if I cannot perceive them (which I cannot) we can be assured that they are there. An object that I perceive is therefore fundamentally unknowable; I can speculate on it and give it a name, but all I can be certain of is that it is mysterious precisely because it is 'worlded'. I can experience the thing in its full force without actually sensing that influence, but talk of knowledge is only minimally useful when we are considering it. I am no more familiar with any one thing than if I had never encountered it. Indeed, I experience an aspect of the worlded thing and its mystery when I meet the limits of my ability to say much about it, or when I realise that I cannot fully know it. Perception is given rise by the formation of the self with the full force of all things in the world.

Moreover, I can talk *about* the thing, or, more precisely, I am discussing it as if I am a part of it. As I make an observation about it, I am obviously using language. Language does not just talk about things, and I am not actually using it as such; like any other entity, it is also the sum of the world (Mika & Tiakiwai, 2016). As an indigenous writer, if I could I would express myself so that all things are given the space to fully engage with each other within one entity. I would also discuss a thing as if I were an aspect *of* it, not separate from it. At least from a Maori viewpoint, I am in the thrall of language so that, when I express myself, I am manifesting the world as a whole (Mika, 2007). I am hence less its master and more of a participant with it (and here we are more in synchronicity with Heidegger's version of 'world'). Things in the world orient themselves to me in a particular way, and I answer with those things similarly present. This ability to speculate about, and discuss, a thing in its full nature is another facet of education. To represent things in the world holistically ensures that the sway of all those things retains its shape, and assures for the human self a type of well-being. Incidentally (but most important), this subsequent step I raise here is only possible because of my relationship with the totality of the world. Education from an indigenous perspective would emphasise that I have to consider all those social and philosophical obstacles and reinforcements that open up a thing for me to consider it as a fully worlded one.

But there is another set of philosophies that has the same consequences in terms of how I propose education yet differs quite significantly from those I have outlined earlier. The thing seems tasked with a formidable enterprise, having to appear as a result of the 'all' within it as it does, but its attunement with the rest of the world is quite plausible for Maori thought at least. What does seem untenable, though, is the opposite: a set of philosophies that dictate an object is caught up in a static 'thereness' and hence displays rigid properties that make it what it is. It is this more recent, colonising metaphysics that insists a thing is solitary and highly positive, and importantly the indigenous self is not immune from its influence. It makes any talk of traditional worlding difficult; indeed, it makes any description tortuous, because whilst discussing worlding, presence is present, and vice versa. Presence encourages me, quite tacitly, to think of any object or idea as that object or idea, not as a traditionally worlded entity. In a very broad way, this proposition meets with Spivak's idea that 'worlding' is coupled with the normalisation imposed by colonisation. This colonising metaphysics, which is a recent phenomenon for Maori, urges me to use particular sorts of language and notions of time to support itself. I am therefore caught in a slippage between my desire to express the worlded entity and the restraints imposed by the language I use and by the layout of logic that does not allow a full demonstration of the All. It would seem that *presence*, in its manifestation as discipliner of text and thought in general, prohibits the simultaneous resonance of the past and the future within perception and expression; presence ignores the continuous coming-to-be of my ancestors and all others within my work; and in its pursuit of rationalism it renders potential terms to describe my culturally specific metaphysics, off-limits.

Presence in a general sense may not be a problem for indigenous holistic perceptions, especially when used to convey that a thing emerges in front of the self with its relationship to the whole world. But when spoken about in the context of a horizon of thinking that originates from Plato, where a thing is 'stuck' for the self's regard, it takes on a different hue altogether. The metaphysics of presence is an inherited, colonised ground of perception that is more than just an abstract problem; it is overwhelmingly a material one for indigenous peoples. The basis of thought for indigenous peoples, then, cannot be reduced to an uptake of the mind, or a mere Kantian regulative ideal. The phrase 'metaphysics of presence' problematises the unquestioned, crucial turn towards "a present under the heading of that which endures and persists, near and available, exposed to vision or given by hand, a present in the form of . . . presence-at-hand" (Derrida, 1982b, p.32). The label *presence* is a useful one for this problem that arguably lies at the base of all colonised thought and expression, but I contend in later chapters that, although the phrase 'metaphysics of presence' can be speculated on from a holistic perspective, the ground that it highlights is at times elusive. This difficulty we encounter when discussing what appears to be an ultimate ground of colonisation 'becomes perhaps even more confounding' when we consider that presence is indeed formed by a notion of worldedness and vice versa.

The indigenous self is therefore formed or educated by a contrary view that an object is 'there' in all its presence. The self in the world or the self in the classroom are both constituted by that 'thereness' (Mika, 2015d). If we think about the classroom context, we can note that education is like other institutions, such as law and medicine, because it takes an approach to its objects as if they are immediately visible. In its dominant mode, it can at least be said that education in schools does not, or perhaps cannot, account for the possibility that any one student is always one with the place that they originate from, or with time and space as a combined entity. The ability of the indigenous self to slip beneath the surface, under the dreadful, everyday aspects of colonisation, is a further facet of education. Education for indigenous peoples is thus the problematising of colonisation generally, but, in specific relation to this book, it is the critique of the static relationship of the self to an object and its world, and of the self and his or her worlded nature to the colonising proposition that such a metaphysical critique is irrelevant. Writing a book or article must also therefore be an educational exercise, not simply because of its ability to add to thinking and knowledge but also, more importantly, because of its interface with both presence and worldedness.

But what is it about an essentially mysterious view of things' immediately collapsed nature that urges me to call it 'education'? I am not suggesting that the more conventional approaches labelled education are not so, simply that the fact that things in the world constitute other things is a form of education deserving to be thought about in its own right. Deloria (2001) is especially clear that what he calls metaphysics as a "set of first principles" (p.2) is to be given priority when discussing education. Admittedly, it is hard to find these fundamental ideas on their own merits being considered as education, without them forming the basis of a more concrete text on teaching and learning of some sort. Ahenakew et al. (2014) do allude to the possibility that the world on its own is educational. In referring to the problem of the "universalization of Western/European thought" (p.217), they emphasise the reality of the entire world in one's learning. What is important in this view of educational construction is the prospect of one's immediate, reflective immersion within/ as part of the world. Ahenakew et al.'s seminal article approximates my own view here: that education is not necessarily a conscious act and a thing's collapse with all others forms that thing and hence that thing is both informed by, and informs, all those other things. Those authors note that "[t]here is knowledge that cannot be known or described" (p. 227), and although I might diverge from the term *knowledge* on the grounds that it is problematic with its immediate source in presence itself, I take from those authors that they are referring to a wellspring of infinite connections and co-constitutive realities that are beyond our perception but that we are nevertheless indebted to (which, as I discuss later, is a worlded sense within the Maori term *whakaaro* often reductively referred to as 'to think'). The "grammar of interdependence" (p. 224) that Ahenakew et al. argue is necessary to an indigenous worldedness may underpin a generally indigenous view of education, with its continuous mention of things' interconnectedness.

An aspect that contrasts this notion of education from more orthodox approaches is the possibility that one is constructed entirely, or is formed, by how one represents the world and its discrete entities. One also constructs the world in turn, thus influencing its well-being. Far from being unique to indigenous cultures, these ideas also exist in some European traditions in varying degrees, and they may have existed in an everyday sense, if Wildcat (2001b) is correct when he states that Western views of the world were at one stage highly pragmatic. Of concern to German existentialism, for instance, is the notion of *Dasein*. This term generates interest for its innate depth and for its multitude of interpretations. Most literally, it refers to existence, or the phenomenon of 'being-there', and it thus exceeds the term *human* for its reclamation of the self's active involvement in the world. Amongst its scholars, Dasein is complicatedly diverse. The early German romantics banish any possibility of arriving at a conclusion, preferring instead to romanticise the static objects that appear to be final. The early German romantics' dismissal of finality is crucial in any discussion about how the self encounters other things in the world and, moreover, the interdependent nature of those things. In this, they foreshadow Heidegger's (1962) ontological difference. Heidegger, who is perhaps the most well known for using the term *Dasein* in place of 'humanity', seeks to overturn the highly visible idea of the self, derived from Platonic thought, and attributes 'thrownness' to Dasein. Dasein for Heidegger is always in the world, and is confronted by its many possibilities. What is of concern to the self is Being, in the sense that the self is determined by Being and is always inquiring into it. Banal, conventional beliefs and interactions with the world are inauthentic modes of comportment towards it, and so Heidegger bases Dasein on what is historically important for one's world.

It is perhaps the philosophies offered by Friedrich von Hardenberg (Novalis), a key member of the early German romantic movement, that prove most exciting for the indigenous philosopher. Featuring infrequently in the English-speaking academy, Novalis is highly challenging for his emphasis on a sort of political holism, where fragmentation of the world's components is imperceptibly destructive for the individual. His thinking corresponds with an indigenous metaphysics of worlding – not only for his own particular critique of presence as we shall see later, but equally for his more positive statements about how the self reverberates with the external world. Developing an aspect of *Bildung* (educational formation), Novalis proposes most essentially that the self comprises the world: "the world is materially influential on the self even when it cannot be perceived . . . the unseen is responsible for the educational experience" (Mika, 2015c, pp.10–11). To the extent that he prefers the invisible realms for Bildung, he corresponds with Herder, who emphasised that the unknowable working of nature is more important than the overt acts of education which we commonly see now (Horlacher, 2016). We act *within* and as constituted by the world whilst proclaiming something about it. One is educated *as* the world; one simultaneously educates the world. With 'world' Novalis refers to materiality and hiddenness as well as appearance. The dual constructive activities between world and self take place at once, and in order to reflect the true flux of the world, the self is encouraged to avoid banality at all costs – pedestrian thought and representation discipline things, for Novalis – and to convene with the world as if it is mysterious. Novalis's emphasis on the materiality of the world suggests that he is a believer in a thing's essence, which is impermanent and likely to contain to it aspects of nothingness as much as positivity. He thus thinks of the Bildung, or education/formation, of the self as both self-conscious or agentic and dependent on the full influence of the outside world.

This view of education places us within the world, as part of it at all times, preferring that we do not think of it solely as a conscious act. In general terms, indigenous belief seems to insist that one does not leave things in the world as one speculates. Whether involving human-mediated teaching and learning or as a mode of construction of/by the world, education is meant to ensure that thinking takes place within the full interplay of the world, and so a statement about the world is actually a worlded statement. A Maori approach to language, for instance, is linked with the idea that indigenous thought prefers a view of knowledge where things are immediately resonated along with speech, as opposed to them being given as a concept (Whitt et al., 2001), evident for instance in the Maori term *mea*. I move to a more thorough philosophising about language and representation in the context of 'Ako' (teaching and learning) in Chapter 3; however, *mea* is an interesting homonym in the context of our current discussion about presentational thought as it quite clearly places an entity and speech within each other (Mika, 2016c). *Mea* means both 'to say' and 'thing', and these two meanings, which seem to be utterly separate and unrelated, do indeed tend to refer to separate concepts. It will be recalled that this sort of distinction marks an unusual facility of the Maori language, whereby if I intend to use *mea* in the context of 'to say' I do not mean to obliterate its other references, including 'thing'. The hidden aspect of the word through 'thing', to be sure, is unannounced but nevertheless at work within the word. With this undisclosed facet taken into account, 'to say' becomes 'thing' at the same time.

When I am uttering, I am invoking a thing. More than that, though, the thing is an active participant in the utterance, and is thus continually presencing – not in a static way. Heidegger (2001) invents some useful wording to deal with what is being suggested about mea, although without an indigenous/Maori conception of the thorough world within a thing. He considers that an entity comes into its own true nature when it resonates centrally as the Fourfold. A Maori approach to *mea* would acknowledge that an entity is energetic and active, and that language is immediately constituted by the thing's vitality.

My second but related element of education – the worlded phenomenon innate to contemplating worldedness and its complications through presence – is perhaps more familiar to the orthodox educational standard. At least, the declaration that one can reflect on one's immersion in the world and the aspects that thwart both that immersion and one's reflection on it is more familiar but not necessarily that the worldedness of a thing and its relations are responsible for that reflection to begin with. This step is a critical one because it is here that we have some agency to actively reflect on our relationship with things in the world and those colonised realities which stifle that relationship. One's freedom to think is clearly at stake here but only because of the self's makeup by the world. As I go on to describe in Chapter 5, it is extremely difficult to speculate on the thoroughgoing extent of the world in academic writing because the limits of what one can say are already tightly prescribed and policed. It is probable that poetry and art come closest to being able to carry out that heavy lifting, but even those forms of expression are likely to have been restricted by what rests outside them, undeclared and hidden, as much as any internal template they may now have to fit.

There is no shortage of indigenous theory that deals with decolonisation, though, and various indigenous writers have emphasised the creative element that is necessary for a critical reflection on one's existential dimension: Smith (1999), for instance, argues for a decolonisation of one's research approaches, through a process of questioning imperialism; Ahenakew et al. (2014) suggest that we should destabilise long-held truths and renew our relationship with mystery by reminding ourselves of our place amongst other things in the world; and Wildcat (2001a) thinks that a theorising of metaphysics can help put Western science in perspective. Green (2011) has drawn on Foucault to disinter what orients indigenous people towards the world in a colonised way, in relation to sexual and reproductive health policy. Anne Waters (2004) identifies problems that the language of positivism brings for indigenous peoples, arguing that indigenous groups resist that mode of description because it established binaries between things, and Kovach (2009) similarly conducts a type of dialectic when indicating that there is both an appropriate knowledge for indigenous peoples and one that tends to suppress it. She continues that "[w]hen Cree and Saulteaux Elders talk about the world as being alive, as of spirit, it makes sense because this is reinforced on a daily basis in the language" (n.p.). In all cases these writers describe a means of examining one's ability or freedom to reflect on oppression and carry that method of reflection out at the same time. What is also striking in indigenous counter-colonial literature is the degree to which the first principles arise as a topic of discussion. In most of this writing, the author acknowledges the existence and presence of the hidden realms that are necessary to indigenous knowledge.

This reflective mode is double-edged insofar as it tries to account for indigenous existence against its colonised counterpart. It reflects mystery as much as hard-nosed rational critique. Other notable writers in this vein are Freire, Heidegger and Hölderlin, to name a few. Freire is well known to indigenous scholars for his overt drive to liberate the oppressed, and his theorising around banking education is especially popular for the decolonising writer as he also proposes some solutions. Heidegger, contemplating Being, adopted a profound line of Hölderlin's (1961): "poetically, humanity dwells on earth" (p.372), and interpreted its message in relation to one's philosophical colonisation by the essence of technology. Hölderlin was a contemporary of Novalis's, who similarly advocated that lyrical thought was ascendant. In all cases one is constructed as much by the materiality of colonisation as by traditional utterances.

Thinking about terminology

So far, I have considered worldedness, presence and their educational slant. There are some other conceptual and technical aspects to consider before continuing. First, this book speculates on the impact of what I variously call 'metaphysics of presence' and 'presence' on *indigenous* worlded perception and education. It should be noted that rigid definitions of 'indigenous' sometimes appear to be problematic. To begin with, to label and define a group as 'indigenous' is, in a certain way, a non-indigenous practice (Battiste & Henderson, 2000) because it may not sit that well with an indigenous worldview (Corntassel, 2003). Indigenous writers' concerns about names certainly coincide with those of many Maori who resist the label 'Maori' itself. Rangihau (1992), for instance, defies the label as one that was imposed by the coloniser to render the various iwi or tribes of Aotearoa homogeneous, and thus easier to deal with. As to the term *indigenous*, there are anecdotal accounts of Maori expressing their discomfort when it arises in various settings. It may well be that the term is the most extensive leveller of them all, given its almost phenomenal ability to glide over highly varied landscapes and their inhabitants – to gloss globally over difference. When coupled with 'knowledge', the term is also a potentially difficult one because "it is so much a part of the clan . . . that it cannot be separated from the bearer to be codified into a definition" (Battiste and Henderson, 2000, p.36). Corntassel (2003) writes of the global debate that exists around the definition and highlights the various debates that range from peoples' uncurbed self-identification as indigenous to legalistic criteria to be met in order to be termed indigenous.

Despite these obviously valid concerns, indigenous peoples are to be thought of as different to their colonial counterparts because they are engaged with struggles to overcome oppression (Alfred & Corntassel, 2005), alongside the fact that they are from the lands that are simultaneously their concern. They are as focused on the process of resistance as they are on the fact of their status as first on their lands; indigenous people's experience of the multifaceted aspects of colonisation is part of being indigenous. This more straightforward characterising of 'indigenous' simplifies the debate in many ways whilst complicating it with a discussion of how indigenous peoples tend to be affected by colonisation. The United Nations Permanent Forum on Indigenous Issues (n.d.) has outlined characteristics that would disappoint anyone seeking a rigid definition, describing some of the key indicators of indigeneity, which include: self-identification, strong connections to their geographical locations, distinct language, culture, practices and beliefs. One might add to this list that colonisation has occurred and that this process includes the potential change in how one views an object and then, on the strength of that perceptual mode, how one's well-being may have been detrimentally affected.

A key problem with discussions about indigeneity and metaphysics is that metaphysics cannot be seen or sensed as such. It is a lens through which the world is apprehended. We cannot say definitively that *that* is a non-indigenous metaphysics and *this* is not. What also makes it a difficult task is that indigenous groups have been integrated, colonised or assimilated. In the current Aotearoa context, for instance, Maori knowledge – which is linked to a particular view of the world – has been undermined. The traditional element of Maori knowledge has hence been weakened. As well as being a problem in itself, this loss has created trauma; colonisation must therefore shoulder most of the responsibility for the undeniable decline in well-being of indigenous people in Aotearoa (Lawson-Te Aho, 2013). More globally, the impact of colonisation on indigenous identity has only acted to highlight the problems that indigenous knowledges face. In her report to the Commission on Human Rights, Daes (1994) explains indigenous knowledge as "a complete knowledge system with its own concepts of epistemology, philosophy, and scientific and logic validity" (para. 8). She further argues that one needs to interpret, abide by and transmit through indigenous knowledge systems in order to protect them and continue them. It is only the local ceremonies and practices that can assist with that process. It is the role of each indigenous individual and community to ensure that the view of the world is retained and to revive the deeper meanings that reside within each indigenous language. Decolonisation is said to be crucial here: it is a necessary process to regain the former integrity of indigenous knowledge (Battiste & Henderson, 2000; Brown, 2011; Mankiller, 2011; McIvor, 2010; Smith, 1999). This is no easy feat as the hegemonic dominant discourses are rooted firmly within individuals and communities through forces such as media, education organisations and governments and at the much more microscopic level, such as rational discourse. Indigenous knowledge is then framed by, and embedded with, those dominant discourses.

While I have noted that we cannot definitely say that *here* is indigenous metaphysics and *there* is its apparent opposition, we can note that the literature does theorise their difference and that we do have to make some claim to those differences. Indigenous codes of viewing the world have been threatened and not just lost (in some cases) but replaced at least partially with something else. It is to be acknowledged that amongst indigenous peoples there may be different ways of explaining their own modes of perception, but their general resistance to a view that the world can be apprehended in its pure visibility means that, despite the plurality of indigenous experiences, an 'indigenous' deconstruction of the metaphysics of presence is possible, in much the same way as a cautious *indigenous* response to research that Linda Smith (1999) noted can be identified. In respect of research, she warns that anthropological, scientific and academic research "brings to bear, on any study of indigenous peoples, a cultural orientation, a set of values, a different conceptualization of such things as time, space and subjectivity" (p.42). The same holds true for metaphysics: as Calderon (2008) indicates, "[w]hile indigenous metaphysics are diverse . . . it is important to provide descriptions of the shared components of indigenous metaphysics" (pp.109–110). I write from the central premise that there is a common problem for indigenous peoples with a key philosophical premise that was introduced through colonialism into our very perceptual ability. The relationship of indigenous self to the world within an object characterises the sort of discussion that removes 'indigenous' from the solely political (i.e., institutional and social in a human sense) towards what De La Cadena (2010) advocates is a politics based on a relationship with the non-human world.

However, there is a fine line between suggesting an indigenous worldview and, in reality, speaking from one's own local (but indigenous) perspective. To suggest that there is an indigenous perception of the world in general, I refer to and interpret the nearly universal indigenous remark, expressed at conferences, in traditional practice, and in general conversation, that 'the world is one'. The explanations for this incredibly complex maxim are numerous. Hence, although I am Maori and thus indigenous, I am unable to speak for indigenous peoples apart from very broadly. I can branch out in my theorising from that statement of oneness and speculate on its very general implications, but at certain points that are indefinable I have to return to examples from my own, Maori experience. It is moreover entirely likely that the Maori lens is at work even when it is not being explicitly mentioned (and here we meet a tantalising possibility: one's essential and ancestral influence imbues thought and writing, sometimes perceptibly, although it may not be explicitly mentioned!). The discourse of indigeneity does indeed reach its limits at crucial times, perhaps throughout one's indigenous theorising. As in the case of much *indigenous* discourse, the indigenous reader is asked to remember that I am adopting a *speculative* approach to that worlded comment that insists things in the world are one. I do draw on indigenous literature to adumbrate that broader indigenous speculation, but ultimately one's human and non-human ancestors will always guide one's theorising.

Not quite incidentally, as indigenous writers in philosophy we may have observed that mainstream philosophy is rarely compelled to visit its roots or core influences to the same extent. To those of us who work within aspects of dominant Western philosophy but also crucially sit outside it, it is frequently represented as normal. It does not have to take into account any indigenous, feminist or similar tome of thought because it simply *is*. Only if mainstream philosophy deigns to refer to something other than itself, does it have to mention itself. Of course, many writers do name it as something different and hence identify it so that it is not so monolithic: 'Western' philosophy is "critical" (Peters & Biesta, 2009, p.82); Western philosophy is critiqued on the basis that it is separate from culture (Peters, 2015); and Heidegger, Derrida and Foucault all signal various characteristics about the origins and tendencies of *Western* philosophy or discourse. In most cases, though, Western philosophy is self-sufficient because it does not declare that it is one philosophy of many. Indigenous philosophy, on the other hand, must constantly reflect on itself as relational to dominant Western philosophy. This includes looking back on its own self-description as 'indigenous' and being mindful that, in calling itself that, it must also account for its local origins. It can never simply assume that it *is*.

Nor, I suggest, should Western philosophy. Dominant Western philosophy's self-assuredness spills over into what will be taught in philosophy departments, as well as who can comment on Western philosophy. In relation to the first problem, Garfield and Van Norden (2016) critique philosophy departments for not including other philosophies besides 'European and American philosophy'. Tackling the second issue, Wildcat (2005) reflects on Deloria's lack of popularity among the U.S. public. It seems that Deloria's main affliction was being Sioux Indian; he was not authorised to comment on Western society. He could be expected "to be angry" (p.421) and even to reflect on his own culture, but casting his gaze to "the internal coherence, assumptions, and practical consequences of Western civilization" (p.421) was annoying for mainstream America, including its philosophers. Paralleling that problem is that indigenous peoples are meant to be performers; they are not meant to know about the assumptions of the coloniser. With these critiques, we see that dominant Western philosophy quite simply needs to branch out, not in a tokenistic way but with a genuine dialogue in mind that means it is no longer "fortified . . . against even the mention of other forms of thinking" (Mika, 2015b, p.2).

Our indigenous powers of speculation

The indeterminate character of the world as a whole that is an inevitable outcome of the perceptions of Kovach and others sets in train a significant approach for this book. From the outset, the stream within which the thinking of this book takes place calls for a disclaimer of sorts so that the reader is clear about the nature of this discussion. Because a solid ground of thinking – quite possibly a metaphor for the metaphysics of presence – asserts itself in indigenous communities, we are often involved in making some counter-colonial assertions about this ground on the one hand, and being reluctant to do so for various reasons on the other. Indigenous writers may certainly be aware of this predicament, particularly in light of such complicating declarations as those by Raerino (1999), who describes an inseparability of the self from the natural world, leading "a great chief [to] speak of himself as the mountain or the river; these cannot be objectified or externalised. They are not 'out there'; but 'in here'" (p.73). I suggest that this mode of expression is not solely that of a chief but is related to everyday conceptions of things as well. One's expressions present what is apparently 'out there'. If this introductory chapter doesn't firmly grasp the opportunity of crystal clarity that its kind is normally meant to, then I have achieved my aim, because from the outset I note that any talk of a root to colonisation is contingent on another. This book is therefore speculative: ultimately, no grand claims are made about the solid properties of either a colonising ground of truth or an indigenous ground of understanding, if indeed those elements exist in themselves. But the opportunity is taken, with that in mind, to theorise the rough and mysterious nature of that which gives life to colonisation to begin with, resulting in an indigenous perspective on the theme. Thus, my aim here is to think through a single problem that has implications for notions of truth and certainty. Its crux is to carry on the thinking – in some measure at least – that is vital in an era of modernity. In our technological age, according to Heidegger (1977), this reflection becomes more important than ever as the 'saving power' against a time that is typified by a discouragement of thinking itself. In other words, we need to look beneath the surface of the 'social' which is often given to us as the crux of the problem and, instead, speculate on what lies at its base.

It is quite likely that indigenous groups have specific concepts that relate to the kind of thinking I allude to here. I theorise that, in academic research at least, thinking has been subsumed under the overall projection of certainty that typifies knowledge: that is, the difference between them is not made explicit, and the loser in that process is speculation (Mika, 2014b; 2016b). In other words, knowledge and thinking have been dealt with by the term *knowledge*. Knowledge – which may certainly contain aspects of thinking – is discussed extensively but thinking is not given its own place, for its own sake. It is the silencing of speculation, however, that should pique the cynicism of not just indigenous peoples but also other groups. In the more conventional vein of education, the problem of epistemic certainty versus the validity of philosophical thought plays out most prominently in the context of tertiary education. In 2013 in Australia, for instance, a funded research project titled 'The God of Hegel's Post-Kantian Idealism' grabbed media attention simply because it *was* funded. Headed by Professor Redding and based at the University of Sydney, it differed from other forms of research because it prioritised philosophy. Its scholastic worth was not disputed (Cosic, 2013), but whether it should have been supported by research money most certainly was, with even the coalition expressing indignation. The issue in the comment's section of Cosic's article then arose as to whether philosophical inquiry constituted research.

This question, I suspect, is more sensitive for philosophy scholars than empirical researchers, and it has no easy answer: the terse and petulant response might be "you can have research but we'll have scholarship"! The question may also arise among doctoral students of philosophical inquiry who are unsure about whether they are conducting 'proper' research or not, and it may surface within postgraduate committees which insist on a demonstrated, visible, data-driven method from the student.

Indigenous students, researchers and scholars are not unaffected by all this to-ing and fro-ing between the research/scholar and knowledge/speculative thought binaries. It means for them that the reservoir of thinking that was so highly valued in precolonial times, while not necessarily reduced in acuity, is simply underutilised. They may feel forced to fit thinking to a rigid method (and arguably it is no longer free thinking once that happens) so that it corresponds with a decree of the postgraduate committee, or they may reject it as a possibility altogether. They engage with the one way of knowing (Markley, 1999), by which Descartes and others proposed that we can ascertain as a divine ability. The stockpile of knowledge that is then added to, born of empirical research, is valid but threatens to become one-dimensional, and indigenous communities eventually inherit the belief that verifiable, solid knowledge is ascendant. To some extent, this process may involve what were formerly mysterious, intangible phenomena. In Aotearoa, for instance, an interesting approach to assessing sustainability exists, with Maori innovators measuring mauri (life force) as part of the process (Mauriometer, 2013). Their aim is to measure mauri with regard to "environmental wellbeing (taiao mauri), cultural wellbeing (hapu mauri), social wellbeing (community mauri) and economic wellbeing (whanau mauri)" (Mauriometer, 2013). Central to this process is the 'mauriOmeter', which assesses "indicators" of aspects that influence mauri. The aim of the innovation is to inform whoever wants to evaluate the gradual effects of those aspects on mauri and, more positively, to provide him or her with alternatives that will eventually lead to the support of the mauri.

For the Maori reader, the name 'mauriOmeter' is undoubtedly an awkward linguistic blend, but more important than the difficult wordplay is whether the inventors of the mauriOmeter believe it is the *concept* of mauri or mauri *in itself* that is being measured. This is also important when we understand that the concept is just as material and important in Maori thought as the entity to which it relates. While its authors are valiantly attempting to introduce a culturally appropriate element to an orthodox, calculative understanding of sustainability, care must be taken not to reduce the mysterious to the banal through measurement. It is in that undeniably dangerous act that what was formerly and heroically beyond our grasp (and yet able to be thought about in a contemplative way) is now apparently knowable to us. Even if it is not really knowable to us, it is still posited *as* knowable or, at the very least, not thought of as still possibly unknowable.

Speculation with the Western thinker

Indigenous writing has not focused a great deal on Western thought apart from the latter's role in colonisation. This is hardly surprising when we think about the role of some Western academics or professionals in historical injustice. The ways in which the colonial anthropologist, scientist, lawyer, doctor and teacher have, throughout history, had an impact on the indigenous social fabric, is well documented and theorised and is beyond the scope of this book. But at the same time speculation can emerge from a number of unlikely sources, or sources that are not widely referred to. Included here is the Western philosopher. Referring to this thinker sometimes asks us, as indigenous writers, to entertain some dual, unclear possibilities about him or her. In fact, the Western thinker is as complex as the indigenous one; he or she cannot be universalised any more than we can be, even though we might call them 'Western' for reasons of description and convenience. With their own sophistication as a backdrop for our approach, we can refer to the Western philosopher to help us coax out some of the problems we face. There is a place for the non-indigenous philosopher in indigenous thinking as long as the latter is privileged and on the proviso that the indigenous writer or critic is familiar with the nature of colonisation in the first instance and can identify where the Western impetus for thinking may have a subtle impact on his or her own thinking.

Introducing the Western voice occurs alongside traditional indigenous discourses and the theorising that indigenous first principles evolve. However, before launching into a conversation with the Western philosopher, we do need to acknowledge some of the problems that indigenous peoples frequently associate with them. Any method of referring to Western philosophers is not without its difficulties, given their reputation amongst certain writers on indigenous thought for prescribing areas of thinking that are, at best, useless for indigenous peoples and, at worst, detrimental to them (Maffie, 2005; Walker, 1996). First, certain Western philosophers have disrupted indigenous people's comportment towards the world. Their impact was probably inadvertent because they were not concerned with indigenous peoples. It should be made quite clear that not all Western thinkers have contributed to the philosophical demise of indigenous metaphysics. Some may have even been horrified at the possibility. But nevertheless, others did indeed contribute in such a fashion. That Descartes is solely to blame for philosophical colonisation of indigenous peoples, as many writers seem to suggest, is unlikely, but it must be noted his epistemology that favoured resisting "the outside world" (Oskal, 2008, p.337) is indeed radically different to that of indigenous peoples. He indirectly opposed indigenous thought; however, a glance further back in time shows Plato had already laid the foundations for Descartes's thinking in his own propositions about the true form. It is important that the wrongdoing is not personalised, even if identifying a source is useful. Descartes, it is true, represents a detachment from things in the world (Fagan, 2008). However, he is *one* product of a set of philosophies that, from an indigenous worlded perspective, are quite detrimental, as they set the self up to be sovereign and separate the self from the rest of the world.

Descartes's and others' incursion appears to have been an unseen overflow from Western institutional practices This is undoubtedly a valid observation to make, although from a standpoint of indigenous metaphysics the influence may be felt as pre-institutional. In other words, from an indigenous perspective those philosophers' very powerful thought might have *given rise* to the very existence of those institutions, but it does not exist *because of* them. The quandary that is highlighted here then revolves around the possibility of a ground of thought that is inimical to that of indigenous peoples and wields an influence, at times outside of anything perceptible. Quite well known are Foucault's arguments dealing with a deeply entrenched paradigm of conceiving the world, which the prison, educational and medical systems operate on, and which thought itself, even if not directly engaged with those institutions, must always aspire to. With all that in mind, some extremely penetrating critiques of Western rationalism, metaphysics of presence, advocacies of final ground and correspondence truth, come from Western philosophers themselves. These can augment the indigenous critic's theorising on a problem, although as indigenous thinkers we have the right to remember that there are also some crucial differences between indigenous aspects of holism and the Western theorist that we refer to.

It cannot therefore be assumed that the Western philosopher has nothing to add simply because he or she is not indigenous. It is true that they may not have experienced the same type of oppression, but they often possess a detailed and unrelenting critique of their own institutions and underlying assumptions. Some Western philosophers have battled with the change to philosophical thinking that has ended up undermining indigenous existence. It is, perhaps, thrilling to imagine that there was at times open and vehement hostility between key figures in Western philosophy, sometimes about the sheer nature of the ground of experience and thought. Such militancy did indeed play out most recently between two intellectual giants of the twenty-first century – Carnap and Heidegger. Carnap, a logical positivist, thoroughly disdained entertaining metaphysics in philosophy, arguing that it could not evolve anything of sense. He was especially incensed by Heidegger's enigmatic proposition that 'the nothing noths'. Heidegger, critical of wholesale logic through and through, noted crisply that precise thinking is simply the re-enactment of whatever is already established (Heidegger, 1949). Carnap and Heidegger's dispute is not expanded on in this book, although it is an example of what I highlight as a problem with presence. The point to be made here is that, at times, fascinating dissent has occurred between leading thinkers in Europe about what may be said with authority in the first instance and what may not. The nature of a ground that lies beneath a thought has been hugely concerning for Western philosophy from Parmenides (and reaching a crescendo with Plato but not abating thereafter) onwards. The differences in thinking between them put paid to any broad-brush attitude towards the Western philosopher. Indeed, their thinking is as polarising and complex as that of their indigenous counterparts.

Whilst Heidegger and Carnap's debate looks like something that only involves their own, in fact they have highlighted what is probably *the* crucial theme for the indigenous philosopher of metaphysics: the role of the 'nothing' in everyday perception. For indigenous peoples, some very useful critiques could evolve on the basis of the disagreement between Carnap and Heidegger, even if we do not conceive of the 'nothing' in the same way as Heidegger. For instance, what, if anything, can be said about the 'nothing'? Is it just a waste of time to think about it, and should one just adhere to talking about what is verifiable through logic? And how would one encourage indigenous students to hold the concept of nothing, valid in its own right, within a statement? Although I raise the issue of the nothing here just as an example of the Western theorist's purpose in this book, more incidentally I also make some immediate and early observations about the possibility of the nothing for indigenous education. Heidegger concerns himself with the issue of the nothing as well as suggesting it "nichtet" (Heidegger, 1998, p.39) – 'nihilates' or 'noths'. It therefore leads us from an indigenous worlded perspective towards thinking that there is an activity that occurs beneath the surface of presence. It may indeed be the nothing, or more precisely its relegation to the mythical in education, which is at stake for indigenous peoples, and Heidegger has succeeded here in bringing its significance, together with its assertively differential process, to confront indigenous educational theory. The nothing would therefore have to be pondered as a credible backdrop to everything that is included in thinking in education, including criticality. Derrida's suggestion that speech is privileged over writing, and that the metaphysics of presence prefers the former, encourages us to come to terms with an indigenous approach to the différance, whereby the meaning of a term is dependent on the interplay of what is its other (Derrida, 1982a). Education, nuanced by its etymology as a process of 'drawing out', would not involve the student producing his or her thinking so that its exteriority connects with the light of reason on its own but would deliberately allow the student to *move back into* a conceptual mode that privileges the equality of presence and absence. The Western philosopher has made the abstract issue an everyday one, and it is up to the indigenous critic to hold what the Western thinker says alongside the existential realities of an indigenous community.

The central and most broadly stated theme of this book – how the indigenous self is influenced through the dual mechanisms of worldedness and presence through colonised philosophy – means that I consider the nature of the object within both traditional and colonised discourse. Eventually some possible solutions are suggested, but these themselves raise more questions than solid connections. Addressing the metaphysics of presence does not rest primarily on conventional forms of knowledge; instead, as Heidegger believed, it is owed to the sheer possibility that arises with an inquiry into Being. With this in mind, it is not so much the repair of the rift between the past and the present that is sought in this book but the bringing to the fore of both Western and indigenous critique and holism, a combination that offers a tantalising glimpse of what lies beneath the expected and foreclosed realms of thought forced by colonisation through presence.

The metaphysics of presence: an introduction

I have described the metaphysics of presence briefly at certain points, but for many indigenous and Western readers unfamiliar with Western metaphysics it is likely to be an unfamiliar phrase. This is a book that both traverses a deep philosophical problem – or, perversely, even threatens to fortify one – and straight away reads education alongside it, as if education and metaphysics were one and the same. The quick but somewhat incomplete supplement to that dual aim of this book is that indigenous peoples, generally speaking, have not been performing well in what are fundamentally Western education systems. The book could therefore be seen as highlighting one explanation of many for that underperformance. It would add to the squadron of reasons that have already been frequently proposed, including language medium (whether lessons and concepts are delivered in the native tongue or not), socio-economic influences, lack of government funding for indigenous initiatives, and so on. An answer closer to the truth, though, is that education from an indigenous perspective needs a sustainedly philosophical approach, and that indigenous peoples simply did not conceive of entities in the same way that settler institutions propose. Indigenous peoples, it is generally suggested, do not buy into the idea that the world is fragmented. This latter notion has its roots in the sinister triad of Descartes, Newton and Bacon (Kincheloe & Steinberg, 2008), whereas for indigenous peoples the complexity of the world lies in its thorough interconnectedness. Moreover, indigenous peoples understand the world not just as interrelated but animate. By this, I mean that its entities are animate as well. Thus, "the rivers, mountains, land, soil, lakes, rocks, and animals are sentient" (ibid., p.151). The view of these entities decides how education in a conventional sense takes place. The indigenous concern, then, may not be so much with the school as with the issue of perception. Whether indigenous peoples are performing well in colonial education systems is of secondary importance to a more deliberate assertion of indigenous epistemological and ontological integrity.

Colonisation is a direct consideration in both possible answers. It has many guises, including one that heralds a change in philosophy for its victims. The indigenous individual is grappling not just with the colonisation of *knowledge* (although knowledge is a philosophical concern) but of the very basic comportment of the self to other things in the world, or of how the self turns to those objects, as it were, before knowledge evolves. In the West, various thinkers have identified the Western self as the object of a certain kind of impoverishment that pre-exists the inequities that occur in social or political domains. Chief among these were the early German romantics who identified that seemingly plausible conceptions of the world resting on logic and reason were not timeless, despite what was commonly thought, and that, instead, a feel for Being, a primordial substance that infused all things in the world, was preferable. This privileging of the unknowable would be voiced in many ways, with Hölderlin (2002) at one stage bringing to the fore the poetics of darkness and obscurity when he implied that there is more to be had from the "night of the unknown" and the "cold strangeness of any other world" (p. 10) than the visible realm. The ideologies of certainty were not always so influential, affecting European communities as they were at the time of the German romantics' writings. Thinking about what lies behind reasoned thought, though, was already at that time becoming unacceptable, even in Germany, where the Enlightenment was not so invasive (Wellek, 1965). Thus, language was turning towards a sort of prescriptive ontology, leading Novalis to react by saying that "if [someone] wishes to speak of something determinate, temperamental old language makes him say the most ridiculous and mistaken things" (Bowie, 1997, p. 65). Terms themselves, the fundamental components of an utterance, were losing their ability to hint at what was not epistemically certain about a phenomenon. What these terms could hint at, and indeed their source in something beyond the perceptible, was fast receding into the background, in favour of a 'higher' octave of language that favoured clarity and precision. The question of the role of the world in education, which is itself an educative and formational question, carries as a huge burden the task of proposing what language is in a philosophical sense and how it is to be valued *as* this or that entity. It is thus complicit in colonisation, not just by dint of what language a lesson is delivered in or what social class it tends to prefer but also through how it dictates language and its objects are to be anticipated in the first instance.

With these issues in mind, I recognised that I would have to refer to an economical phrase that would describe this most primordial of colonising forces at some point in my writing. I return here to the phrase 'metaphysics of presence', which is a label originating from Western philosophy but is hugely useful as a means of identifying a problem for indigenous peoples. In general terms, it can be summed up as follows: an approach to a thing that enables one to conceive of it *as* this or that, as stuck in time, without incursion by any other thing. It is made a definitive thing because "[the privilege of the present] is what is self-evident itself, and no thought seems possible outside its element" (Derrida, 1982b, p. 34) and it is established as that thing in the present time.

We can make some preliminary remarks about the metaphysics of presence here. With that comes a disclaimer, but only of sorts. The qualification I raise is a *partial* one, in that it addresses what *appears* to be my preference of beings in favour of Being. Here we encounter a key problem that consists in my resistance to the metaphysics of presence but, at the same time, appears to privilege it. I appear to have committed a grave error in trying to identify a final, unifying ground (Thomson, 2002). But I am quick to repeat what I believe are certain important mitigating factors: these being that the 'final, unifying ground' is constituted by all things in the world to the point of not really being final and unifying at all, and, secondly, that, although I am inquiring into the essence of Being as I consider beings (and hence committing an equally cardinal sin), I am only conducting that inquiry because of my active constitution by those things in the first instance. My inquiry into a broad, general nature of things is not at all separate from those things. It may seem as if my preference for discussions about 'things' and their essence refers them to an unchanging, permanent idea of Being. If this were true, then I would certainly have fallen into the trap that presence sets, and I do devote space to that possibility when I come to Derrida's views on the inescapability of either absence or presence in Chapter 5. Certainly, I am proposing an indigenous *metaphysics*, but it is one that is predicated on the 'idea' – I scare-quote that word because, as we have seen, an idea for indigenous peoples is a construction by the world and indeed *is* the world – that the final ground is one that is indivisible from the discrete thing we see before us.

In the metaphysics of presence, the thing is there to be studied and considered in its abstract form (Miller, 2012), from the perspective of the cognitive self. It is alone; it is divided from other things in the world; and it has permanent, identifiable characteristics that make it possible to be represented as here-and-now. It is no longer constituted by the drive of all other things within it, or it is no longer infused with active Being. This last point is highly relevant to indigenous peoples. But the issue of presence for indigenous peoples is not straightforward in some of its detail. Although indigenous metaphysics may disdain the view of the single, highly positive thing as much as Heidegger or Derrida, there are subtle but significant points of divergence. White (1996) argues that so-called primitive peoples do not have a notion of Heidegger's present-at-hand or ready-to-hand. For Heidegger (1962), Western humanity treats an object as present-at hand when they become aware of it in a theoretical sense, and consider its properties and the facts associated with it. According to Heidegger, this approach is deficient when compared to the other, ready-to-hand, in which the user of a tool, for instance, is involved in an everyday relationship with it. The tool is not made self-conscious or isolated. White devotes much of her article to the idea that "primitive" peoples probably do not have an approach of present-at-hand because of their explanations for how any one thing is constructed. The "myth and magic" (p.150) that characterises indigenous thinking removes present-at-hand entities in a far different way to how Heidegger argues a ready-to-hand orientation does for the West. For White, present-at-hand in indigenous thought aims to bring forth the hiddenness of other worlds.

Of course, White's terminology is itself potentially an example of present-at-hand as it renders indigenous peoples essentialised entities, to be anthropologically contemplated. If we leave to the side all issues with those loaded terms, though, we see she has identified that the nature of Being for indigenous peoples is vitally different from that of Heidegger's. It is *vitally* different even though there are some overlaps: Being from an indigenous perspective may be conceived of as the culmination of the world within any one thing so that it is never actually one, yet Being for indigenous peoples is, I suggest, the chief question of one's existence. Heidegger's notion of Being, different to the culminating aspect, nevertheless attaches directly to it: Being reveals things and their concern for the self *as* a culminating force or entity. There is both Being itself, as a thoroughly changing and nebulous entity, and being in indigenous thought about both. One thing becomes clear: the indigenous scholar should be aware that the works of these philosophers are extremely useful but incomplete. They form the substantial basis of a critique and it is up to the indigenous scholar to contemplate them in terms of what is more proactively or positively a metaphysics of worldedness. At that same point, we are considering how the indigenous person is educated as a constructed participant with the *isolated* thing in the world.

An indigenous notion of education that is based on worldedness needs to consider the formational force of the metaphysics of presence. In particular, the fragmentation that it augurs is impactful. First, however, it is useful to think about the nature of presence as a theme. From Plato onwards, things, including the human self, participate in a permanent, unchanging Being. Therefore, whatever is *present* – 'here and now' – is what is true (Miller, 2015). What is in the now is what is true because I am convinced of my own existence only in the current time: I am present (and Descartes helped show this) because of my own thoughts. An object is therefore only valid in terms of its 'here and now-ness'; its past or future reality is unreliable, and it needs to be represented as if it is before me. Gumbrecht (2004) abbreviates what are frequently long explanations of the metaphysics of presence to the following: "what is 'present' to us . . . is in front of us, in reach of and tangible for our bodies" (p.17). Culler (1982), having listed the ways in which presence comes to bear on modern society, states that "[t]he authority of presence . . . structures all our thinking. The notions and practices of 'making clear,' 'grasping', 'demonstrating', 'revealing,' and 'showing what is the case' all invoke presence . . . the metaphysics of presence is pervasive, familiar and powerful" (p.94). The fact that it *is* so widespread (in fact, replete throughout thought) makes it the "troublemaker" (Ankersmit, 2012, p.160) for indigenous metaphysics because the two are largely opposed to each other. As we shall see through the works of Novalis, Heidegger and Derrida, dominant Western thought has prioritised what *appears before the self* rather than considering the fact that it appears at all and the contexts responsible for that appearance. An indigenous proposition that a thing is made possible by the interplay of all other things makes the metaphysics of presence a problematic entity in many respects, as presence poses "the origin itself . . . as pure, simple, normal, standard, self-sufficient and self-identical" (Biesta, 2010, p.75). The object, having appeared before us and possessing the properties that that object should, is hence all there is to the object; to the indigenous onlooker, it is meant to be permanent, unchanging and alone.

It is helpful to provide a concrete example here. Peller (1985) uses the instance of a tree, and discusses it in light of its 'thereness' or its fact of standing out among other things. When a tree is represented through an idea, it is given definition *as* a tree. The idea of the tree is given absolute emphasis even for a split second. According to Peller, "a substantiality of being is assumed to fill up the realm of treeness" (p.1169). This approach of imbuing a thing with its thingness happens to everything at any given time. But just as important for our current discussion, this complete endowment of being to a thing in our mind's eye does something else: it disregards everything else that constitutes the tree. It "pushes other concepts out of the realm by giving positive content to the concept 'tree'". Language further entrenches this active but completely unrecognised act by representing the tree. It seems that the tree has been specifically recognised through the profound 'defriending' of all other entities. The defriender is not aware at all that he or she has acted it out because it is an embedded act that has its genesis in Plato. A deeply unconscious and instantaneous preference for one object over another, it is called metaphysics by its critics because it proposes a ground of orientation towards things in the world. One can only utter the word 'tree' if one has predetermined how it is to appear in the first instance – possessed of certain properties that determine its 'treeness' (Mika, 2015a). That predetermination occurs before facts and knowledge.

So much for the theme of metaphysics of presence itself, but what could all this possibly signify for indigenous peoples? Here, we should recall the opening few sentences of this chapter where I asserted that the conception of an object is all-important to a colonised group. For how the indigenous, colonised self *turns* to an object in the first instance and then refers to it in language is an act of education. One quite simple term – *ground* – may especially resonate for some indigenous peoples as an aid to discuss the nature of ultimate knowledge of a thing. 'Ground' has the ability to be highly paradoxical, especially in indigenous thought. On one hand, it can suggest a physical phenomenon that things rise from and sink into. On the other, it can highlight a conceptuality: a finality or solidity in thinking, for instance. In that reading, it foresees a notion of metaphysics of presence because it is the origin of conception and "*always amounts . . .* to reconstituting, according to another configuration, the *same* system [of Being of presence]" (Derrida, 1982b, p.60). Or the term can somehow refer to a mysterious conception and phenomenon, one that lacks the certainty that it at first seems to hint at. Even more strangely, it can herald uncertainty due in part to the 'coming to bear' of phenomena that one has no control over. In that interpretation, ground as earth in Maori thought would never be realised (Mika, 2016a; 2016b; 2016c). Thinking itself would rest on an ever-newly-disclosing ground that reveals itself as soon as we think we have alighted on a final outcome. Our thinking "is called by a ground . . . that we widely believe to be solid and rationally antecedent" (Mika, 2014a, pp.54–5) but to our eternal consternation we never reach that final ground. If we did, we would finally be able to say we know what any one thing is in absolute, totalising terms. Talking about the ways in which theology and metaphysics are often equated, Adorno (2001) stated that "[t]o put it somewhat more crudely, the widespread equating of metaphysics and theology . . . can be traced back simply to mean something which pre-exists and predominates in the mental formation of all of us, even if we are not directly aware of it" (p.6). Preferring to synthesise metaphysics and its entities – although making no bold claims to any links between what I want to discuss and theology – I can invoke the term *ground* as a useful one because of its capacity for indigenous theorising to incorporate both realms of physical existence and thought that cannot, as Adorno identifies, be brought out into the opening with stunning clarity but that remain behind a veil.

The consequences that the notion of a ground anticipates for Peller's tree are many and are explored (not necessarily with the tree as a continuing example) throughout the book. But given the all-encompassing nature of the Earth Mother, or the originator of the notion of 'ground' for many indigenous peoples, it is unlikely that the tree is perceived as ever being free of the influence of other things, even if this ground has receded into the backdrop of discussion about the tree. It is likely, though, that the concept of a 'tree' was not to be approached without the influence of the ground. In other words, just as a metaphysics of presence encourages an approach to things in their utter positivity, an indigenous worldedness that highlights a ground of uncertainty encourages an approach to things as if they are to be discussed in their relationship with each other. The ground, an aspect of the Earth Mother (if we wish to make that connection even for conceptual thought), is an uncertain, not a solid, one that may even presuppose an ethics of encounter between self and thing. As Barad so colourfully put it, "[w]hat if the ground is not made of bedrock but rather oozing slime molds and other protean forms that lack determinate identities?" (Kleinman, n.d, p.80). What, moreover, if the matter of one thing oozes into the other, thus revealing a non-foundational ground that has to it all things in the world? In the instance of the tree, it is entirely possible that conceiving of a tree requires that one hold the possibility of the 'ground of All' in one's utterance. The tree for the indigenous person has a vestige of everything else in its conception and reference. Where it becomes fraught for indigenous peoples is in how we have undoubtedly inherited a set of philosophical assumptions from another set of metaphysics through colonisation, dictating how we are to turn to the object. This tree/ground relationship is different to what Western critics argue metaphysics of presence governs: a truthful conception based on the idea of the 'tree', in all its positivity and its certain distinction.

The tantalising possibility of oneness in one term – that in uttering the word *tree* one has already and necessarily brought with the utterance a whole set of unstable contingencies – is more fully explored in Chapters 2 and 3 when I discuss an indigenous and indigenous/Maori concept of metaphysics as it relates to the object and the self respectively. Despite the potential of that holistic metaphysics, indigenous peoples have been forced to play on a field of distinctions that is not their own. It is telling that, in indigenous literature, the phenomenon of metaphysics of presence has been covered over with terms such as 'rationalism', which, although an intimate bedfellow with the former and indeed sometimes indistinguishable from it, is really one of its primary offshoots. In other words, it is argued throughout this book that rationalism in its many guises would not have evolved if there had not been a drive in the first instance to approach the world in a particular way. But talk of this ground is problematic because one is asserting the final ground. Schelling (1856) raised the problem of talking about a final ground with his fascinating play on the word *thing*. The nature of the thing for Schelling was apparently what was most sought after in philosophy. One tries to make something a thing, but at the same time the thing resists being made such. It is hence an "unconditioned thing". If we use the terminology of thing-liness, it is 'unenthinged' ('Unbedingt', as Schelling calls it) – a contradiction. It is by its very nature not made into a thing, because its thingliness has dissipated from the outset. Our final ground that rests in making the thing a definite thing has suddenly dissolved towards yet another *apparent* finality. The metaphysics of presence must also share in this ever-regressive ground. If we entitise it, either through our indigenous worldviews or simply by mentioning it as what it is, we soon realise that it hides part of itself just as Schelling suggests it would. It would reveal other grounds of conception in turns, ironically evading any strictures of 'truth' in the sense of logic.

Education in its orthodox manifestation pays scant attention to the possibility that an indigenous conception of things links immediately back to that initial and dually conceptual and real ground that is hidden from immediate access. But how is this ground retained in an indigenous conception of one thing, as it is being focused on? In order to clarify what is at stake in this question, let us turn to a very quickly sketched scenario. An indigenous student, at junior or tertiary level, utters the word *tree* in a sentence, either in his or her own native language or in another. What are the possibilities for that word and the self as far as the indigenous student is concerned? From an indigenous metaphysics, the self is one with the tree through genealogical links. So is the utterance itself. A tree is tied to other things in the world also, and so is the utterance. Thus, the utterance always already contains to it something of all those other entities, even though they are not declared in the sentence. All those other things emerge from a ground that infuses throughout everything and so that ground, as I have suggested, is indeterminate. But that ground additionally persists throughout the utterance – as both a separate entity but simultaneously as the totality of all those entities. By attending to these factors, I already must have considered the ancestors and those to come in the deep gathering that the utterance anticipates.

What may be clear to anyone familiar with educational practice and theory is that there is a deep tension between the colonial educational positing of a thing and the indigenous conception of the thing as a silent representative of all other things. The complexities of this scenario are immense when the pursuit of clar-ity, logic and precision in education is privileged, with the result that "Western knowledge [is] . . . premised on the ideal of making visible the entire natural and social world" (Jones, 1999, p.311). Where to make an utterance about a thing, from an indigenous perspective at least, is in fact to be with the thing (Mika & Tiakiwai, 2016; Whitt et al., 2001), it seems that a sort of disciplining occurs whereby the indigenous student is made to consciously dismiss the possibility of those other entities in that utterance, for the sake of that clarity. This very last act of constraint is also seen as a form of education by a particular view of the world. Moreover, what does a metaphysics of presence propose for indigenous reflection on his or her speculation, as an aspect of education? Kant, for instance, is hugely important in Western philosophy, and his indirect impact on indigenous peoples through colonisation by the West, although not provable, is likely to be profound. Fuchs (1976) identifies that Kant's destruction of metaphysics ironically demonstrates that "all that is possible is Appearance, which is precisely *other than* the presence of Being itself" (p.8). Despite Kant's resistance to Being and his rejection that we cannot know the thing-in-itself, "Being is presence". Kant's categories would propose that those entities that indigenous propose as 'more-than-cognitive' should indeed be reducible to the cognitive. For instance, the Maori term *whakapapa*, now sometimes referred to as a "fundamental form of knowing . . . [whereby] it functions as an epistemological template" (Whitt et al., 2003, p.5), plays a similar role to the Kantian *a priori* categories. It can be theorised, however, that the 'problem' with indigenous conception for this proposition is that an idea is both at once conceptual and entity. Like all other things in the world, it holistically retains the sum of things to it. It then becomes less a mode of conception and takes on aspects of other things.

López (1998) highlights these sorts of vulnerabilities when discussing the responsibility of the indigenous scholar in "writing against the mainstream" (p.226). Briefly, he asserts that the problem lies in "engaging non-traditional epistemological forms in research" which he undertakes to be audible against "scientistic frameworks". I take 'epistemological' to also be tied up with 'ontological', and in that case the metaphysics of presence is likely inescapable. Heidegger, its most ardent critic, saw it as the key mistake of Western thought but would himself be criticised by Derrida for not being able to free himself from its influence. What may seem like a pessimistic stand on the matter is actually both depressing and contributory: it acknowledges the long inheritance of a particular tendency in dominant Western philosophy that has, in turn, affected indigenous peoples, and it therefore makes no grand claims to disband that ground of fixity. But I do bring an important subject into the discussion for indigenous peoples. In addition to announcing the theme of primordial colonisation through a basic concern for truth that the West privileges, I highlight the following possibilities: Can indigenous creation stories or explanations for existence, alone, counter a Western notion of truth, as some indigenous commentators imply? Or is there another element that needs to be not only accounted for but, indeed, *sustained* in any critique? These and other problems filter throughout the book, but no firm solution is envisaged on my part.

These possibilities are further vexed by the issue of language. Presence is so widespread that even the most innocuous terms are imbued with its fixity. I discuss an example – *is* – in Chapter 5, but I offer another here. I can ask the following, seemingly innocent question: could metaphysics – that 'certain something' that cannot be fully experienced – be the most pressing issue facing indigenous peoples? More urgent, even, than the retention of language, the staving off of ill health, or the instituting of indigenous legal systems? My position is certainly that it is most pressing, but already I may have betrayed an indigenous metaphysics in my language, for what matters here is the assumption underpinning *most*. *Most*, of course, is *the* necessary superlative, and superlatives are useful devices for an introduction but there is no doubt they are risky: they provide a captivating inroad for the reader and are valuable in that sense, but they are potentially dicey. If they are used wrongly, they can cut out other possible participants in the quality being described. They can have social and political implications: one thing becomes preferred or abhorred in comparison to others, and bodies of knowledge are placed in traction or released, graded and categorised, according to whether they live up or down to a measure. The stakes are high for indigenous peoples because any claim to the biggest, best or worst of anything has the capacity to isolate a characteristic of an idea, a person or some other being, and in turn that assertion fixes that characteristic and the being. For instance, if I state 'that mountain is the most beautiful', then both the idea of beauty and the mountain are centred on and influenced. Other realities are created, other states of well-being reconfigured, even in that simple assertion, in which one aspect of an originally whole entity has been singled out.

This problem is an aspect of the crux of this book. The claim to the 'most' of anything is no different from any other, where writers must necessarily isolate a characteristic out from its environment in academic work in order to indicate its significance. Saying that metaphysics is the *most* pressing issue for indigenous peoples and their beliefs around education brings it into stark reality. It becomes reified, which as we shall see has particular consequences from an indigenous perspective. The second problem, though, is often left unchartered and goes to a much wider but related issue. As an indigenous teacher, learner or writer, I am called on to continuously represent a nature, perception or characteristic that makes sense for the text. This holds true even when I am critiquing that very call. To make the critique I have about that fragmentary practice, I have had to draw on that very field that gave that practice vitality in the first instance. I reiterate here that as indigenous writers, educators, students, or researchers, we are prone to academic representation by the fact of its underlying, silent nature: we are susceptible as much when we are critiquing it itself as when we are writing generally. The stakes for indigenous peoples are high when we consider that any one thing is meant to be composed of all others, in a state of interconnection. Simply saying that the superlative is a problem, then, does not suffice: I am caught even as I protest by the very ground that gave life to the superlative in the first instance.

At a number of levels, the indigenous self is educated through the apparently external world, not primarily by the other human. This approach to education is not mine alone, but it can be made more evident through a radical encounter with both indigenous metaphysics, which almost universally privileges interconnection and animacy, and its antithesis – the metaphysics of presence.

Book outline

The book can be thought of informally as comprising two parts. The first part, or Chapters 2 and 3, excavates into the oft-cited indigenous and Maori metaphysics of worldedness and considers its referencing indigenous notions of education that I have already alluded to earlier. This part sets the stage for the second, which describes how the metaphysics of presence runs counter to that indigenous metaphysics (but may simultaneously be thought of as an aspect of worldedness) and its implications for that indigenous notion of education I have theorised.

Chapter 2 – An indigenous philosophy of worldedness

Indigenous writers often describe their communities' worldviews as holistic. This chapter devotes itself to expanding on the features of that written and spoken metaphysics and is therefore firstly contextual because it sets the scene for the reader. It is also productive, however, as I continue to add to philosophies that propose indigenous education as a world-given phenomenon. I deviate from positioning education as a primarily human-centred event and instead emphasise that education is primordial – it is the construction of the self through the positing of entities, and it is also the working of the world on the self. Cajete (1994) has argued in favour of indigenous education being viewed simultaneously as "endogenous education" (p.34). As he emphasises, knowing the self is a fundamental aspect of any education. This version of selfhood is not to be confused with the tightly individual self espoused in capitalist societies because it must recognise that what appears to be individual in the current sense is in fact completely implicated by all other things. Thinking about and reflecting on one's relationship of the self to an object, and the kinds of relationships encouraged/discouraged by education, are hence paramount to the health of the self and the self's community for indigenous peoples. At the most fundamental level, well-being for indigenous peoples is predicated on the perception of an object and the possibilities an object is allowed to hold. The constraint of an object through its appearance as merely present, I argue, has implications for what is often cited as a 'holistic' metaphysics in indigenous circles.

Chapter 3 – Ako: a Maori example of worldedness

An 'indigenous' explanation needs to be further specified through the cultural lens of the author. I speculate on the Maori term 'Ako', which is often simply referred to as 'teach/learn'. Having discussed the implications of worldedness in Chapter 2, I consider Ako in the light of the working of all things in the world. I explore various Maori terms and their concepts that display the idea that the world works on the self at all times, such that the self along with any other thing is indivisible from other things.

Chapter 4 – An indigenous dialogue with Heidegger: the consequences of presence

The metaphysics of presence is articulated in a very general sense by Martin Heidegger, and for the indigenous critic of presence his works are useful as we formulate our own response to the problem. This chapter draws heavily on his works on enframing to pose an indigenous response. I discuss the theoretical impact of presence on the indigenous notion of worldedness, and consider from that perspective how presence reconfigures objects so that they are no longer all within any one thing.

Chapter 5 – Presence for the Maori student and writer/critic in Ako: Novalis and Derrida

The indigenous student and writer/critic are both impacted on by presence. This chapter discusses the theoretical impact of presence on the Maori student and writer, and I return to the notion of Ako, building on the previous chapter which has illustrated what the metaphysics of presence means for indigenous peoples and the notion of worldedness. Novalis was especially keen to critique any notion that the self was ontologically self-sustaining, and he therefore alludes to a sort of presence of the self to the self. I establish a dialogue with him from a Maori worlded perspective, focusing on the Maori student, who is caught up in presence as he or she learns as an unmysterious character. And like Heidegger, Derrida was critical of the metaphysics of presence because of its rejection of absence. In some ways indebted to Heidegger's conception of 'Destruktion', Derrida's 'Deconstruction' engages more with the misconception that something is indeed purely present. It aims to highlight the forms of text and meaning that are hidden or suppressed, although with the knowledge that one is always already influenced by presence. Deconstruction thus acknowledges an already established opposition between essential presence and absence and aims to intervene to re-establish some degree of absence in writing.

This chapter provides concrete examples of presence's influence on the self-reflective and logocentric aspects of Ako. For instance, I shall suggest that dominant Western assumptions in education rest in the first instance on the idea that an object can be described in isolation from other things. In short, a Maori student or critic/writer is hence expected to know what a thing *is* when they mention it. While this may give rise to a Platonic correspondence version of truth and is not altogether invalid, an indigenous reaction to an object is much more likely to hold the possibility of other things in the world even as one apprehends the one object. How this correspondence of perception and object is not encouraged in an indigenous notion of education, even subtly, forms the basis of this chapter. Heidegger's fusion of orthodox, compartmentalised segments of time is relevant here, because the presence of a thing is complicated by the collection of past events in relation to a thing, its label in indigenous languages, and its promise for future events. These, I argue, make up the approach to a thing from an indigenous perspective, but I set out to show that the metaphysics of presence does not at its base acknowledge this indigenous comportment to things.

Those problems all have repercussions for what one can say about them. This chapter largely looks at the dual futility – but also, importantly, the possibilities – of language that attempts to critique the problem of presence from an indigenous perspective.

Chapter 6 – Cause for optimism?

I conclude by thinking through the challenges that Western metaphysics offers in light of what I have discussed. There are possibilities for transformation offered by both Western and indigenous philosophers here that need to be taken into account to see whether innovative forms of indigenous resistance can be achieved.

Bibliography

Adorno, T. (2001) *Metaphysics: Concept and Problems*. Stanford, CA: Stanford University Press.

Ahenakew, C., Andreotti, V., Cooper, G., et al. (2014) 'Beyond Epistemic Provincialism: De-Provincializing Indigenous Resistance', *AlterNative* 10(3): 216–31.

Alfred, T. and Corntassel, J. (2005) *Being Indigenous: Resurgences against Contemporary Colonialism*. Oxford, UK: Blackwell Publishing.

Ankersmit, F. (2012) *Meaning, Truth and Reference in Historical Representation*. New York, NY: Cornell University Press.

Aranga, M., Mika, C. and Mlcek, S. (2008) 'Kia Hiwa Ra! Being Watchful: The Challenges of Student Support at Te Whare Wānanga O Awanuiārangi', *MAI Review* 1(6): 1–12.

Arola, A. (2011) 'Native American Philosophy', pp. 562–73 in W. Edelglass and J. Garfield (eds) *The Oxford Handbook of World Philosophy*. New York, NY: Oxford University Press.

Battiste, M. and Henderson, J. (2000) *Protecting Indigenous Knowledge and Heritage: A Global Challenge*. Saskatoon, Canada: Purich Publishing.

Biesta, G. (2010) 'Witnessing Deconstruction in Education: Why Quasi-Transcendentalism Matters', pp. 73–86 in C. Ruitenberg (ed) *What Do Philosophers of Education Do? (and How Do They Do It?)*. West Sussex, UK: Blackwell Publishing.

Bowie, A. (1997) *From Romanticism to Critical Theory: The Philosophy of German Literary Theory*. New York, NY: Routledge.

Brown, M. (2011) *Decolonising Pākehā Ways of Being: Revealing Third Space Pākehā Experiences*. Unpublished doctoral dissertation, The University of Waikato, New Zealand.

Buss, J. and Genetin-Pilawa, J. (2014) 'Introduction: The World Is Not Enough', pp. 1–12 in J. Buss and J. Genetin-Pilawa (eds) *Beyond Two Worlds: Critical Conversations on Language and Power in Native North America*. Albany, NY: SUNY Press.

Cajete, G. (1994) *Look to the Mountain: An Ecology of Indigenous Education*. Durango, CO: Kivakí Press.

Calderon, D. (2008) *Indigenous Metaphysics: Challenging Western Knowledge Organization in Social Studies Curriculum*. Doctoral dissertation, The University of California, Los Angeles.

Corntassel, J. (2003) 'Who Is Indigenous? "Peoplehood" and Ethnonationalist Approaches to Rearticulating Indigenous Identity', *Nationalism and Ethnic Politics* 9(1): 75–100.

Cosic, M. (2013) 'Is Philosophical Enquiry a Waste of Taxpayers' Money?', *The Drum*. Available at http://www.abc.net.au/news/2013–09–10/cosic-university-research-funding/4947744 (accessed 2 July 2016).

Culler, J. (1982) *On Deconstruction: Theory and Criticism after Structuralism*. Ithaca, NY: Cornell University Press.

Daes, E.-I. (1994) *Preliminary Report of the Special Rapporteur: Protection of the Heritage of Indigenous People* (No. E/Cn.4/Sub.2/1994/31 Commission on Human Rights, Sub-Commission on Prevention of Discrimination and Protection of Minorities, Forty Sixth Session, Item 15 of the Provisional Agenda, UNESCO). UNESCO.

De La Cadena, M. (2010) 'Indigenous Cosmopolitics in the Andes: Conceptual Reflections Beyond "Politics"', *Cultural Anthropology* 25(2): 334–70.

Deloria Jnr, V. (2001) 'American Indian Metaphysics', pp. 1–6 in V. Deloria Jnr and D. Wildcat (eds) *Power and Place: Indian Education in America*. Golden, CO: Fulcrum Resources.

Derrida, J. (1982a) 'Différance', pp. 3–27 *Margins of Philosophy*. Chicago, IL: University of Chicago.

Derrida, J. (1982b) 'Ousia and Grammē', pp. 29–67 *Margins of Philosophy*. Chicago, IL: University of Chicago.

Fagan, K. (2008) 'The Delicate Dance of Reasoning and Togetherness', *Studies in American Indian Literatures* 20(2): 77–101.

Fuchs, W. (1976) *Phenomenology and the Metaphysics of Presence: An Essay in the Philosophy of Edmund Husserl*. The Hague, The Netherlands: Martinus Nijhoff.

Garfield, J. and Norden, B. (2016) 'If Philosophy Won't Diversify, Let's Call It What It Really Is', *The New York Times*. Available at nytimes.com

Green, J. (2011) *A Discursive Analysis of Maori in Sexual and Reproductive Health Policy*. Unpublished masters thesis, The University of Waikato, Hamilton.

Gumbrecht, H. (2004) *Production of Presence: What Meaning Cannot Convey*. Stanford, CA: Stanford University Press.

Heidegger, M. (1949) *Existence and Being*. Chicago, IL: Henry Regnery Company.

Heidegger, M. (1962) *Being and Time*. Oxford, UK: Blackwell.

Heidegger, M. (1977) *The Question Concerning Technology and Other Essays*. New York, NY: Garland Publishing, Inc.

Heidegger, M. (1998) *Was ist Metaphysik?* Frankfurt am Main, Germany: Vittorio Klostermann GmbH.

Heidegger, M. (2001) *Poetry, Language, Thought*. New York, NY: Perennial Classics.

Hölderlin, F. (1961) 'In Lieblicher Bläue', pp. 372–4 in F. Beissner (ed) *Sämtliche Werke: Gedichte Nach 1800: Text*. Stuttgart, Germany: W. Kohlhammer.

Hölderlin, F. (2002) *Hyperion and Selected Poems*. New York, NY: The Continuum Publishing Company.

Horlacher, R. (2016) *The Educated Subject and the German Concept of Bildung: A Comparative Cultural History*. New York, NY: Routledge.

Jones, A. (1999) 'The Limits of Cross-Cultural Dialogue: Pedagogy, Desire, and Absolution in the Classroom', *Educational Theory* 49(3): 299–316.

Kincheloe, J. and Steinberg, S. (2008) 'Indigenous Knowledges in Education: Complexities, Dangers, and Profound Benefits', pp. 135–56 in N. Denzin, Y. Lincoln and L. Smith (eds) *Handbook of Critical and Indigenous Methodologies*. London, UK: Sage.

Kleinman, A. (n.d) 'Intra-Actions: Interview of Karen Barad', *Mousse* 34: 76–81.

Kovach, M. (2009) *Indigenous Methodologies: Characteristics, Conversations and Contexts*. Toronto, Canada: University of Toronto Press.

Lawson-Te Aho, K. (2013) *Whāia Te Mauriora-in Pursuit of Healing: Theorising Connections between Soul Healing, Tribal Self-Determination and Māori Suicide Prevention in Aotearoa/New Zealand.* Unpublished doctoral dissertation, Victoria University of Wellington, New Zealand.

López, G. (1998) 'Reflections on Epistemology and Standpoint Theories: A Response to "a Maori Approach to Creating Knowledge"', *International Journal of Qualitative Studies in Education* 11(2): 225–31.

Maffie, J. (2005) 'Aztec Philosophy', in J. Fieser and B. Dowden (eds) *Internet Encyclopedia of Philosophy.* http://www.iep.utm.edu/aztec/

Mankiller, W. (2011) *Every Day Is a Good Day: Reflections by Contemporary Indigenous Women.* Golden, CO: Fulcrum Publishers.

Markley, R. (1999) 'Foucault, Modernity, and the Cultural Study of Science', *Configurations* 7(2): 153–73.

Mauriometer. (2013) *Mauriometer.* Available at http://www.Mauriometer.Com/ (accessed 2 July 2016).

McIvor, O. (2010) 'I Am My Subject: Blending Indigenous Research Methodology and Auto-ethnography through Integrity-Based, Spirit-Based Research', *Canadian Journal of Native Education* 33(1): 137–55.

Mika, C. (2007) 'The Utterance, the Body and the Law: Seeking an Approach to Concretizing the Sacredness of Maori Language', *SITES* 4(2): 181–205.

Mika, C. (2012) 'Overcoming "Being" in Favour of Knowledge: The Fixing Effect of "Mātauranga"', *Educational Philosophy and Theory* 44(10): 1080–92.

Mika, C. (2014a) 'The Enowning of Thought and Whakapapa: Heidegger's Fourfold', *Review of Contemporary Philosophy* 13: 48–60.

Mika, C. (2014b) 'Maori Thinking with a Dead White Male: Philosophizing in the Realm of Novalis', *Knowledge Cultures* 2(1): 23–39.

Mika, C. (2015a) 'The Co-Existence of Self and Thing through "Ira": A Māori Phenomenology', *Journal of Aesthetics and Phenomenology* 2(1): 93–112.

Mika, C. (2015b) 'Counter-Colonial and Philosophical Claims: An Indigenous Observation of Western Philosophy', *Educational Philosophy and Theory*: 1–7.

Mika, C. (2015c) 'Novalis' Poetic Uncertainty: A Bildung with the Absolute', *Educational Philosophy and Theory.*

Mika, C. (2015d) 'Thereness: Implications for Heidegger's "Presence" for Māori', *AlterNative* 11(1): 3–13.

Mika, C. (2015e) 'The Thing's Revelation: Māori Philosophical Research', *Waikato Journal of Education* 20(2): 61–8.

Mika, C. (2016a) 'The Ontological and Active Possibilities of Papatūānuku: To Nurture or Enframe?', *Knowledge Cultures* 4(3): 58–71.

Mika, C. (2016b) '"Papatūānuku/Papa": Some Thoughts on the Oppositional Grounds of the Doctoral Experience', *Knowledge Cultures* 4(1): 43–55.

Mika, C. (2016c) 'Worlded Object and Its Presentation: A Māori Philosophy of Language', *AlterNative* 12(2): 165–76.

Mika, C. and Southey, K. (2016) 'Exploring Whakaaro: A Way of Responsive Thinking in Maori Research', *Educational Philosophy and Theory.*

Mika, C. and Stewart, G. (2015) 'Maori in the Kingdom of the Gaze: Subjects or Critics?', *Educational Philosophy and Theory*: 1–13.

Mika, C. and Tiakiwai, S. (2016) 'Tawhiao's Unstated Heteroglossia: Conversations with Bakhtin', *Educational Philosophy and Theory.*

Miller, V. (2012) 'A Crisis of Presence: On-Line Culture and Being in the World', *Space and Polity* 16(3): 265–85.

Miller, V. (2015) *The Crisis of Presence in Contemporary Culture: Ethics, Privacy and Speech.* London: Sage.

Mobein, S. (2011) 'Interconnectedness of Mind, Body and Nature in the Traditional Healing System of American Indians', *International Proceedings of Economics Development and Research* 5(2): 57–61.

Oskal, N. (2008) 'The Question of Methodology in Indigenous Research: A Philosophical Exposition', pp. 331–45 in H. Minde (ed) *Indigenous Peoples: Self-Determination, Knowledge, Indigeneity.* Delft, The Netherlands: Eburon Academic Publishers.

Peller, G. (1985) 'The Metaphysics of American Law', *California Law Review* 73(4): 1151–290.

Peters, M. (2015) 'The Humanist Bias in Western Philosophy and Education', *Educational Philosophy and Theory* 47(11): 1128–35.

Peters, M. and Biesta, G. (2009) *Derrida, Deconstruction, and the Politics of Pedagogy.* New York, NY: Peter Lang.

Raerino, N. (1999) *"Pure" and "Karakia" as a Window to Maori Epistemology: Koi Rō Pure Me Karakia E Oke Ana.* Unpublished masters thesis, The University of Auckland.

Rangihau, J. (1992) 'Being Maori', pp. 183–90 in M. King (ed) *Te Ao Hurihuri: Aspects of Maoritanga.* Auckland, New Zealand: Reed Publishing Ltd.

Schelling, F. (1856) 'Vom Ich Als Prinzip der Philosophie oder Über Das Unbedingte Im Menschlichen Wissen', pp. 149–244 in K. Schelling (ed) *Sämmtliche Werke.* Stuttgart, Germany: Cotta'scher Verlag.

Smith, L. (1999) *Decolonizing Methodologies: Research and Indigenous Peoples.* London, UK: Zed Books.

Spivak, G. (1985) 'Three Women's Texts and a Critique of Imperialism', *Critical Inquiry* 12(1): 243–61.

Thomson, I. (2002) 'Heidegger on Ontological Education, or How We Become What We Are', pp. 123–50 in M. Peters (ed) *Heidegger, Education and Modernity.* Lanham, MD: Rowman & Littlefield.

Walker, S. (1996) *Kia Tau Te Rangamarie. Kaupapa Maori Theory as a Resistance against the Construction of Maori as the Other.* Unpublished masters thesis, The University of Auckland, New Zealand.

Waters, A. (2004) 'Language Matters: Nondiscrete Nonbinary Dualism', pp. 97–115 in A. Waters (ed) *American Indian Thought: Philosophical Essays.* Oxford: Blackwell Publishing Ltd.

Wellek, R. (1965) 'The Unity of the Romantic Movement', pp. 45–52 in J. Halsted (ed) *Romanticism: Problems of Definition, Explanation, and Evaluation.* Boston, MA: C. C. Heath & Co.

White, C. (1996) 'The Time of Being and the Metaphysics of Presence', *Man and World* 29: 147–66.

Whitt, L., Roberts, M., Norman, W., et al. (2001) 'Belonging to Land: Indigenous Knowledge Systems and the Natural World', *Oklahoma City University Law Review* 26: 701–43.

Whitt, L., Roberts, M., Norman, W., et al. (2003) 'Indigenous Perspectives', pp. 3–20 in D. Jamieson (ed) *A Companion to Environmental Philosophy.* Oxford, UK: Blackwell Publishing Ltd.

Wildcat, D. (2001a) 'Indigenizing Education: Playing to Our Strengths', pp. 7–20 in V. Deloria Jnr and D. Wildcat (eds) *Power and Place: Indian Education in America.* Golden, CO: Fulcrum Publishers.

Wildcat, D. (2001b) 'The Schizophrenic Nature of Western Metaphysics', pp. 47–55 in V. Deloria Jnr and D. Wildcat (eds) *Power and Place: Indian Education in America.* Golden, CO: Fulcrum Resources.

Wildcat, D. (2005) 'Indigenizing the Future: Why We Must Think Spatially in the Twenty-First Century', *American Studies* 3(4): 417–40.

Chapter 2

An indigenous philosophy of worldedness

As a preface to this chapter, we can reiterate some fundamental ideas about worldedness. The concept of worldedness relates to the fact that one thing is constituted by all things in the world, to the problem of perception and worldview, to the place of an utterance and thought in the life of a group, to how landmarks will influence the self, and to whether one decides to label a phenomenon or not. Posed in various ways, phrases and utterances such as 'worldedness' and 'one thing is constituted by all others' are easy to place in the abstract realm, and there they will remain largely under-theorised and will have very little impact in everyday activities, simply existing as tired sayings to invoke at particular times. But the concept is not so easy to manage, and indigenous writers such as Calderon (2008), Smith (1999) and Wildcat (2001) have identified – perhaps without continuously naming that very phenomenon but having mentioned it in various places in their works nevertheless – that there is a link between the idea of worldedness and the ethical demands placed on the indigenous self (Mika, 2015c). The challenge delivered by worlding is one that does not sit easily with the belief that education is necessarily either directly delivered or negotiated by the human world. Most tellingly, the indigenous educationalist is compelled to mediate between the belief that the learner is taught largely through the effort of another person on the one hand, and the more originary thought that comes with the philosophy of worldedness on the other. In the philosophical thinking of worldedness, the human being may not be addressing education in its common guise.

In this chapter I offer some preliminary remarks about a very broad notion of 'education' within the context of indigenous metaphysics, but the initial aim is to philosophise about the nature of the world and the thing. The constitution of the self by the world, and vice versa, is educational, as I noted in the Introduction. The general nature of indigenous relationships with the world is complex, abstract and often paradoxical. Furthermore, one must account for the limits on what can be said with complete authority about any one entity, given its thoroughgoing collapse with the self. What follows is a radicalising of the most fundamental idea that one thing is composed of all others.

The hidden and perceptible world

Raerino's (1999) observation I recounted earlier – that landmarks are internal to the self – means that the representer of them is indeed those landmarks. Deloria (2001) has found a way of articulating that thinking, too, when he speaks of a "unified world" (p.2), with power and place at the heart of indigenous existence. One could not exist without the other, and indeed both elements for Deloria operate in synchronicity with each other to form indigenous identity and well-being. Both came into being before human consciousness of them, and we can speculate that both contained to them the potential for human existence. Quite what characterises power and place is mysterious as they are in some sense indistinguishable from each other and are highly mercurial to the self's perception. Power and place figure largely in indigenous thought: so prominent are they, in fact, that Vine Deloria Junior saw fit to title his book with those two nouns. There is nothing straightforward about power and place, however, and indigenous literature tends to stress their importance as living entities that implicate humanity and all other things in the world. They can – and perhaps should – be described in broad terms. They could be simply equated with power and place as 'human influence or agency' and 'land', respectively, yet those explanations do not do them justice. Power in indigenous thought consists of life force, which infuses throughout the world and all its objects. Place gives rise to a general understanding of the world; it structures horizons of thought, physically and spiritually. It is also the totality of all entities, seen and unseen, that reside there and that are emotionally and cognitively meaningful for tribal members. Deloria (2001) identifies that Native American metaphysics is primarily related to an awareness of the complexity of the world as one entity. In this fully enmeshed realm sits the human self, but humanity is merely one aspect of the world's social nature. As everything was so thoroughly interrelated, then immediately everything else was social as well. Deloria rejects the fragmented approach to the world that western science advocates, although he believes that aspects can be transferred as long as they are familiarised with Indian thought. But ultimately it is power and place that resonate for Deloria. The energy of power and place influences humanity, who can become familiar with other things in the world through their own proper resonance with power and place. All things are united through these two phenomena. The response of humanity to the entities of the world is an ethical one in at least two ways. First, one must be attuned to power and place as the means of guidance to deal with things. Additionally, there are ethical aspects of behaviour to be maintained, such as the preservation of life, the conservation of sacred areas, and the ceremonial and silent ways of conveying knowledge. Place informs discussions about Being as a holistic possibility. Indigenous ontologies are sourced in the deep connection with land and with the ways in which that land and its totality come to bear on those whom it chooses to claim. Land thus *acts* on the self (Mika, 2016a). Most profoundly for the idea of the individual, all things and their relationships constantly accompany the indigenous self, in turn, with all things. The indigenous self is never quite alone, even if acting individually: he or she bears the full mantle of the world in total.

There is a thorough construction of self and thing through their immediate association and unity with each other. This curious ontological makeup is further complicated by the position that place is influential in a bodily sense. Whitt et al. (2001) appear to have this link in mind when they describe that "the natural world is alive, spiritually replete" (p.702). They recount the words of a Dineh woman who, when faced with relocation to another area from Big Mountain, was concerned that the flora and fauna of the new region would not know her. She would be strange to those things; she herself would be unrelated to that land as a whole. An indigenous explanation thus privileges how one resounds in a bodily sense with a place and with what are conventionally taken to be external phenomena in general. The self, an entity thoroughly related with all other things, is utterly dependent on the constitutive nature of power and place. There must therefore be a subtle change that takes place in the self across different terrains: we are not essentially the same, in other words, in one part of Aotearoa as we are in another. This alteration is probably imperceptible – it undoubtedly should be, given that power and place and their sum activity are likewise unbounded – although it may manifest as an individual's well-being if we think of power and place in their accord with holistic models of health (Durie, 1994). The individual is also changed by other entities that have inhabited those places and by others that are yet to manifest. In social practice, this phenomenon may be acknowledged by various names given to a newborn, and to the reference and placement of the deceased self to their landmarks. Power and place are immediately part of the self; the self is de-individualised, despite appearing to be alone.

Crucially, power and place link intimately with notions of time and thence with Being. For indigenous communities, all of these facets intermesh to the extent that they allow the self to act in certain ways, to give voice to issues, and to maintain states of well-being. Power and place are essential for other peoples as well, but indigenous peoples often see the need to reiterate them because their perception of them is in direct contrast to the worldviews that drive colonisation. Being – the totality of all things in the world – is also influential and at work when it is beyond the direct experience of the indigenous self. Within its vast domain, however, indigenous peoples have the ability to transform, and act in concert with, the world. For the indigenous writer, scholar or researcher, Being foreshadows the overly empirical focus of measurement: it stands behind all entities, making them comprehensible for a time but, overall, unknowable. The indigenous scholar is to rethink knowledge as a relationship with Being (Mika & Southey, 2016), and an individual's or group's encounter with the external world is at all times mediated by Being, which is a consistently primordial and mysterious event.

The counter-colonial indigenous 'Being': beyond the human

Why is it important, from an indigenous perspective of power and place, to begin discussions about Being by focusing on the process of *thinking* about Being? In academic text, there appears to be a rush to define the limits of an entity and detachedly regard it rather than discuss its impact on one's thinking. In other words, there is little concern for what I hold to be important to my writing as I write: terms and ideas are either credible or they are fallible. In specific relationship to Being, there would be a galvanic impetus for me, from academic convention, to define Being in this book *as* this-or-that, rather than be primarily concerned with its relationship to anything I represent or how it enables me to represent anything in the first instance. But for an indigenous writer, Being is not so straightforward because I am only writing this chapter, or reflecting on metaphysics, to begin with because of some interaction in the world, past, present and future, that I am probably not aware of (Mika, 2016b; Mika & Southey, 2016). These sorts of reflections originate from the discord that frequently arises between knowing and Being. Instead, there must be a conversation between self and other thing whereby one is attuned "to the other's modes of being – its ontological presence" (Kincheloe, 2011, p.340). Furthermore, but relatedly, there may be guidance from ancestors in the work any of us do (Ahenakew et al, 2014), and undoubtedly I am influenced by the sway of what may most economically be called my 'tribal landmarks'. Additionally, my own and other people's ideas, histories and experiences act in some unknowable way to allow me to respond. The thinking that I refer to here is linked with vitality to all other things in the world (Ahenakew et al, 2014) and is not just confined to the materiality of entities – or their 'nothingness' – but is also intimately connected to my reflection on them. And further still, my representation of those entities may (or may not) be influential and useful at a cognitive level. This latter scenario, however, does not adequately explain from an indigenous perspective how important representation is. Many indigenous peoples may say something that does not have logicality as its primary intent. Far more likely, given our adherence to a worldview in which everything is living, is that my (and others') representations through language, debate, weaving, carving and so on somehow have a material effect outward.

Few words are as central to an indigenous worldview as 'Being', which immediately invokes the possibility of all other things outside of (but not excluding) the person. There may presently be widespread discussion about what constitutes indigenous knowledge (commonly acronymised to IK, so frequently does it figure as a concern), but I suspect that 'Being', the more mysterious counterpart to knowledge, takes priority in indigenous thought without necessarily being labelled. One cannot claim to know Being, but it encourages indigenous speculation within its uncertainty. Being is thus a deeply obscure issue for indigenous peoples, and a standard declaration of its properties would run counter to its own tendency to withdraw from certainty. A common theme among indigenous writers is that worldedness (as I have termed it) relates to the confluence of all things in the world, such that there is an underlying, driving move of all those things to be in conversation with each other. Senghor (2010) tells us that there exists among "the African" (p.479) a complex notion of the relationship between matter and Being. Senghor asserts that African perception is more deeply attuned to the materiality of things. Things, however, are important both for themselves but also as a much more fundamental sign of the All that resides everywhere in the world. African philosophy does not confuse the individual manifestation of a thing with all that there is to that thing. Whilst things may appear different and hence limited, they are all part of the "same reality". Things in the world are only the presentation of the singularity of "the universe: being, which is spirit, which is life force" (p.479). When discussed in that context, humanness is constructed within an infinite schema. The ontological description extends immediately to other phenomena alongside the human self, and to their astounding and overwhelming convergence with each individual entity. The total activity of all things in the world, a concept that cannot be fully grasped for any particular group of people, can be thought of here as an ontological *substance* that infuses or defines all things. But even here, 'substance' is a problematic term because it carries with it an Aristotelian sense of overwhelming positivity, of thorough solidity and of an entity that is to be thought of as comprising overly visible properties (Mika, 2015a). Because of the infinite nature of things in the world – the endlessness of their connections with other things, as well as of their potential to be composed of all other things – Being is also negative or 'void' (Mika, 2013b; Mika & Southey, 2016; Mika & Stewart, 2015). It is a non-foundational, negative substance.

In that process, Being is implicit in (although not constrained by) thinking. It is not always explicit in name. That it is not named should not encourage the non-indigenous reader into expecting that Being has somehow withdrawn from thought, or that indigenous peoples are not contemplating it. It can indeed sometimes be labelled, but this may be purely tactical. For instance, it may be overtly highlighted to draw attention away from what is currently a grand narrative, such as epistemic certainty. For those who are fascinated by Being, the term does not do full justice to its enormity, and some cautions need to be voiced in discussions where Being is mentioned. First, as Cajete (2000) identifies when discussing indigenous North American peoples, there exist important distinctions in cultural expression between the separate groups. He goes on to note, however, that there are also significant similarities between them and that they all express interconnectedness between things in the world. The similarity exists for indigenous peoples generally, with a worlded notion contending that Being is totally linked to power and place. More vitally, Being is not foremost a human attribute (Mika, 2013a). Being does incorporate human knowledge and experience within it but this is not its origin. To place it in the self is insufficient and dangerous, even when the indigenous self is capable of inquiring into the notion of Being. Instead, Being is a notoriously difficult phenomenon to discuss because it is ultimately elusive. As we do inquire into it, we are made aware of our limits in that act because we are sourced within it. The indigenous scholar, who is particularly intent on isolating Being as a point of concern, may be acutely aware that Being cannot be 'gotten around' and discussed from a distant, all-knowing vantage point.

Being from an indigenous vantage point is therefore ultimately unknowable. Claims to grasp Being would need to rely on having a thorough knowledge of all things in the world, their place and their innate, and often hidden, aspects. Indigenous peoples would meet such far-reaching claims with scepticism. We can *speculate* about Being, however, and thus that act of thinking calls out to be considered. Far transcending the being of the human, Being moves throughout the words and general expressions of indigenous existence, although it may not be a focus. An indigenous notion of Being is thus expressed even *within* Being, and Being conceived in that way is rendered further unknowable and unequatable with anything else. If I make a statement about Being, the act of making such an utterance is indebted to Being itself (Mika, 2016c). Furthermore, the term *Being* may appear to have more in common linguistically with ideas of permanent essence or characteristics, but in fact it is probably better thought of as constant activity. The indigenous self or collective operates within this continuous state of flux and Being is never fully proportionate to the human self. Raerino's (1999) suggestion that there is in Maori belief "an oppositional counterpoint" (p.32) to everything is evident in the dual but intertwined nature of, for instance, life and death, darkness and light. Being both acts within *and* outside of those experiences, even allowing for them to manifest in the first place.

Being, I suggest, does not simply exist because of the fact that we think; it is not confined or limited by our thinking, because it is responsible for our thinking in the first instance. But it does reverberate with thinking. As indigenous peoples, when we think, we are in fact giving some acknowledgement to Being. Being in its own right is evocative, and it draws the indigenous self on to ponder it, regardless of whether it is a conscious theme in a discussion. This proposition about Being is Heideggerian but only partially so, because unlike Heidegger's earlier ideas of Being it relies on a fundamental decision that Being is a force substantially within things, drawing out of power and place. Curiously, though, Being takes place throughout the world, whether thought about or otherwise. Thinking *about* Being is therefore an expansive and unsettling process. A common term approximating 'to think' in my own, Maori vocabulary is *whakaaro*. *Whakaaro*, I suggest, is to immediately have regard for Being but not as an object of a clinical gaze: instead, this thinking arises *as* a response to Being, even in thought that is seemingly not related to Being. Thinking must therefore be a kind of immersion in the world, as part of all things. Here, Kincheloe (2011) identifies in relation to Andean culture that the vitality of all things ensures that one is "in relationship to the world" (p.339). For Maori, as with the Andean self, one converses with the world, with the result that the delineation between subject and object is dissolved. This complex conception of thinking infers that Maori thinking is more than human evolved; it is connected with the notion of place that Deloria highlights and is intimately connected with the self's absorption in the full extent of the world. Here we can see some human agency in the act of thinking, but the phenomenon which one is casting attention to has much greater sway in that Maori version. Even if we approach whakaaro in its capacity of the self to do something, we soon encounter a different notion of the self. The self is existentially enmeshed in the world, to the extent that the world is responsible for the self's existence to begin with (Mika, 2015a). The connection between self and world is a thoroughgoing one, greater than just an abstract idea, with Cajete (2004) indicating of indigenous peoples that "[t]he physical, cognitive, and emotional orientation of a people is a kind of 'map' . . . [it] is multidimensional and reflects the spiritual as well as the mythic geography of a people" (p.46). He assigns this conceptual framework to the 'mind', but in an indigenous interpretation, 'mind' could well become 'body' as a whole and vice versa.

Thinking in an indigenous framework sets out to re-emphasise a spiritual approach (Deloria & Wilkins, 2012). Relatedly, the term 'spiritual' carries with it its own limitations, chief among these being that it seems to discourage further inquiry simply because it self-sufficiently describes a state of being. It is therefore useful to peer beneath the surface of that word to uncover what it refers to when thinking is involved. Where thinking in the West has been dominantly premised on a notion of truth that seeks to grasp an objective conception of a thing, indigenous thought valorises a number of other factors. Thinking for the latter is sourced in a set of complex, fundamentally unknowable but ultimately unlimited relationships. At the source of my proposition here is the philosophical belief that one is immersed in and constituted by the world but that one's ancestors and forthcoming generations, even if not immediately related genealogically to the self, have the ability to constitute what one thinks. To the Western reader, the possibility that any future events are influential on the present is perhaps a difficult one to tolerate, yet the irrationalism it suggests synchronises with the paradoxical nature of indigenous thought itself. Set against that material connection between past, present and future is the idea that the world is a precise, rational phenomenon. Indigenous approaches do indeed acknowledge the validity of that form of thinking, but it is after all only one way of thinking among others. Indigenous thought hence seems able to transcend the rationalism of Western metaphysics, transforming it by placing it among other paradigms and ideas.

Furthermore, indigenous thinking prizes the relatedness of the self and the world. Royal (2005) discusses the Maori term *aroaro* (sensory field) and its implications for well-being, highlighting the importance of a balance in the senses. Reminding us that thinking conjoins what we do in everyday life, he suggests that the aroaro can be either broadened or limited. The latter occurs when we spend too much time on one task. Royal suggests that the way we orient ourselves towards a particular task, for instance, has direct consequences. He lists "texts" and "screens" (p.16), which help to "narrow the aroaro". In other words, too much of one kind of focus does not bode well for our peripherality. I would add to Royal's discussion here by indicating that the physicality of place also orients one's thinking. Corresponding with that possibility, Calderon (2008) avers that the world is comprised of a complex web of genealogical connections that are dependent on physical and metaphorical location. Calderon, drawing on Deloria's philosophies, devotes some space in her dissertation to the indigenous notion of power and place. One's personality, indeed one's self-formation, ultimately depends on one's tribal identity. Landscapes have the capacity to shape how we think. Tau (2001) argues here, in line with Maori epistemology, that Maori knowledge reflected the self onto the landscape. In that act, place and self are inseparable, being immediately informed by each other. Calderon continues that 'truth' is contextual and concretely formed by our embeddedness within the landscape. Deloria (2001) notes that humanity is similarly reliant on this immersion in one's terrain. Mika (2012) suggests that Being for Maori is indeed a supernatural entity but, unusually for Western metaphysics, constitutes the self and his or her everyday experiences, and also contains to it aspects of nothingness. Marsden (2003), a Maori philosopher and theologian, had earlier stated of the creation accounts that there was a real emphasis on the dual phenomenon of essence/nothingness. Thinking for indigenous peoples hence calls for a tentative approach to a topic or concern that takes into account the interconnectedness, obscurity and imprecision of the world.

Being, beyond the highly positive

From a counter-colonial indigenous perspective, it seems useful to conceive of Being in a way that deliberately opposes how we are normally taught in colonisation to conceive of things. With that counter-colonial glance towards the undesirable as we think proactively about Being, we would understand the latter as a non-positive phenomenon, because we are constantly urged in the Academy to apprehend the presentation of an object in its complete positivity (Mika, 2016c). This latter attempt to grasp an object does not accord with much indigenous literature on Being. In its different names, Being for some writers (Cordova, 2007; Marsden, 2003; Mika, 2012; Sharrad, 2003) is underscored instead by its nothingness as much as its positivity. Cordova stresses that the nothingness is not simply emptiness but can be likened to a void: it is what she hyphenates as "No-thing" or "without definite characteristics" but "it is the void out of which arise 'the ten thousand things'" (p.103). Being from a Maori perspective may also be an actively nihilating force that evokes an emotional response to Being's finite things in the world. In other words, Being's voidness is the source of my emotional response to the world because it veils phenomena and keeps me from rendering them completely knowable. I therefore react to Being – it is uncertain, and it claims me in its mysteriousness.

There is a curious and largely inexpressible process at work here while we write as indigenous scholars, though. If indigenous peoples do in fact commune with things in the world or, as Whitt et al. describe it, "live or keep company with" (p.734) them, then they have to be especially reflective on how they refer to those things. They have to think ontologically even as they describe its many constitutive entities. The indigenous academic is not outside of the obscurity that Being poses, despite what one thinks. The undesirable aspect of this phenomenon is that academic writing lures us into ignoring the hiddenness of Being and leads us to believe that we have somehow transcended its call to be emotional. Even if Being is inclined to make us respond emotionally, we can at least treat a thing that we are contemplating coolly, as if it is divorced from its 'parent'. There are therefore some dangers lying in wait for representing Being as if it is removed from the world: if Being does infuse and give rise to all things, then how Being is conceived of must also dictate how its things are understood. Being is both greater than, but utterly within, all its things and should be envisaged in exactly the same way as any other entity. Academic, scholarly representation encourages us to replace the primordial – and both indeterminate and definite – Being of things with the human being and with that sets us above the things that share at once with Being.

This difficulty is one of many that the indigenous writer encounters. Being is to be thought about within a colonised context, not solely a traditionally rarefied one, and the indigenous writer who wants to engage with Being in their own thinking should, I argue, take account of power, place and Being themselves as historically and politically constructed. They are participants in history even if they still retain something essential to themselves. If power and place are not exactly *constructed* by their own history and the decisions made on and about them, they are at least *influenced* by it. Power and place are themselves not outside of or unaffected by colonisation, and that realisation calls for a set of approaches beyond what traditional knowledge can offer on its own. To describe this as concretely as possible: if there has been a massacre on a piece of land, then most indigenous peoples will know that the land has been changed, along with the power that it both has and that it interchanges with other entities. This problem is an unlimited one, to be sure, because indigenous peoples may insist that there is an unchanged essence to power and place even when, historically and contemporarily speaking, various atrocities have occurred in relation to them. Areas where precolonial battles occurred, or which were confiscated by settler government, are undoubtedly altered – but not thoroughly – in that argument. It follows, then, that traditional indigenous knowledge is sufficient to engage with a discussion of Being. However, even if Being does have a certain resistance in that scenario, there are particular blockages to our access to that pure strain. Traditional knowledge, although important, cannot replace thought that tries to account for the full experience of indigenous existence whilst that thought makes some assertion about Being in its traditional guise. If we are to dichotomise traditional knowledge and counter-colonial thought, then, as Wiredu

(1998) suggests, we must bring them together again; it is at this point that we can think about Being-as-total.

Colonisation is as much an entity as the self or any other if we are to refer to worldedness in its fullest form. Colonisation is therefore to be thought of in its true worlded form, not as if it is socially constructed or just emotional, physical or even spiritual. In some indigenous contexts, this nature of colonisation is acknowledged through various ceremonies, such as prayers and chants: usually these are addressed directly in order to be dealt with. It may be uncomfortable to think of colonisation as a worlded entity with as much validity in that respect as the human self or the animal or natural worlds, yet here is the starting point for thinking about problems facing indigenous peoples in general. Colonisation is an entity that both detrimentally and productively influences the worlded proposition. It is destructive because, as we shall see in Chapters 4 and 5, it asks indigenous people to turn to the world as if it comprises distinctly separate elements. In that act, the indigenous self is proposed as an entity capable of being apprehended as separate from all others. Science seems to loom large here in this drive, as do law and rational discourse in general. With indigenous worldedness, these disciplines have already been located on something far prior that insists that one's current idea of an object is sufficient. The representation of the object is then supported by how one turns to the object itself – separate, fragmented and self-sufficient. And, as I also go on to discuss, there is potential thought to be had from colonisation, despite its own attempts to dampen down contrary thinking.

Colonisation is therefore grafted onto all other things as part of them. It may be that it calls for our attention more than other entities, though, and it is significant because it still retains some aspects of itself, but it shows itself up through all entities so that they are all colonised. Yet these worlded entities are also simultaneously traditional things, in the sense that they are also what they were earlier. There is no place that is free from colonisation (and this horrifying prospect exists even in our thinking and writing) – but there is also no place that is free from our precolonial thinking, either. This uneasy co-constitution of colonised and uncolonised entity shows up in ceremonies, where the apparently traditional event is backdropped by deeply colonising events that are apparently unrelated to it, or distant from it. If a blessing for a house to clear it of spirits of the dead is performed, for instance, it appears to be a traditional ceremony – and it is, even though the individuals of the group carrying the ceremony out are, in completely different spaces and times, signing tribal registers or engaging in blood quantum DNA tests (as examples). What are taken to be 'completely different spaces and times', in fact, are constructively the same as the ceremonial space. Here I am not talking about a moral defect in any of these individuals but simply that we are forced to act in colonised ways in one space or another that is immediately constitutive of the traditional realm we are now choosing to act in.

But as I have suggested, the converse of that formidable problem is that colonised relationships with the world are never free from the presence of a more traditional indigenous element. Some more commonly written about examples can be recounted here (and doubtless there are several more). Current Western scientific knowledge, for instance, is indebted in a major fashion to non-European knowledge for its existence (Loomba, 2015). The latter is implicit within it, from a worlded perspective. Additionally, whilst indigenous knowledge was contrasted with rational knowledge and appeared to be thoroughly separate at times of colonisation, in fact the former had already been constituted by the latter, showing itself in the coloniser's consternation at never being quite able to exterminate the presence of indigenous thought. Even as Europe thought it was making that contrast by diffusing its knowledge to the lesser episteme (Blaut, 1993), it was being influenced in a profound manner by the backflow of indigenous existence itself. This attempt to normalise the indigenous self by promoting rational knowledge resulted in a tainting of its apparent purity. It is here that we see postcolonial literature as being particularly powerful when it writes about the constitution of the coloniser by the unknown 'Other'. The coloniser, according to Sardar et al. (1993), has long been plagued by the thought about the Other, starting with a fear of the Other's body: a dread of it remains and forces itself throughout the subsequent thought of the coloniser. It is quite a conscious fear and, to deal with the problem, a conscious effort was made to tame the Other (this project was actually one that aimed to deal with quelling the *fear* of the Other as much as the Other themselves). The Other grew more hideous the more distant they were from Italy or Greece, and the indigenous self especially would be associated with untameability, Otherness and overall indecency. They would continue to lurk peripherally in the selfhood of the coloniser, with one result being that the coloniser would describe and depict them through art as inhuman and hence *not* a part of the coloniser's self. In more contemporary times, the current fascination of coloniser knowledge with traditional ceremony may be a sign of that same quandary. The 1990s saw a rise in non-indigenous interest with spiritual ceremonies (Smith, 1999) and language; it may have been seen as an antidote to a particular void that some commentators have suggested exists in their thought (Abrams, 1996; Huhndorf, 2001; Mander, 1992; Mika & Tiakiwai, 2016). It should be noted, not quite incidentally, that the assertion of a void is itself backdropped by both void and its apparent opposite: as I make that assertion, in other words, I acknowledge that it is a somewhat murky statement, underpinned by as much complexity of the world as its meaning.

Time: the 'always-already'

Whether the indigenous self was always already constituted by the world, whether the colonised or traditional entity was forever grafted onto by its other, or whether the indigenous self became aware of the world which *then* constituted him or her, are issues to do with time. Deloria's observations about power, place and Being have implications for indigenous notions of time as well. That the past somehow builds up to and shows itself in a future event is tenable for most mainstream thinking. That the apparent future conducts the same for the past by somehow having already been conceived of in some way, however, hints at a much more complex and unclear metaphysics. Ideas about future, past and present become deceptive. We would be thrown into a more extreme state of uncertainty than ever, and would have to accept that all things, including ourselves, are participants in a thoroughly fluid and unlimited event, in which the self is never quite definite. The self would then be at the directive of power and place, not just in their current form but in their sheer historical and future togetherness. Indigenous holistic thought does indeed suggest that apparently different stages of time are, in fact, co-instantaneous. Events do occur separately, but they are contained within a certain potential, and that potentiality is of utmost consequence for indigenous philosophy. That potential is non-linear (Mika, 2015d; 2016c; Mika & Stewart, 2015). Something had *always already* occurred, and its occurrence always already constituted other things (Mika & Tiakiwai, 2016). The *always-already* was a latent specific event waiting to unfold but is at the same time real, and this anticipation – yet assured fulfilment – of future time was held to be extremely important, for instance, for the idea that humanity evolved later than power and place. Humanity may certainly be dependent on, and chronologically follow on from, power and place as Deloria describes them, but humanity was always possible as one event of many within the fabric of that sublime combination. Power and place, in turn, are entirely contingent on what has seemed to follow them. Dominant notions of linear time have already been dispensed with in different ways by writers such as O'Connor (2007), Pihama (2001) and Whitt et al. (2001). In a tangential relationship with their thinking, I propose that the indigenous individual has *always* been constructed by power and place as well as their ancestors. They were constituted in this way beyond our current understanding of time. Power and place in the past construct the individual of now; power and place of the future likewise manifest within the current individual.

Time is hence an untidy and non-constraining phenomenon in indigenous holistic thinking, and its nebulousness would mean that parallel dimensions existed alongside the one currently being experienced. As unconventional and undesirable as this might sound to stalwarts of academic orthodoxy, it is highly plausible for indigenous metaphysics but it loses its potency when explained in specialised academic language – destined, perhaps, for science fiction or new age–speak. What may be discerned here is a deeply ingrained move in academic convention to render the idea itself silly, by making the language delivering it untenable; such language does not accord with what Foucault (1984), in his own context, called "a set of ordered procedures for the production, regulation, distribution, circulation, and operation of statements" (p.74). Conversely, an indigenous metaphysics of time would undoubtedly resist the proposition that our current experience is all that there presently is. It is not unusual for indigenous healers, for instance, to speak of entering other dimensions, including past and future ones, for an outcome. These dimensions are in fact part of the present one but need to be brought to awareness. Moreover, this tendency of one point in time to encroach on another (or, more correctly, to have *always* participated in that way) is a matter for everyday observation; time, with its perplexing lack of strict boundaries, is not to be confused solely with ceremony. The indigenous scholar in the act of writing, which is an apparently straightforward undertaking for those who are used to it, for instance, would then have to contemplate that it is more complex than it seems, as he or she is constructed by the holistic reality of time as well.

The nature of this interlinking between space and time is made available for some human speculation through the use of genealogies. From an indigenous worlded perspective, *genealogy* is, in fact, a deeply unsatisfying term to represent the complexity that is being alluded to in their various indigenous equivalents. We can accept the term *genealogy* for the time being, though, and note that it arranges places and the various dimensions of time that arise within those landmarks and people. Genealogies depict how things in the world are brought together continuously and in an ever-evolving fashion (Whitt et al., 2001). They are not focused on the human world, and time and space are entities *within* which all things are positioned. Place and time are brought together in genealogies. One's ancestors and descendants are already implicit and this fact is acknowledged through the world that is disclosed through genealogies. Time is incredibly complex because things unfold within it as a permanent presencing. The Australian Aboriginal term *Tjukurpa*, for example, holds that what are commonly thought of as separate stages of time are, in fact, collapsed. Klapproth (2004) explains that existence, or Tjukurpa, is the confluence of all dimensions of time. We could infer here that the suggestion of separate times, even to then explain them as a confluence, would immediately undermine what we wanted to say about the oneness of time; this predicament displays one of the key aspects of the metaphysics of presence which we come to in Chapters 4 and 5.

Language and its materiality

Speech, including song as well as everyday utterances, is constructed as much by what is not yet vocalised as what is stated. Again, time is implicated with language. This important facet to an indigenous view of time begins at the large level and moves towards a finer granularity. To begin at the macro level, an indigenous metaphysics would suggest that the speaker is claimed equally by the term and the full extent of the utterance that follows (Mika, 2016c). Curiously (for a teleological perspective), the influence of the world that is hinted at in the forthcoming words has always 'turned back' to the speaker, and the speaker is hence captured by the sublime that resides within the utterance *as a whole* from the outset. The unusual aspect of language here is that indigenous notions of time and place dictate that an utterance in total is influential before the words are encountered, or before the self is cognitively aware of them. Moreover, any speaker will be constructed in some way by speech without ever being aware of what is stated. There are several concepts for that phenomenon in Maori parlance: one of them, *wana*, conveys a continuity of mystery throughout things in the world through their enduring presence that is simultaneously an 'unshowing'. By that latter term, I mean that the hiddenness that the term *wana* signals is a powerful lure because it may draw the speaker on towards further speculation (Mika, 2013b; 2014a). It also demonstrates that the self, along with other things in the world, is a participant in what is not present.

The indigenous self may be constructed in a substantial way by the world that is presented at once from the outset of an utterance such as a song or a speech. Silence is also a phenomenon that constitutes things in the world (Mika, 2012; 2014a; 2015b). Mosha (2000) observes that "[f]ew other virtues have as many proverbs [as silence]" (p.122) among indigenous Africans. It may be because it is a precious entity that it tends to be revered among indigenous peoples. For Maori, silence could be ruined by questions (Smith, 2007); silence is a thing that is prone to injury by something verbalised, and it needs tending. It appears to have been privileged enough to be allowed to manifest as a thing that was both positive and absent. It is hence not uncommon to participate in discussions in Maori forums, only to find that silence suddenly prevails. This sudden lapse in the audible is itself full of meaning, and one way of perceiving silence is that it is an entity immediately constituted by all others. Silence is curious in that it also allows speech to emerge: here, Mosha (2000) continues that "[e]ach thing gives birth to its child: speech gives birth to its mother (that is, silence)" (p.122). If we theorise on those words, we might conclude that silence and speech occur at the same time, to the extent that they may well possess difference (they give rise to each other) yet sameness. While it is tempting to think that silence exists as a supporting actor for the grand entrance of speech, in fact they always attend each other. Silence may indeed be construed as a language of sorts. This equality of language and silence should not lead us to think that silence has to be language in order to be of any worth, however. It declares itself by virtue of its own taciturn presence; it coalesces as itself and thus expresses itself to all other things in the world. Silence's own brand of clamour is not the same as loud speech – it is not as direct and forthright – but it is no less demanding for all that. Silence can also stand for the work of things in the world in general where they are imperceptible. As I have suggested, the indigenous self is produced by the worlded thing and its relations, but we need to constantly remind ourselves that this influence of the (apparently) external world does not need to be felt in order to be valid. Mosha (2000) identifies that silence for African indigenous peoples is "mighty, creative, and productive. It is not a vacuum or a sign of weakness" (p.124). The unfelt or imperceptible is just as engaged with the self as its sensed Other; even the proposition that a thing is unfelt or imperceptible is itself a working of silence! Without a reverence for silence, the world would simply be comprised of what is able to be heard or felt.

Speech may also be a version of silence, inasmuch as whatever is uttered contains to it a sort of darkness that may de-emphasise the idea being represented. The "bifurcation point" of thought that Cajete (2004, p.48) talks of, for instance, applies to a notion of the hidden sense of the All that adheres to even one singular term or utterance. Cajete refers to the phenomenon in relation to boiling water and adapts it to a moment of truth for the indigenous perceiver. The spaces of change that occur between boiling and its tempering stabilise into an overall pattern. The "stable pattern of vortices" (p.48) can be thought of as the tendency of all things in the world to inform and implicate each other. Of course, there may simultaneously be further realms of these vortices that are suggestive of instability. The point of this as it refers to silence and speech is that they have always already constituted each other before speech has been uttered or silence has manifested. The vortices may be the coexistent but unseen worlds that gather and graft themselves to the silence and speech. Already, then, both speech and silence have been augmented by the full potential of those other realms. In a more concrete sense, when one utters something, as I have suggested it is backdropped by what is not stated. Its silent counterpart exists within the utterance but, at the same time, obscures it so that what is *not* spoken of takes on as much important as the stated.

If we use the language of clarity and murkiness, then we might be able to have an insight into what is an admittedly abstract proposition. In the Maori world it is likely that language in general is an obscurer of an entity (Mika, 2014a) protecting things from any possibility of being left as "dead, quivering remnants" (Novalis, 2005, p.27). This enveloping tendency, of course, is not perceptible; it operates in pure silence. A sound therefore also hushes by its nature. Pihama et al. (2004) refer to the function of the word (*kupu*) as the "*kakahu* [cloak] of sound" (p. 21). As an entity is cloaked, its intelligibility is concealed, and often it is other entities that come to the fore even when it is intended that a particular thing is to be made precise. This process has the capacity to lead to a great deal of creativity for the Maori individual because the highlighting of the 'incidental' through the silencing of the word's sound takes on importance for the self. The true nature of that new thing, in turn, recedes into the background by the utterance (which can be written, not necessarily verbalised) and both that withdrawal and the appearance of the even more recent entity become the new 'bifurcation point'. Also, as I speculate in the following chapter, the self is itself cloaked, not just the entity that is being spoken of. The self can be silenced by the very entity that is meant to be clarified.

The multifarious nature of things' language

In dominant academic discourse it is often assumed that inanimate things in the world do not possess language. Yet, indigenous peoples argue strenuously for a type of expression that things possess which may be called 'language'. Language in this sense is not the same as that of humans, which is not to say that humans are special for the fact that they have a unique sort of language: I suggest that all things in the world vary in their type of language from each other. Language may be the sound that forms from the manifestation or recession of a thing. It is the lure of a thing as it either withdraws or appears; in Maori philosophy, this movement of an object is considered to be fundamental even to human speech, as it is the orientation of the natural world to the human self that urges one to talk (Mika, 2016c). But even when not perceived by humans, things arrange themselves and thus form tensions with other things, thereby creating their own distinctive voice. Things say by their flaring up. The language of things is predicated on their ongoing interlocking with the world, and depends on their freedom to merge with others, de-emphasise themselves to other things but also retain those other entities as constitutive of themselves.

How can something that is apparently part of another thing yet be external (and thus cause language, for instance)? Indigenous thought recognises that things are simultaneously distinct from, yet the same as, each other. Extremely difficult to convey in academic English, this paradox is at the heart of indigenous dealings with an object. However, as Loutzenhiser (2008) suggests, paradox is not the most apt term for talking about indigenous philosophy. Loutzenhiser refuses to use the term *paradox*, because for him it suggests that there are "truths that seem to oppose each other" (p.13), but he resists that notion that underpins the term, arguing instead that these truths sit with each other as "coemergent wisdoms". Ahenakew et al. (2014) and Cooper (2012) similarly allude to a set of concurrent phenomena that may not stack up against normal logic. The Maori notion of *kore* or negativity that has always been simultaneously positivity, references another set of truths that cannot be resolved through rational means. Reflecting on the panentheism of the Lakota, Callicott (1997) notes that this group of people did not have an issue with the apparent problem that rests with thinking of a thing as both differentiated and yet collapsed with the "Great Spirit". They simply are both at once, but never is the differentiated object outside of this supreme, entity. With the interlocking of one thing with another, one thing can have its own form but be completely one with all other things.

The human self: inseparability from the materiality of the world

From an indigenous worlded viewpoint, if there is an incongruent logic at all, it is the one that emerges as a clash between the tendency of Western thought to iron out varying truths and the indigenous insistence that those contradictions are truthful. In other words, indigenous peoples may not have a problem with the simultaneous separateness/togetherness of all things, but they may do with the Western attempt to banish that apparent illogicality. The ability to retain a sense of one's traditional utterances whilst considering their problems or their benefits is the task of critical ontology. It is insufficient to simply rely on straightforward statements originating from traditional discourse; one must also peer beyond them to see how snugly they may sit with another (colonising) set of beliefs. These latter philosophies often run counter to what was intended in the traditional ones. Yet, there are some essential messages within traditional discourses that one should start with, particularly those that represent the self and the world as one. Despite the various approaches that indigenous peoples take to their knowledge, they accept that humans are inseparable from all that exists, a view which is conceptually at odds with those forms of knowledge that tend to fragment things from each other. Some aspects of disconnection emphasise, for instance, that the knowledge and its creation occur externally to that deeply embedded relationship of the self with the world. The human mind, its thoughts and its depictions of the world are completely one with the processes of nature and the cosmos. Thus, fragmentation is quite alien to indigenous experiences of the world (Kincheloe, 2011). According to Ahenakew et al. (2014), Latin American indigenous narratives that highlight the non-human world assume that interconnectedness and difference co-exist. However, at some point – those authors indicate a "cataclysm" (p.224) – humanity started to delude itself that forms were static. Resembling in some ways Heidegger's warnings on Western humanity's inability to distinguish beings and Being, these creation narratives unearth a more authentic way of thinking in the form of a critique and casting one's mind back to a time when things were apprehended in terms of how they are linked. This forgetting of various forms and the persistent flux of the things led to some catastrophic social events, where things in the world started to deceive themselves that they were distinctly themselves. Entities were separated from each other in their frozen forms. The antidote to this problem exists in the conversations that can take place between those (humans and non-humans) who are aware that authentic notions of forms once prevailed. Ahenakew et al. continue by exposing the political implications of such stories. 'Self-determination', they cite, is a widely acknowledged goal of indigenous peoples, but it is rendered far from straightforward when thought about in light of its ontology, which throws into doubt the notion of 'self' as complete and self-governing, and 'determination' as resulting in totalised existence.

The fact of the indigenous self's interconnection with the world highlights some additional difficulties of rational language in conveying the depth of that relationship. We are reminded, yet again, of Kincheloe's insistence on viewing our representations carefully. Gillett (2009), drawing on Heidegger's propositions around facticity, argues that the indigenous self is confronted by the world and all its possibilities. He or she is an active participant in the totality of the world. For indigenous metaphysics, this 'thrownness' assumes further importance because the human world is *materially* connected to all other things in the world through genealogical 'oneness'. 'Material', though, cannot cater for what is really meant by the shared connection with the world; it may approximate the indigenous belief that there is an expressible 'oneness' to the world, but it diverges from the permanent, highly positive properties that can be identified through science (Mika, 2015a). Similarly, a term such as *genetic* is a poor word to deal with the complexity of this arrangement, although it may be used for the moment to adumbrate that there is a shared essence between the self and the world. In relation to that term, Western science has tended to emphasise the importance of physical tissue to discuss one's genetic phenomena, but indigenous worldedness would counter that the deep relationship between self and world is only available through speculative thinking, or thought that privileges uncertainty, not through empirical study (Mika, 2015d). Indigenous thought, contrary to Western science, places a great deal of emphasis on the *collapsed* nature of things, which may be expressed as genealogical links between one entity and all others. As associations that are dependent on each other, the links are active and always existent, reaching up from the totality of the world and ensuring that all things – again, visible and imperceptible – are one. They are not immutable, however; an indigenous worldedness instead suggests that they are convergent on, but inseparable from, the world, in the sense that they continuously maintain the sum of all things.

Several indigenous languages display the oneness of all things in a single term, and there is little distance if any between the self, as an interrelated entity with other things, and the oneness innate to that term. Sometimes, especially where colonisation is evident, these terms have to be excavated in order for that holistic sheen to be recovered, but in many indigenous groups the possibility still exists for both a recovery and a reaffirmation of that deeper texture. The Maori term *Papatuanuku*, for instance, may be grasped either as a nice, neat and orderly 'Mother Earth', capable of being conveyed economically, or it can be more disruptive than that (Mika, 2016b). It can assume force even within written text. The latter prospect is the more difficult to deal with because it asks the indigenous self to suspend the field of expectation that academic language draws and relies on, but it sits easier with indigenous notions of time and the thoroughgoing unity that is often said to exist between things in the world. Due to language's infusion with the voice of all things in the world, a statement of fact is further complicated with the possibility that the utterance is not just a hollow set of words that carry the internal wishes of the self. Language is imbued with life force, and whilst the terminology itself is inadequate – a shell for something much greater than it can contain, and one that indigenous writers will undoubtedly recognise as reductionist – the possibility that a set of words contains to it something highly influential, imperceptible and undeclared, is of huge consequence to indigenous thought. An utterance such as "The mountain and I are one", in that vein, is 'worlded' in itself, not simply in a way that relates to intellectual or social construction but essentially through the world's drive within the words. Statements therefore contain to them the activity of things in the world. Admittedly, I may indeed have intended to refer to the mountain and myself; however, within those very words and inside that intention lies the hidden "clear overplus of meaning" (Otto, 1958, p.5) that cannot be satisfactorily accounted for by the indigenous self.

It is therefore unsurprising that indigenous thought privileges the animate character of the non-human world. Where the human self's perception is privileged in relation to other things in Euro-Western philosophy, indigenous thought places the human and the non-human on equal footing and attributes a mysterious activity to the external world (Cajete, 2004; Klapproth, 2004; Miller, 2009). Fixico (2003) discusses that the physical world is inseparable from the supernatural, and cites the experiences of Black Elk, of the Oglalas. What the latter witnessed surpassed his knowledge and demonstrated the delicate relationship between one's human agency and the world in its totality. Black Elk recounted a vision, in which he witnessed "the spirit" (Fixico, 2003, p.4) that gave shape to everything in the world. This spirit simultaneously imbued all those things, and to him it was "holy". But the 'holy' that Black Elk recalls is not to be reduced to something manageable or attributable to humans. According to Otto (1958), its meaning has become nothing more than signalling that something is perfect – a nuance that he argues is detrimental to its primordial and mysterious texture. Otto is a useful source for considering mystery here because, as an ardent devotee to notions of the sublime and its reclamation in ancient and modern thought, he advances on the field of modernity and speculates on the different forms mystery previously took and may assume in current contexts all at the same time. That mainly religious sense that 'holy' has taken on, according to Otto, does not do justice to its original intention. Initially, he avows, it related much more personally to the limitations of knowledge that can be had about a thing. Black Elk, and indigenous metaphysics of holism more generally, similarly appear to acknowledge that what is referenced through the senses cannot account for the full nature of the phenomenon. One's emotional experience can provide some insight into it, but although Black Elk may well have perceived more than he could describe, he does not take the more outrageous step of suggesting that he himself is immutable throughout the vision. He is altered by the experience in ways he cannot perceive; the 'sacred hoop' was relevant to him and claimed him – not as a detached, knowing bystander but as an immediate participant. Of equal importance, the unknowability of a thing in a colonial setting must be taken into account, alongside the precolonial inheritance of the entities engaging in the vision. All these things' immersion in the full history of Black Elk (as just one participant) and his lived experience, throws the entire vision into a realm of incomprehensibility. Fundamentally, Black Elk himself is materially changed by (and through) the vision and its characters. Fixico also notes that "[i]t is acceptance of a fact that a relationship exists between a tangible item like a mountain and a dream" (p.3). He makes a distinction between one thing and another, although by announcing that there is a relationship between them he may well be reciprocating their respective characteristics between them as well. Duran and Duran (1995), however, add that intangible templates (such as attitudes, habits and so on) are material; they occupy space in the world as a whole. Intangible phenomena here are endowed with power and place as much as those of the visible, concrete world, and so ideas, habits, aspects of well-being, disease and so on are formed as both entities and activity. Where Foucault argues that discourses are material insofar as they are influential at the human level (Mika & Stewart, 2015), an indigenous metaphysics after Duran ascribes their own life force to them. Discourses may in fact have always existed but a dominant practice amongst the human world could have made them more pronounced, bringing them to a point of concern. Discourses from this mysterious perspective fill the world and are amalgamated with its tangible entities.

Well-being through worldedness

The potential for discourses, ideas and dominant worldviews to occupy the world as material entities has direct and unnerving consequences, from the viewpoint of indigenous metaphysics, for notions of well-being and education *at the same time*. Many propositions about health and well-being (and indeed education) in indigenous literature argue for a holistic view (see Duran & Duran, 1995; Durie, 1994; Smith, 2016); thus, common ways of describing the nature of a thing, for instance, will have an influence on one's health. Put most simply, indigenous writers insist that the human self is composed of spiritual as well as physical, emotional and mental aspects. For the person to be in a state of good health, he or she must have all of these elements in balance. Alongside having access to appropriate food resources, being free from environmental pollutants and so on – all of which are commonly recognised as necessary in mainstream health policy – one must be able to resonate properly with one's place, perceive other things in the world as if they are all connected and living, acknowledge and name the self as one animate entity among many others with essentially no separation from them, and label a concept along holistic lines. Furthermore, the indigenous body is moulded according to how the self is restricted or free to represent and make an utterance. Those common approaches and processes become relations of the indigenous self that he or she must deal with as much as any ceremonial or traditional being. Duran and Duran (1995) thus relate that a habitual belief or practice – they cite alcoholism as one example – is a spiritual entity and must be engaged with in a different manner than if it were simply a medical condition. Illnesses are beings and become materially part of the person's essence; as Mika and Stewart (2015) propose after Duran and Duran, entities give rise to trauma which will constitute the self. Duran and Duran's argument may be broadened to include instances where the positing of a practice or concept is likewise entitised, becomes material and impacts the body of the indigenous self. The belief that all things are intertwined, one, interconnected and animate, for instance, is an entity. Metaphysical thought is hence a material substance that influences subsequent practice, selfhood and well-being. *How* one apprehends the world is crucial for one's continued health.

The first principles that dictate how the indigenous self proposes what education is, therefore, are of utmost importance, and the critical question then arises: Is education human-centred, or is it derived from the external world, with the self merely one element in the process? In a major sense, for indigenous meta-physics education can be viewed as the very representation of how something is to appear, or what form it may take. This 'creature' of education evolves from a deeply originary orientation to things in the world; it must then ask for unrivalled attention from the indigenous critic, because whatever is proposed as most fundamental will then dispense itself into how one teaches, learns, and represents an object in writing and in speech – all of which themselves take on entitial form. The possibility that these more familiar practices in the classroom, as offspring of that metaphysical entity, have always already existed incidentally raises a further issue of whether time is similarly material. Basso (1996), reflect-ing on the relevance of Bakhtin's chronotope for Apache explanations for time and space, identifies that humanity, time and space converge on the earth. In that act, stories that are told are acknowledged as always having force. Basso cites Bakhtin: "time takes on flesh and becomes visible . . . likewise, space becomes charged and responsive to the movement of time and history" (p.62). Time and space merge: "[t]he Apache landscape is full of named locations where time and space have fused and where, through the agency of historical tales, their inter-section is "made visible for human contemplation". Time and space, far from being mere geometric phenomena, are one's ancestors, cohabit the world with other entities, and call to be represented in that light.

Summary

To say something is indeed to say a thing in a worlded philosophy, and as we have seen a thing is constituted by the world. There is hence a very strong ethical dimension to what may best be described as 'uttering an entity as a worlded entity' in educational terms. That the world can be affected by what the self proclaims about it is common to many indigenous groups, and the ways in which settler governments have required the indigenous self to frame the world often proves problematic. While one commonly sees social issues being framed as political and ethical ones in indigenous literature and activist works, less frequently will the philosophical be seen as at once thoroughly political. The philosophical gravitas of indigenous presentational thinking needs to be considered as relevant in terms of power. In other words, the act of *saying* her-alds something profoundly different for the indigenous self in social realms and political institutions. Whitt et al. (2001) thus highlight the consequences of using language and knowledge that is engraved with the world for legal disputes; Mika (2007) theorises that cross-examination in legal proceedings constrains the full, true disclosure of things in the world because it preordains what language is to be used as a response; and Cajete (1994) talks of language as a 'breath' that is linked to entities and that has profound implications for education, the closest translation for which in Tewa traditions is *"Hah oh'* or 'breathe in" (p.34). What one proposes the world to be is therefore linked intimately with one's ability to draw life from the external world.

Indigenous writers Ahenakew et al. (2014) referred in their article to a communication of an indigenous elder and her daughter. The authors asked the latter two who should be cited as the originator of that communication. In a response that diverges thoroughly from modern conventions of academia, the elder and her daughter reminded the authors that "[t]his knowledge was passed down from teachers including specific plants and mountains" (p.227): it was not of human origin. The question then arose as to whether a self-conscious philosophy of education was *ipso facto* necessary in a global education incentive that had been started by a Quechua community, given that priority of things in the world attributed to education. They are not precluding the process of human-mediated thinking here, and, as I have suggested, a step in the direction of world-located, world-constituted speculation would ask the thinker to reflect on the fact that their speculation was made possible by the world in the first instance. There could hence be a strong metaphilosophical aspect to indigenous thought, because the individual is made to theorise about thinking *whilst* making some statements about the influence of the world, seen and unseen, on both those phases of philosophising.

According to Illich (1971) and Oliver (1998), education has tended to become equivalent with schooling or contingent on what occurs in the classroom. This strict and reductive approach is the converse of a holistic mode of education that can be proposed through an indigenous worldedness. Whilst schooling is a rendition of education and is certainly an element of the greater process that occurs for indigenous peoples, it neglects the possibility of the world and the individual amounting to one. With things' active and continuous construction of the self, indigenous concern emphasises the consequences that arise in education as an activity that allows for some agency of the self but also acknowledges and represent the totality of the world in any expression. This latter call to attention should take place within the familiar concepts of one's own cultural group. It is to a specific Maori example of worldedness through the educational term *Ako*, and its infusion throughout specific Maori terms, that I now turn.

References

Abrams, D. (1996) *The Spell of the Sensuous*. New York, NY: Vintage Books.

Ahenakew, C., Andreotti, V., Cooper, G., et al. (2014) 'Beyond Epistemic Provincialism: De-Provincializing Indigenous Resistance', *AlterNative* 10(3): 216–31.

Basso, K. (1996) *Wisdom Sits in Places: Landscape and Language among the Western Apache*. Albuquerque, NM: University of New Mexico Press.

Blaut, J. (1993) *The Coloniser's Model of the World: Geographical Diffusionism and Eurocentric History*. New York, NY: Guilford Press.

Cajete, G. (1994) *Look to the Mountain: An Ecology of Indigenous Education*. Durango, CO: Kivakí Press.

Cajete, G. (2000) *Native Science: Natural Laws of Interdependence*. Santa Fe, NM: Clear Light Publishers.

Cajete, G. (2004) 'Philosophy of Native Science', pp. 45–57 in A. Waters (ed) *American Indian Thought: Philosophical Essays*. Oxford, UK: Blackwell.

Calderon, D. (2008) *Indigenous Metaphysics: Challenging Western Knowledge Organization in Social Studies Curriculum*. Doctoral dissertation, The University of California, Los Angeles.

Callicott, L. B. (1997) *Earth's Insights: A Multicultural Survey of Ecological Ethics from the Mediterranean Basin to the Australian Outback*. Los Angeles, CA: University of California Press.

Cooper, G. (2012) 'Kaupapa Māori Research: Epistemic Wilderness as Freedom?', *New Zealand Journal of Education Studies* 47(2): 64–73.

Cordova, V. (2007) *How It Is: The Native American Philosophy of V.F. Cordova*. Tucson, AZ: University of Arizona Press.

Deloria Jnr, V. (2001) 'American Indian Metaphysics', pp. 1–6 in V. Deloria Jnr and D. Wildcat (eds) *Power and Place: Indian Education in America*. Golden, CO: Fulcrum Resources.

Deloria Jnr, V. and Wilkins, D. (2012) *The Metaphysics of Modern Existence*. Golden, CO: Fulcrum Publishing.

Duran, E. and Duran, B. (1995) *Native American Postcolonial Psychology*. Albany, NY: State University of New York Press.

Durie, M. (1994) *Whaiora: Māori Health Development*. Auckland, New Zealand: Oxford University Press.

Fixico, D. (2003) *The American Indian Mind in a Linear World*. New York, NY: Routledge.

Foucault, M. (1984) *The Foucault Reader*. New York, NY: Panthcon Books.

Gillett, G. (2009) 'Indigenous Knowledges: Circumspection, Metaphysics, and Scientific Ontologies', *SITES* 6(1): 1–19.

Huhndorf, S. (2001) *Going Native: Indians in the American Cultural Imagination*. London, UK: Cornell University Press.

Illich, I. (1971) *Deschooling Society*. London, UK: Calder & Boyars.

Kincheloe, J. (2011) 'Critical Ontology and Indigenous Ways of Being', pp. 333–49 in K. Hayes, S. Steinberg and K. Tobin (eds) *Key Works in Critical Pedagogy*. Rotterdam: Sense Publishers.

Klapproth, D. (2004) *Narrative as Social Practice: Anglo-Western and Australian Aboriginal Oral Traditions*. New York, NY: Mouton de Gruyter.

Loomba, A. (2015) *Colonialism/Postcolonialism*, 3rd edn. New York, NY: Routledge.

Loutzenhiser, M. (2008) *The Role of the Indigenous African Psyche in the Evolution of Human Consciousness*. New York, NY: iUniverse Inc.

Mander, J. (1992) *In the Absence of the Sacred: The Failure of Technology and the Survival of Indian Nations*. San Francisco, CA: Sierra Club Books.

Marsden, M. (2003) *The Woven Universe: Selected Writings of Rev. Māori Marsden*. Otaki, New Zealand: Estate of Rev. Māori Marsden.

Mika, C. (2007) 'The Utterance, the Body and the Law: Seeking an Approach to Concretizing the Sacredness of Maori Language', *SITES* 4(2): 181–205.

Mika, C. (2012) 'Overcoming "Being" in Favour of Knowledge: The Fixing Effect of "Mātauranga"', *Educational Philosophy and Theory* 44(10): 1080–92.

Mika, C. (2013a) *Reclaiming Mystery: A Māori Philosophy of Being, in Light of Novalis' Ontology*. Unpublished PhD dissertation, University of Waikato.

Mika, C. (2013b) 'Western "Sentences that Push" as an Indigenous Method for Thinking', pp. 23–6 in A. Engels-Schwarzpaul and M. Peters (eds) *Of Other Thoughts: Non-Traditional Ways to the Doctorate. A Guidebook for Candidates and Supervisors*. Rotterdam, The Netherlands: Sense.

Mika, C. (2014a) 'The Enowning of Thought and Whakapapa: Heidegger's Fourfold', *Review of Contemporary Philosophy* 13: 48–60.

Mika, C. (2014b) 'Maori Thinking with a Dead White Male: Philosophizing in the Realm of Novalis', *Knowledge Cultures* 2(1): 23–39.

Mika, C. (2015a) 'The Co-Existence of Self and Thing through "Ira": A Māori Phenomenology', *Journal of Aesthetics and Phenomenology* 2(1): 93–112.

Mika, C. (2015b) 'Counter-Colonial and Philosophical Claims: An Indigenous Observation of Western Philosophy', *Educational Philosophy and Theory*: 1–7.

Mika, C. (2015c) 'Thereness: Implications for Heidegger's "Presence" for Māori', *AlterNative* 11(1): 3 13.

Mika, C. (2015d) 'The Thing's Revelation: Māori Philosophical Research', *Waikato Journal of Education* 20(2): 61–68.

Mika, C. (2016a) 'The Ontological and Active Possibilities of Papatūānuku: To Nurture or Enframe?', *Knowledge Cultures* 4(3): 58–71.

Mika, C. (2016b) ' "Papatūānuku/Papa": Some Thoughts on the Oppositional Grounds of the Doctoral Experience', *Knowledge Cultures* 4(1): 43–55.

Mika, C. (2016c) 'Worlded Object and Its Presentation: A Māori Philosophy of Language', *AlterNative* 12(2): 165–76.

Mika, C. and Southey, K. (2016) 'Exploring Whakaaro: A Way of Responsive Thinking in Maori Research', *Educational Philosophy and Theory*.

Mika, C. and Stewart, G. (2015) 'Maori in the Kingdom of the Gaze: Subjects or Critics?', *Educational Philosophy and Theory*: 1–13.

Mika, C. and Tiakiwai, S. (2016) 'Tawhiao's Unstated Heteroglossia: Conversations with Bakhtin', *Educational Philosophy and Theory*.

Miller, B. (2009) 'Sami Shamanism Today: The Spirit Helper in Sami Epistemology', pp. 476–84 in P. Bennett (ed) *Capetown 2007: Journeys, Encounters: Clinical, Communal, Cultural*. Einsieldeln, Switzerland: Daimon Verlag.

Mosha, S. (2000) *The Heartbeat of Indigenous Africa: A Study of the Chagga Educational System*. London, UK: Garland Publishing Inc.

Novalis. (2005) *The Novices of Sais*. New York, NY: Archipelago Books.

O'Connor, T. (2007) *Governing Bodies: A Māori Healing Tradition in a Bicultural State*. Unpublished doctoral dissertation, The University of Auckland, New Zealand.

Oliver, R. (1998) 'The Ideological Reduction of Education', *Educational Philosophy and Theory* 30(3): 299–302.

Otto, R. (1958) *The Idea of the Holy: An Inquiry into the Non-Rational Factor in the Idea of the Divine and Its Relation to the Rational*, 2nd edn. New York, NY: Oxford University Press.

Pihama, L. (2001) *Tihei Mauri Ora: Honouring Our Voices: Mana Wahine as a Kaupapa Māori Theoretical Framework*. Unpublished doctoral dissertation, The University of Auckland, New Zealand.

Pihama, L., Smith, K., Taki, M., et al. (2004) *Literature Review on Kaupapa Maori and Maori Education Pedagogy*. ITP New Zealand, The International Research Institute for Maori and Indigenous Education.

Raerino, N. (1999) *"Pure" and "Karakia" as a Window to Maori Epistemology: Koi Rō Pure Me Karakia E Oke Ana*. Unpublished masters' thesis, The University of Auckland.

Royal, T. (2005) 'Exploring Indigenous Knowledge', in *The Indigenous Knowledges Conference – Reconciling Academic Priorities with Indigenous Realities*. Wellington, New Zealand: Victoria University.

Sardar, Z., Nandy, A. and Davies, M. (1993) *Barbaric Others: A Manifesto on Western Racism.* Colorado, CO: Pluto Press.

Senghor, L. (2010) 'Negritude: A Humanism of the Twentieth Century', pp. 477–83 in R. Grinker, S. Lubkemann and C. Steiner (eds) *Perspectives on Africa: A Reader in Culture, History, and Representation.* Malden, MA: Wiley-Blackwell.

Sharrad, P. (2003) *Circling the Void: Albert Wendt and Pacific Literature.* Manchester, UK: Manchester University Press.

Smith, C. (2007) 'Cultures of Collecting', pp. 65–74 in M. Bargh (ed) *Resistance: An Indigenous Response to Neoliberalism.* Wellington, NZ: Huia.

Smith, J. (2016) *Australia's Rural, Remote and Indigenous Health.* Chatswood, Australia: Elsevier.

Smith, L. (1999) *Decolonizing Methodologies: Research and Indigenous Peoples.* London, UK: Zed Books.

Tau, T. (2001) 'The Death of Knowledge: Ghosts on the Plains', *New Zealand Journal of History* 35(2): 131–52.

Whitt, L., Roberts, M., Norman, W., et al. (2001) 'Belonging to Land: Indigenous Knowledge Systems and the Natural World', *Oklahoma City University Law Review* 26: 701–43.

Wildcat, D. (2001) 'Indigenizing Education: Playing to Our Strengths', pp. 7–20 in V. Deloria Jnr and D. Wildcat (eds) *Power and Place: Indian Education in America.* Golden, CO: Fulcrum Publishers.

Wiredu, K. (1998) 'Toward Decolonizing African Philosophy and Religion', *African Studies Quarterly* 1(4): 17–46.

Chapter 3

Ako

A Maori example of worldedness

Although I am not chiefly concerned with how worldedness influences peda-gogy, I do indicate here that the first principles reflecting an indigenous world-view, outlined in Chapter 2, have consequences for both how one teaches and learns, and for those discussions that take place around those practices. A con-scious effort to articulate the tensions between mainstream schooling and Maori metaphysical approaches was made in 1982 by Maori scholar, Rangimarie Rose Pere, who penned the groundbreaking book *Ako*. The first of its kind, it theo-rised that teaching and learning (which is how the Maori term *Ako* is most commonly defined) must account for the external world. Pere moves through some of the abstract concepts that steer Maori thought *from the outside* and retains within her work the deep idea that the human self is indebted to the spiritual and physical world for thought, language and perception. In a Maori worldview, 'Ako' therefore is enacted through a continual inclination of one thing towards all others. This chapter lays out a specifically Maori speculation on that infinite, moving orientation between things and the ways in which the self is involved in that activity. By 'orientation' I mean that there is an activity that takes place between the self and the world, predicated on a predisposi-tion toward and between all things; this idea of motion rejects one that privi-leges physical movement within three dimensions and instead engages with the imperceptible potential of all things. For Maori, there is a complexity attached to this suggestion because 'orientation' means the coalescence of all things in the world within just one object or idea (Mika, 2016c). In other words, if I am speculating on an object, I am actually engaging with the totality of all things even if they do not announce themselves to me. Ako is a prime example of worldedness; it is most broadly the act of education through constitution by the outside world, and it identifies with the possibility that the Maori self is free to perceive an object as if it is holistically comprised of all others and as if it is connected to, and constitutive of, the self.

Crucial to Ako is how the self is related to all things. In the metaphysics we are exploring, language contains to it the full nature of the world, arranged through the self-organisation of Papatuanuku, which is commonly known as Mother Earth but could also be considered primordial Being (Mika, 2016a;

2016b). Teaching and learning are practices that retain the totality of the living world – visible and imperceptible; through an interpretive reading of the world as an interrelating, diffusive phenomenon, learning and teaching are exercises that involve the self as constructed by, and constructive of, things in the world. Importantly, statements *about* Ako relate to this materially affective nature of Ako as well, where expressing an idea about a thing generally is tempered with the notion of vulnerability that Ako depicts (Thrupp & Mika, 2012). Seen in this light, Ako, whilst certainly capable of pertaining to teaching and learning within a classroom context, refers to education in a much broader way. As we shall see, Ako is thus identified through the following features: one is constructed by the whole of the activity and nature of things in the world; statements about a thing are, in fact, constituted by the totality of things and are hence characterised by uncertainty; and making propositions about Ako is itself a precarious act as those utterances are rendered opaque because of the fullness of the world within them.

Ako: an introduction

Ako has proliferated in Maori educational literature as a discourse that attempts to encompass a specifically Maori concept of teaching and learning. Because it is so widely reported on, there are numerous interpretations of how it can be resorted to within different classroom contexts. In its most frequent use, though, Ako can be said to commonly refer to the reciprocal nature of teaching and learning, where both acts take place simultaneously (Bishop & Glynn, 1999). In this practice of Ako, the teacher is said to be a learner and the learner is the teacher. Government policy, such as that disseminated by the Ministry of Education, sums it up in the following way:

> The concept of ako describes a teaching and learning relationship, where the educator is also learning from the student and where educators' practices are informed by the latest research and are both deliberate and reflective. Ako is grounded in the principle of reciprocity and also recognises that the learner and whānau cannot be separated.
>
> (Ministry of Education, 2009, p.20)

Serving as the backdrop to this human activity are certain Maori concepts such as *whakapapa* (genealogy), *wairua* (spirit) and *manaakitanga* (hospitality). One's connection to another person, witnessed through the display of these terms, can vary the degree to which one can learn or teach: the role of self-esteem in the relationship between learner and teacher and hence to knowledge, the openness of the classroom as a whole to the dissemination of knowledge and thinking, and the point at which one is related to the Other – teacher or learner – are all hugely important in the educational process for Maori. Some of these elements may be said to exist across all educational settings, but it is perhaps the aspect of 'connection' that contrasts Ako with general practice in schools because what are often taken to be ideas are, in fact, material, recitable (in the sense of genealogical) links. Ako emphasises that the self and other are one, and because of that collapse of the world with the learner or teacher, knowledge, thought and language are emphasised as relations (*whanaunga*).

Thrupp and Mika (2012), however, expand further on the ontological dimension to the term and its concept through its other meanings. The Williams Dictionary (1921) gives the following meanings of *Ako*:

(1) To learn, teach, instruct, advise
(2) Split, have a tendency to split
(3) Move, stir.

As Thrupp and Mika note, these terms are not commensurable for common sense approaches to language and meaning. It is not unusual, though, for terms in the Maori language to incorporate these apparently disparate ideas. *Whenua*, which is commonly taken to mean 'land', for instance, also means 'afterbirth', and asks that one resist thinking of them as two entirely different meanings. When thought of with an irrational twist, *afterbirth* corresponds with the notion that whenua (land) gives rise to, sustains and claims its entities. This disruptive, uneven influence of whenua – which is really one participant of many in the world – can be seen in Greenwood and Wilson's (2006) suggestion that "the land surrounding us/proclaims its wonder" (p.89). Similarly, Ako for the writer about it displays its hidden relationship with mystery and interconnectedness through its incongruent meanings. Like whenua, it needs to be encountered through a view of the thinking self as a participant in a worldedness that cannot be accounted for solely by a linguistic study of language, which tends to be empirical (Fromkin et al., 2000). Unsurprisingly for the Maori theorist, Ako is not unrelated to whenua; both have the same capacity of subsuming the self within a phenomenon that cannot be adequately explained by its discrete components.

With that underlying sense in mind – and emphasising that this ontology is not knowable but may be speculated about – Thrupp and Mika theorise about the possibilities of the homonym "have a tendency to split" in order to explicate something about Ako that transcends simply 'teach and learn'. They suggest that it indicates more than simply a physical fragmentation and that it accentuates one's vulnerability in the face of things in the world. Ako insists that the self is somewhat 'chipped away at' by other phenomena. In relation to one's emotional state, Thrupp and Mika then consider the nature of the movement that underpins Ako. The principle of Ako does indeed involve the human self but no more than any other entity in the world. But Ako with reference to humans must acknowledge that one is only moved or stirred as a result of the external world. One is provoked, moved on, stirred up by things in the world. Ako is thus not just a process of teaching and learning through the human realm;

education for Maori is instead necessarily an instruction from the outside world which the human self (teacher or learner, for instance) can mediate but which originates prior to the teacher or learner. Indeed, teaching and learning may not involve a human teacher – although they may, occasionally. Moreover, that the entire perceptive capacity of the human self derives from the unknowable workings of the external world suggests there is an emotional aspect to learning. A human learner is premised on all things, and one's response accords with that fundamental lack of control with a sense of mystery as a result. It would seem that the world is meant to be held in mind as an essentially mysterious entity, one that forms the self but is similarly integrated with all other things and hence, at times, perceptible. The worlded self (and here I address education in its more conventional vein), in order to authentically learn something, must be in awe of it. He or she must be essentially mystified by the fact that it simultaneously constitutes the self and yet appears outside of the self; the learner must be thoroughly rapt with the possibility that an object is retaining an element of the unseen to itself; and he or she even needs to forego learning about the object and instead involve him- or herself with the deep uncertainty that comes from a lack of knowledge about it, brought about because of the thing's self-retention and its constitution of the learner.

Some counter-colonial thoughts and contexts

Ako and 'world'

At this point, it is useful to reiterate what 'world' can refer to, this time in a more determinedly Maori sense. The most commonly used Maori word for world is *Ao*. Despite its diminutive form, it holds in its active store the totality of all things. Ao, which I frequently have in mind whilst I write *world*, defies a thorough explanation but can be summarised as the world's 'coming-to-bear' on the human self, allowing some form of understanding (Royal, 2008) and an ability to reflect on aspects of existence. This description of the world's influence does not privilege the world's seen aspect, and implicit here is a refusal to reduce its scope to whatever is tangible. World does indeed represent itself to humanity, but as we shall see in this chapter it does so from outside of the self's perception as well as offering itself up for direct experience. World is the expression of all things in one entity; within any one entity, the world reorganises itself (and hence all other things) so that the one entity we speak of is continuously reconstituting itself. A 'thing' from a Maori perspective can be conceived of as 'world' because, although it presents itself as individual, it is composed of all other things in the world. 'Things', in turn, may be beings, ideas, histories and experiences. Royal gives the example of a *rākau* (tree). Echoing Kant, he states that the word *rākau* comes to mind, not the actual rākau, and that this is a form of, as he calls it, *mātauranga* (knowledge). Whilst I agree that most rational philosophical conventions would disdain the decidedly mystical proposition that a tree has manifested in one's mind in its totality, a Maori notion of a thing does not readily distinguish between the conceptual shell of a thing and its full materiality (Mika, 2015d; Mika & Tiakiwai, 2016). Any one dimension is comprised of coexisting ones, with the result that one thing is constituted by the presence but invisibility of all others. There is a complicated issue of mystery at stake here which may well coincide with irrational or mystical thinking. This conception of a thing and its world *may* be evidence of what Heidegger (1962) would drily describe as a problem relating to method, but Maori (and indigenous) writers generally are not unfamiliar with a kind of worlding that curbs creative speculation (see, for instance, Smith, 2003). Attempts to get at a ground that does not resemble a rational one and that allows beings to show up, as Heidegger continues, are not sustainable through epistemic certainty but rather through meditative thinking. Such is an alternative world of ontological thinking, in which things are allowed to show up – for Maori, even in one entity. Ao, together with Ako, is hence a colonial issue.

The restricted notion of Ao, however, affords us with the capacity to speculate on an alternative world. For Maori, the suggestion that an entity stands alone and that it is not materially composed of the fullness of all other entities is quite possibly one of the most implausible that colonisation forces on indigenous peoples. Similarly, the idea that a world is an opening up of Being in a Heideggerian sense but that this disclosure is not achieved through the total organisation of all things, is untenable. Speculating on the disclosure of the world, even on the prospect that the world comprises entities that are able to be represented as if solitary, can be overwhelming for the self; hence, the self is engulfed by the possibilities these colonizing propositions provide. In colonisation, then, there lies the potential for a sharp intake of the unknown. With Ako, a teaching and learning exercise could include this very sort of speculation – of being constructed by the world whilst, paradoxically, making representations of it. This approach to Ako sits well with the dual noun/verb properties of the word *Ao*, in which the entire plethora of phenomena reverberate within any one thing. Equally, whoever is making proclamations about the world is encouraged to consider the possibility that they are not exercising some sort of thoroughgoing autonomy; the Maori scholar, thinking about an idea, is never able to fully grasp it because it is also influential on, and constructive of, him or her.

Mystery and mysticism

In much indigenous literature in the 1990s, there arose a great deal of resistance to the New Age movement, with its intrusion into indigenous spiritual philosophy. Not only was an indigenous worldedness feasible as far as its acolytes were concerned; it was *desirable*. Linda Smith (1999) observes that indigenous peoples frequently fall afoul of the ways in which the spiritual packaging would express indigenous metaphysics. She is suspicious of "the mystical, misty-eyed discourse that is sometimes employed by indigenous people to describe our relations with the land and the universe" (p.12). With that warning in mind, indigenous scholars are encouraged to consider the language they use to describe other dimensions that are taken to be active in the world. Exactly how we talk about other realms, whilst avoiding accusations of mysticism, raises a difficult issue indeed. I agree with Smith to a certain extent but am interested in how such talk became off-limits to begin with. It may be that the so-called spiritual utterances she refers to tend to be automatically relegated to a transcendent realm without any anchoring, even though we never intended them to be put there. Thus, 'Mother Earth', expressed in that way, is too free-floating and nebulous. The relegating agent in this instance is likely to be the Enlightenment, which deems "that which does not reduce to numbers, and ultimately to the one, becomes illusion; modern positivism writes it off as literature" (Adorno & Horkheimer, 1997, p.7). Alternatively, it is a problem of language; expressed in English as 'Mother Earth', the expansive phenomenon that underpins all things in the world simply sounds trite. Whether this problem rests in the denotative or connotative aspect of language is uncertain. I discuss these challenges posed by language in greater depth in the following chapters.

But there are several aspects of indigenous philosophy that simply cannot avoid the so-called supernatural realm. (Again, incidentally, we are no better off with the word 'supernatural' than if we continued to talk of 'mysticism'). The indigenous philosopher should therefore not try to skirt around some of the key beliefs that appear to coincide with spiritual belief – such as the idea that supposedly inanimate elements are living, for instance – otherwise, the result will accord too neatly with the 'positivism' that Adorno and Horkheimer identify. At this point, it suffices to say that there seems to be a very fine line between a metaphysics of worldedness from a Maori perspective, and mysticism from a more orthodox philosophical one. Some renowned individual philosophers have been accused of moving too far away from convention, too, in their attempts to articulate an unpositivistic philosophy. Heidegger's later work, for instance, has been accused of being overly mystical (Plebuch, 2010). Quite what is meant by *mysticism*, though, is unclear, and although I acknowledge that it is never adequate just to make a spiritually inclined assertion and leave the topic there, it is not necessarily unphilosophical to theorise about what that same utterance might mean in an everyday context. Moreover, whether this position continued to be mystical or not becomes irrelevant; our thinking *may* be mystical, even so-called primitive, but our sustained reflection on unseen connections between things in the world is an ethical call that cannot be discouraged by pejorative terminology.

Ako is concerned with these mystical propositions about the concrete phenomenon, including the self. That Ako is mystically oriented yet concrete suggests that another word is needed to describe the nature of an object or idea through Maori philosophy, however. *Mystery* and its various permutations could be workable. In the Maori language, one term that equates with the sense of mystery is *huna*, which simply means 'hidden'. Here, we can think of 'mystery' in its conventional way – engaging with an astonishment at the unknowable. Otto (1958) describes one of its types as "Mysterium tremendum", which is broken down into "awefulness", "overpoweringness" and "energy" (p.5), which all herald a feeling of uncertainty and vulnerability. His categories are useful to keep in mind when we are thinking about the teaching and learning process, or the self's implication by the world. With Ako's tendency to emphasise the self's construction by things in the world, the self is indeed overpowered by the vast, active extent of all entities. Not only is this susceptibility perceivable, however; it is also beyond experience, with the self being continually constituted whilst not feeling particularly mysterious at all. Speculating on that phenomenon of constant flux, on the other hand, is particularly evocative of mystery. Learning is associated with this process, and with that in mind we would need to ensure that indigenous processes of education take into account the complex and mysterious element of things in the world. Participating in "a sacred realm (of both visible and invisible realities) that is both elusive and tangible and where multiplicity and uncertainty are natural givens" (Andreotti et al., 2011, p.46) is central to the teaching and learning process, and such an indigenous worldview, entrenched in learning, results in "intellectual freedom", with an "ontological responsibility". The latter of these two elements is interesting for its ethical dimension and implies that there is an appropriate mode of world representation. Placed within a much more expansive notion of ontology than merely positioned as an epistemological exercise, Ako concerns itself less "with a self-conscious situation of learning and teaching" (Mika, 2013a, p.243) and instead is interpreted as highlighting one's uncertainty within the flux of the world and its collapse with the self. I suggest that the ontology that Andreotti et al. speak of is independent of teaching and learning but is, at the same time, completely linked with those exercises when they do take place.

Ako is one term of many that privileges an unknown perspective of an object. Yet Ako is dual-natured; we have seen that it is underpinned by reciprocity, but I am arguing that its mutuality involves the external and internal worlds. Thus, as Novalis would have it, we are expected to teach nature (Schrock, 2006). Yet even here the direct constitution of the world by the self is itself mediated by things in the world. The self is moved to action by these phenomena; the self is linked with the external world by the term *whakapapa*, which I discuss presently. All entities have, and participate in, whakapapa (Cherryl Smith, 2000). Through the display of things in the world, one can make a representation about the world and respond: whakapapa enables "the speaker and listeners to negotiate the terrain of both seen and unseen existence" (Cherryl Smith, 2000, p.45). The back-and-forth between world and self is reflected in various Maori terms that underpin phenomena allowing Ako to take place. Whakapapa, ira, whenua, and kore, the terms that I choose to talk about as aspects of Ako, are in fact interrelated, not separate. And if we were to choose another, such as whakapapa, an ethics of interconnection and animacy would suggest that Ako forms part of its constellation for discussion. Yet, we can explain these terms in relation to their specific importance for instruction and teaching by and through the external world. Possibly the most widely cited of these is whakapapa. Before we come to that concept, one of this term's key components – Papa, which, in turn, is derived from the Maori phenomenon Papatuanuku – must be considered due to the fact that it gives rise to all things.

The non-foundational ground of thought and materiality

Kincheloe's (2011) critical ontology aims to emphasise teaching with indigenous ontologies as both backdrop and central. According to him there is, in teacher education programs, very little emphasis on teachers' awareness of the assumptions that underpin such fundamentals as perception and selfhood. On that basis, analysing why we propose what something *is*, as straightforward as that seems, would need sustained attention. For Maori there is a notion of 'ground' that gives one the ability to make an assertion, but this ground is an entity that the self is reliant on in order to propose anything. 'Ground' in Maori philosophy is both figurative and literal. Insofar as we can quite correctly use the term in everyday speech to either refer to a conceptual foundation or a physical one, this dual character is not particularly remarkable. For Maori, though, the ground immediately invokes the highly complex entity and idea of Papa. As soon as we are talking about a ground of thinking – the basis of our concepts, the most essential framing of awareness that we often speak about when we make an utterance – we are at once dealing with an animate entity (Mika, 2015d). This phenomenon, the "rock foundation beyond expanse, the infinite" (Marsden, 2003, p.22), is more completely known as Papatuanuku or Earth Mother, and the term *Papa* is always derived from that fuller name (Royal, 2008). In turn, Papatuanuku is also thought of as a nurturing entity that draws the self to it – again, conceptually and physically.

Although it is often conceived of as a ground *upon which* one exists, Papa instead denotes a much more omnipotent phenomenon. Papa gives rise to all entities, is hence active, and is in turn comprised of them. In that sense, the idea of primordial Being is attributed to Papa (Marsden, 2003) (note that 'primordial Being' is also equated with other phenomena). With its expansiveness in mind, we could instead think of Papa as the sublime, *within which* one exists. Here, there is a marked distinction between a Maori notion of 'ground' and that of Platonic propositions about the Forms, for 'ground' in the former is that which is forever fused with the self and his or her perception of other things. 'Ground' since Plato (Sweeney, 2015), however, is set out within the etymology of the term *episteme* and relates to the idea that one can only represent an aspect of the world when those "statements [*logos*] 'stand' upon a firm foundation [*epistemi*]" (Grassi, 1980, p.68). A Maori view of ground privileges the idea that the self is thoroughly fashioned by the totality of the world. The marked contrasts between these two metaphysical premises – ground as cognitive, on one hand, and ground as both cognitive and all-consuming/all-creative, on the other – is arguably at the very heart of much misunderstanding between Maori and Pakeha (non-Maori settler) arguments about what constitutes education, as just one example. Ground, both conceptual and entity, must be a colonial issue because it is often reduced in its dimension to refer simply to a foundation of intellectual thought. Whilst it is certainly important that ground be acknowledged as that which accords with the human act of intellectualising and asserting something, for Maori this act is inseparable from the very ground, or Papa, that exists prior to human awareness (Mika, 2016c). For students and teachers, a material, primordial ground that one is dependent on – and that one must acknowledge – during a statement about a thing, poses problems for the solely transmissive practice of knowledge, or indeed for any statement of certainty. For the Maori scholar, consequences arise for assertions *about* Ako as well; he or she would have to be prepared to revisit, deconstruct and reargue his or her assertions and would have to acknowledge that he or she is being constructed by the external world as they are being made. Statements about Ako – or anything, for that matter – are made within a colonised reality that the Maori writer must be prepared for. That colonised ground of thought, as we have seen from Chapter 2, comprises a thoroughly influential entity.

The term *Papa* is much more widely cited than its partner *Rangi*, which is an abbreviation of *Ranginui* and relates to the Sky Father. Yet, the materiality of Rangi quite possibly exists within the concept of Papa even when not mentioned. An interesting homonym constitutes Rangi – what may be called 'tune', which resides as a fuller reverberating constellation of things, within the notion of Papa. Ground is similarly participant with Rangi, despite their separation from each other in dictionary definitions. As for 'tune', Raerino (2000) profoundly notes that the Maori language is incorporated within the music of the world; he discusses that man is bound with the environment through the array of sounds that emanate from the natural world. Approached with an orthodox, straightforward reading, the ground/pervasive entity does not in any way contain to it that of 'tune'. It quite possibly does from a Maori worlded perspective (Mika & Stewart, 2015), however, and there are repercussions here for Maori in the teaching and learning process alongside my wider position on education as world-constructed. The conceptual aspect of ground that a student or teacher holds is bewildered by the refrain that things in the world possess. Brooks (2008) retells the Iroquois story of creation that necessarily involves Sky Woman and states that "the earth materializes through the interrelated activity of its inhabitants" (p.238); in a Maori context, the 'materialisation' depicts the existence of things through their continued harmony. The Maori student or teacher is inclined to be attuned to the sounds that are created by this vast foundation – which, as far as cognition goes, is precariously non-foundational. Ako may therefore signal intense emotional because the self is in a state of susceptibility in the face of the world and the dialogue between all things.

The self's active construction by the unknown

Papatuanuku finds a type of active expression in the concept whakapapa, which is commonly taken to mean simply 'genealogy'. There is, indeed, a notion of genealogy in that Maori term, but whakapapa evinces a Maori ground of worldedness far more deeply than 'genealogy' can cope with (Mika, 2015b). At best, it is left to speculation to establish anything about this phenomenon, because it contains so centrally the full, active nature of Papa. It surpasses certain knowledge. I have thus far suggested that, when teaching and learning are taking place, or the wider sphere of Ako is being thought about in terms of how the self/the world is built, disestablished and fortified by the world/the self, both world and self are influential on each other. The term *whakapapa* is one term of many that embodies this sense, and whilst it may have been reduced in meaning through common use, it still encourages a more primordial regard that prioritises the notion of construction through the world. When whakapapa is not being equated with genealogy, it is sometimes defined as 'to layer' (Ngata, 1972; Royal, 2009). To layer is then commonly represented as a physical event, such as the stratification process of the earth. It can also be related to the layered appearance of a genealogical table, where humans, animals and other entities are connected to each other sequentially. Only occasionally does the potential for whakapapa extend to the accrual of layers to the individual self, and the impact of the self to things in the world, through experience but also simply by the self's location in the world.

Yet, the opportunity for a much more expansive reading of whakapapa as it coincides with worldedness does exist, and such an interpretative approach has a concern for, or cynicism towards, the common discourse of whakapapa as genealogy. More positively, however, reconfiguring whakapapa so that it confers deeply with the mystery of a Maori metaphysics whilst acknowledging that it has an ongoing influence on things in the world, including the self, sits well with Ako as an external (but internally mediated) process. To the extent that the self is identified here with a spiritual inheritance as much as a physical one, in a holistic rendition of Ako the very ground within which the self exists needs to be retained as an ephemeral entity but one that the self can nevertheless speculate about (yet within). There are two main reasons for my point here: first, it is unknowable as a whole. It quite simply shares in far too many dimensions and things for the self in general, and the learning and teaching individual in particular, to cope with. Second, its mystery ensures that the self forecloses against making assertions of certainty about things in the world. Existence for Maori is therefore immediately two-pronged in that it calls for a scanning of a colonising horizon alongside any proactive assertion. The ground or Papa – not thoroughly able to be experienced or grasped – that is related to the self is vital to indigenous thought. A similarly critical but also phenomenological interpretation breaks down another well-known Maori term and concept, *kaupapa*, into the first manifestation (*kau*) of a ground (*papa*) (Marsden, 2003). To the extent that it is something that can solidify or provide a firm ground of thought for the self, it is often referred to as 'kaupapa Maori theory'. This latter approach has been discussed at length elsewhere and is most often asserted as a theory of transformation and liberation for Maori because it opens up possibilities for grounds of thought for Maori (Smith, 1999; Pihama, 2005). Quite a degree of certainty is associated with the phrase and its emancipatory discourse, with 'kaupapa' on its own often referring to an unwavering ground of perception and determination. Despite the certainty associated with it, though, kaupapa is equally a metaphysical term that defies assuredness.

'Papa' thus extends to ethicality, evident in both 'kaupapa' and the more immediately active 'whakapapa' which insist that, despite the disclosure of a cognitive foundation, the full and exhaustive ground is never grasped in its totality. Hence, a thing in the world is approachable *as* an entity but resists being fully comprehended. This revelation of a thing is brought about through the intricate – and itself also inconceivable – arrangement of Papatuanuku and all those other entities that are not immediately discernible in that phenomenon (Mika & Southey, 2016). Additionally, the self is disclosed to any number of other entities: there is a co-instantaneity between the self and other things that remains largely outside of the self's control (Mika, 2015c). The individual becomes aware of any one thing through the expression and organisation of the whole, which as we have seen is fundamentally mysterious. Approached with mystery through the vitality of interconnection as a backdrop, the layering that whakapapa depicts is more closely aligned with how one resonates with the world, including how the learner and teacher, for instance, are influenced by facets of the world that are not immediately accessible. The self's well-being is dependent on the nature of whakapapa, with the entire self being determined by everything that exists, perceptible or otherwise. We might here revisit how one is attuned to the world, or how one is immersed within the omnipotence of the earth. In a concrete context, the learner and teacher both accrue aspects of the entire world to themselves whilst representing any one thing, and so the careful and deliberate treatment of that thing is a key issue for the teacher and learner. To the extent that both the teacher and learner are taught by the world, the reciprocity that is often attributed to dominant discourses about Ako is correct, but whakapapa places greater emphasis on how one 'turns' to a thing, as a related entity to the self, in order to describe it. This orientation towards a thing can be read through a further breaking down of the term *whakapapa*: to become (*whaka*) earth (*papa*) (Mika, 2014). As the learner and teacher are attuned to the fullness of Papa through one thing, they are drawn towards the primordial ground of Papa. They do not take on the form of Papa as such, but they are constantly claimed by it through any one encounter with a thing. In that sense, 'become' encapsulates that Papa continuously 'collects' the self when the self is accosted by a thing.

From the embryonic ground, which the self cannot escape, comes the fragility associated with the dual nothingness and positivity of a thing. In Maori language and concept, these metaphysical characteristics are most often called *kore* or *korekore*, respectively (Mika, 2016a; 2016b; 2016c) in creation narrative, and their influence is to be rethought, through their retrieval from their relegation to 'the deep past' to current times and into all objects, thoughts, and modes of being. That any object or idea can materialise at all is evidence of its positivity, and the term *korekore* carries with it such a strong sense of kore (negativity) that aspects of positivity emerge (Marsden, 2003; Mika, 2012; 2013b). As we have seen, any one entity is constructed by all others, with the positivity meant here being simultaneously backgrounded by the constituting activity of the world. The void that each entity retains is its infinite claim by all others. With that negativity, the positivity of the entity is constantly undermined so that what Maori would call a visible 'thing' is in fact the full amplitude of the world within it, the recession or withdrawal of certain entities in relation to that thing (but the continued resonance of those things with it – and here we are reminded of the active ground Papa and its corresponding activity of whakapapa in particular and the oft-silent but nevertheless influential Rangi), and the past and future phenomena that are unannounced in the thing but with which the thing still has a relationship. Seen through a Maori metaphysical lens, the potential for a thing to be utterly positive is hence at-once annihilated. Maori propositions about the thing, then, are undoubtedly dissimilar to dominant Western ones because the present thing is necessarily thought about in terms of the continuous dissipation of its positivity.

What are the repercussions of nothingness in a Maori sense for the idea that Papatuanuku is the beginning and end of Maori experience? We may have to reconsider the primacy attributed to Papatuanuku here, not least because that entity is participant with kore as are other things in the world. Instead, it may be that Papatuanuku, posited as originary, sits between what Heidegger generally castigates as 'ontotheology', on one hand, and his more optimistic depiction of Being as a dispensing of uncertainty about things in the world, on the other. The non-foundational ground of Papa is indeed primordial Being – it would therefore meet Heidegger's chief criterion for the ultimate entity and hence accord with metaphysics since Plato (Dreyfus, 2003) – but, like other things in the world, it is reliant on voidness as much as the full visibility of things. Maori scholars such as Marsden and Mika argue for the entity that appears to be final – and is often described in final, foundational terms; a further possibility remains, though, that this primordiality is always exiting into the totality of visible and invisible realms, thus suddenly losing its status as 'primordial'. In that context, it does certainly clear the way for beings to be revealed, but its firstness is undermined or negated by other entities that coexist with it.

Neither aspects of Papatuanuku – its dual primordiality but dissipation, and what it heralds for cognition – can be ignored for Maori who are engaging with theorising about Ako. It would be tempting to view the opening up of things for the self's appreciation as the more important facet, but as we saw earlier, this would be to undermine the materiality of things in the world that are given presence and withdrawal within Papatuanuku. To focus briefly on that former aspect: Ako does chime particularly well with the possibility of nothingness, especially with postcolonial/counter-colonial perceptions of an object, and the teaching and learning connected with how an object is to be apprehended. Here, not quite incidentally, we can see a peculiarity about Ako: it is both an active regard for a problem, thing or idea *as a vulnerable self*, but it is also the *teaching and learning* of that regard. Both of these aspects of Ako take place in the suffusion of the All throughout a thing: whilst not discussing Ako, Eckhart and Schürmann (2001) describe the initial active substance as an "indistinct fullness from which flow . . . all oppositions and relations" (p.165). A Maori worlded-ness, I suggest, posits nothingness in a similar way, emphasising both its entity status and the self's inaccessibility to an object because of its infusion with Papa. When one educates or is being educated in a more orthodox sense, then, one is being made aware of the presence of colonised thought which would posit that an object is somehow *not* derived from, or composed of, nothingness – that it *is* fully. That process of regard takes place within the individual learner's or teacher's own formation by that 'indistinct fullness' that Eckhart and Schür-mann speak of. Nothingness is hence quite possibly the ultimate metaphysical issue that is linked with the learning of one's own vulnerability towards the All, because it maintains a veil over a thing, rendering it obscure (*po-uri*, which is said to result from kore, or nothingness, in creation stories) and manifesting in a darkening (also *po-uri*) of one's foundational standing in the world – in short, the overwhelming claim of an object on the self.

Apprehending the object holistically

There are various concepts in the Maori language which reflect the fact that objects reveal themselves and are self-evolving. At the same time, those objects are to be understood as containing to them all other entities in the world. Thus an object is in fact totality. Ako, apart from indicating the self's construction by an object, simultaneously allows for the holistic representation of an entity, with the self being both formed and agentic. The construction of a thing by all others – by Papatuanuku if we think of all things as themselves based on a totality – can be theorised in the light of process philosophy, in which something takes form but through the combined nature of the world. *Whaka*, a particle of speech in the Maori language, conveys this idea by suggesting that an object becomes its outcome (Mika, 2014) but through the complexity that I have discussed. Ako corresponds here because it recognises the self needs to make a representation about an object – has to depict a thing in the classroom, for instance – whilst maintaining that intricacy. *Whaka* is more commonly defined as 'to cause', but with its deeper, non-human element portrayed through its sense of "becom-ing" (Hudson et al., 2007, p.44) it ensures that the self moderates any idea that they are thoroughly the origin of thought, representation and creativity. It may refer to the idea that one is indebted to all things in the world for whatever one apprehends or creates. Moreover, it will be recalled that the creation or idea is not fragmentable from the rest of the world, constructed as it is by the latter.

Thought (*whakaaro*) in Maori metaphysics is immediately connected to this idea that one is both formed and constructive. Whakaaro (*whaka aro*) is a double-sided invitation, where the self speculates on how the world has invited him or her to participate in its disclosure, with the self's fragility before the thing being crucial in that thought. Thinking from worldedness is constituted by an act of acknowledgement, in particular towards the fact that something comes about (*whaka*) into one's regard (*aroaro*). *Whaka* is connected with the possibility that time (*wa*) is non-linear because the self has always already been established by a thing: the full amplitude of any one thing, apparently manifesting for one's regard, always continuously revealed itself to the thinking individual. The phenomenon that gives rise to whakaaro is of central importance in Maori philosophy: one "*cast[s] attention to*" (Takirirangi Smith, 2000, p.58) a thing but not from a position of authority. Smith thus continues that "the stomach is associated with the *ira tangata* [human inheritance] aspect or earthly component of that which forms the basis of action"; moreover, the stomach was the centre of thinking. Maori thought, then, privileges emotional responses and is not confined to "the actual process of rational thought". Instead, as Tau (2001) suggests, knowledge was self-reflective, with Maori conceptually imprinting themselves onto the landscape and answering to that image with sustained feeling. What could be most striking here is that Maori thought, combining outer world and self, prioritises an astonishment at the fact that the self and an external object are related, to the point of their being indivisible.

Alongside that the self acknowledges the thing – and indeed just as important as that material relationship – is the world's devolvement of uncertainty to the self. The self has therefore always acquired a sense of astonishment at the fact of the world's manifestation. Tau's proposition that Maori had mirror thought, and inscribed themselves on the landscape, does concur with the idea that the self is chiefly in a state of wonder at the fact that the world arises (not necessarily in a knowable, sensible way) before the self, as part of the self. The term *ira*, far from referring to 'genetic material' as it is sometimes defined (Mika, 2015a) and frequently thought of, is one that reflects this process. Somewhat similar to the German idea of Dasein in that they both refer to a sort of 'over thereness!' as an existential facet, ira conveys that I am astonished at a thing and its complexity. Indeed, any inheritance through the term *ira* is much more closely associated with the layers of the world to the individual, as well as the renewed ability to be thoroughly surprised at a thing's mystery. Thus, selfhood of the human and non-human realms can be conceptually reflected in the term *ira* because it does imply that one has an essence (another of its common dictionary definitions). Importantly, though, it automatically ascribes to the self all other phenomena (Mika, 2015a) – one's essence is constituted by them. In this more phenomenological conception of the self's wonderment at a thing, the thing can only gain the learner's and teacher's awareness because it is part of the self. To that extent, it is *essentially* bound to the self. Maori scholar Edwards (2009) relates this interconnection to ira also, and cites a discussion with an elder in which the kuia (older woman) explained that lightning in the Maori language – *uira* – is etymologically related to the essence (*ira*) of things in the world. Uira signals "the presence of being" (p.253) and is "the beginning of whakapapa". Here, we encounter one of those examples of 'necessary mysticism' – obligatory, because ira is one of those terms that is too readily associated with a hardened terminology through its equation with static human essence. Reinfeld and Pihama (n.d.) relate ira to the "limitless power of the divine" (p.24); it ensures that the self and the world are given expression. Ideas are also given supernatural status in Maori philosophy, as are memories. The term *u* that precedes *ira*, thus culminating in 'lightning', refers to the collection of an entity or phenomenon, or as Edwards recounts, one's ability to recount the idea of something – which is no less, as he suggests, than the recalling of the actual entity in language.

I turn now to language as a vexed phenomenon – fraught, because through it one seems to discuss a thing as a separate entity rather than as part of the self and, indeed, as a component of an utterance.

Language and agency

Being a hugely important facet of much indigenous discourse, language deserves a preliminary, political introduction. Language in a colonised setting has largely been framed as a sociological or postcolonial issue. From that perspective it is generally a social event, and if it is threatened or diminished then the solution lies in political activism or government intervention. Language plays a role of ensuring the sustenance of a culture, and indisputably it is a vehicle for culture and, in the long run, of self-identity (wa Thiong'o, 1986). Additionally, for the indigenous person language may be one of the most identifiable cultural symbols that distinguish him or her from the coloniser. It is therefore of huge political significance, and there have been numerous and often successful attempts to revive languages that are either endangered or even extinct. In Wales, for instance, language revitalisation strategies have been quite successful (Storry, 2002), leading to a marked increase in the number of speakers. Other groups in Britain, such as the Cornish, have to contend with a very limited number of speakers able to teach that language to begin with. Maori, Hawaiian and certain other indigenous languages in the Americas are experiencing what may be cautiously described as a 'renaissance', although challenges remain there, as they do in Ireland, for instance, in encouraging the use of the endangered language throughout all forums. There is no doubt that indigenous peoples therefore respond emotionally as well as intellectually to the theme of language: it is a topic that intertwines with issues of well-being, pride and political autonomy as much as immediate denotation of the world. What we can say with some certainty about sociological and political advances of language is that the latter is held to be one of the most contested accessories of any culture.

However, the very nature of language itself, and indeed, the extent to which language as a phenomenon may be philosophically different between indigenous and coloniser, is often overlooked in those urgent attempts to revitalise language. In its own way, an indigenous philosophical excavation into the nature of language may be as concerned with language's well-being as the revitaliser's position. This is not to say that setting up language initiatives is an invalid step – clearly it is not – but it is to suggest that more thinking on the tensions between philosophical perceptions of the fact that language actually *is*, are called for. The essence of language, the link between a thing and language, and whether a speaker is outside or within language, for instance, are possible issues to be considered in indigenous theoretical forums. These inquiries into language have mostly been the preserve of philosophy departments and relatedly comprise a formidable stockpile in academic journal writing. The difference in intention may well be stark, though: indigenous peoples overwhelmingly do not want to discuss language as a detached intellectual topic and will need to see some link between these admittedly dense and abstract thoughts, and well-being (both for language itself and for the world). Additionally, having frequently been deprived of access to their own languages, indigenous communities are intent on constructing deeper thoughts about language in response to, and in their rejuvenation of, those threatened languages. Such debates in *indigenous* settings would need to take account of a traditional voice but also, importantly, a highly counter-colonial one, in order to make language a philosophical topic that overlaps with social issues of well-being.

Indigenous peoples and dominant academic conventions have vastly different views from each other on what the nature of language is, and whether (if at all) it is thought to express Being in its own right. For indigenous thought, language is an animate entity that simultaneously reaches outwards from and inwards to the speaker, incorporating the world at all times. It is thoroughly informed by the dynamic activity of Papatuanuku, which is responsible for the fact that things show themselves to the self in the first place. Haig-Brown and Archibald (1996) hence argue for an approach towards things based on reciprocity, in which each thing in the world is respected, resulting in an equilibrium between all things. Language is meant to be the driver of, but also infused with, the completeness of all things. Language is not entirely human derived and, moreover, has importance beyond a unit of meaning. In current contexts, this approach to language is somewhat confusing, given that it has tended to become a defined phenomenon that describes its genesis in the human self. Indigenous belief, however, thinks about language as a thing in its own right and tends to source language in what is not present as much as in the visible world. Even the entity that is discernible for thought is already imbued with the essence of other unseen things. Maori writers Jeffries and Kennedy (2008) hence depict language as the "manifestation . . . of the intrinsic relationship between [humans] . . . and the rest of the natural world" (p.10). The 'rest of the natural world' incorporates the completeness of power and place that Deloria has spoken of.

Language incorporates the hidden

Language is thus an immediately perplexing phenomenon and is paradoxical in various ways for the Maori self. To begin with, when making a statement about language the self draws on language to carry that out, and there was always something already within the statement that he or she cannot arrive at. This confusing relationship of the self with language is permanent and ongoing. Most simply put, in asserting that language is such and such, I have resorted to language itself to describe language. But, more important, I have not attributed language to itself in that statement; I have not declared that language is 'there' for itself. I may have just now declared it so, it is true, but in turn, I have not accounted for language in that subsequent assertion. Language is hence always prior to the Maori self's utterance: one could continue *ad infinitum* proclaiming language's presence in an utterance without ever having the last say over language. This belief in language's primacy is not unique to indigenous philosophy – Heidegger and Wittgenstein, for instance, argued that we can never distance ourselves from language to discuss it detachedly – but Maori attribute its ascendancy (in relation to the self) to different origins. Language resides within other non-human entities including apparently inanimate objects, the dead and those to come; it is a phenomenon that infuses throughout the world and its undisclosed facets. It is always 'there' in the natural world and its demand for the self's attention, as well as in those realms which the self does not have automatic access to, is to be seriously considered. Language for Maori worldedness equates with the revelatory power of all things in the world, and it is beyond human speech because it is so thoroughly linked with the complete possibilities within any one thing, its outward display and its unlimited connection to all other things. The Maori self is incapable of grasping that full interplay of language, and language remains mysterious for the self even in cases of the apparently straightforward utterance.

Relatedly, the self is always urged to consider that he or she is caught up in the thrall of language, with language encouraging the self onwards to think about the fact that the world displays itself in its unlimited way. In Maori ceremony, as I noted earlier, it is common practice to state that "the mountain and I are one". Incidentally, one could just as readily assert that "I am writing in cursive style" or "I am driving to the supermarket": the same basic principles apply to language. Whenever I make any utterance, then I am actually responding to the demand of the world and its corresponding mystery. I am also answering to the mystery that language itself elicits. I am constantly inquiring into the fact that language *is* something beyond what I think it is, as well as that the world has oriented itself in a mode that enables me to respond. As I am connected to the world to the extent that indigenous metaphysics dictates, then this dual response – to things in the world and to the mystery of language itself – makes perfect sense. If we were to venture even further down the dark path of indigenous worldedness, then we might finally decide – for the time being at least – that these two-headed phenomena are, in fact, one because the things in the world may be inseparable from language. That the response appears to be dual when in fact it is now one, is itself cause for excited speculation, and I would then go on to think about the relationship between language once more, the possibility of fragmentation (two-headed phenomena) versus its probable holism and so on.

The fact that one is able to respond is hence as important as the utterance. As we have seen, Maori philosophies of worlded engagement hold that there is no definite answer to that call; one is simply drawn towards it. This astounding phenomenon of response alone is reason for speculation because it is primordial, originating in the world and its self-arrangement, and exists prior to any statement of fact. It would be overwhelmingly enticing to suggest that it was the mountain (or the act of writing or driving) alone that voiced itself, grabbing my attention towards it and reminding me that I am submerged in its influence. This explanation would be closer to a more orthodox one, in which I had an idea about the mountain and that I thereafter expressed my belief about my relationship to it. It is indeed entirely possible that the mountain is somehow connected, in the holistic way I intend here, to my assertion about it; it could certainly have organised my expression in some form. Yet, this would be to oversimplify the totality of the world that indigenous philosophy privileges. Far more likely, the world as a whole (and with this term it should be remembered that the world is as much hidden as visible) has imparted itself to me in a particular way, and I have oriented myself towards its disclosure.

Probably the most concrete element of Ako, at least in relation to teaching and learning, may be discussed at this point. This aspect deals with the representation of an object, all other objects and self as one. Despite the fact that the self is at the mercy of the full intrusion and pervasiveness of the world, he or she is capable of making representations about it and of speculating about the fact that a thing exists. To posit this act in an ethical voice: on the basis of worldedness, the self is encouraged to represent an object as a thoroughly situated, worlded entity. The self inherits the totality of a thing as material relation, and so a thing being considered, in that context, is not a self-contained unit that comprises set properties because it is so thoroughly incorporated with everything else. If one is taught about a thing, one is vulnerable to the materiality of the other's language: here, Cherryl Smith (2000) notes that "a piece of writing or a speech therefore has its own mauri [life force]" (p.43). Accordingly, language is important for Maori as an issue in its own right and as a medium for thinking about the interconnection of the world's phenomena. Language is hence an important facet of the self's agency but, along with the first perception of a thing – whether it is divisible from the rest of the world or not, or whether it is living or inanimate – it is to be conceived of carefully because it can have an impact on the self and whatever is external.

Teaching and learning in a Maori metaphysics are therefore exercises that take account of the vitality of a phenomenon through language, which itself is a living entity. A Maori individual's name, for instance, might therefore have implications for the teaching and learning process. Names in a Maori worldview reverberate with their object, which is always constructed by all others – hence the name is more than a transparent sign for an object. Alongside being feasible in a theoretical, metaphysical voice, this belief is also immediately evident in some indigenous traditional discourse. Maori elder Tikao, for instance, recalled in his accounts with Beattie (1990) that a stand of trees at Akaroa acquired the name, and hence the essence, of a woman. This stand of trees, according to Tikao, could speak. Similarly, Nalungiaq, an Inuit woman, told Knud Rasmussen in an interview that animals and humans shared language, enabling them to take on each other's forms. Language for her was an experience of things in the world, such that "[a] word spoken by chance might have strange consequences. It would suddenly come alive and what people wanted to happen could happen – all you had to do was say it" (Abram, 1996, p.87). If we take the example of a Maori learner's and/or teacher's name, then it becomes evident that even the smallest aspects of language hold vast implications for any relationship to an entity, and for the representation of a thing through language or another medium. A person's name may have ties with an event that is currently being discussed and would then resonate with the entity of that discussion in certain ways; the person themselves may be influenced by the name in certain places; what happens at a distance – "[w]hat is thinking sensing etc. here – is burning, fermenting, thrusting etc. yonder" (Wood, 2007, p.24) – is constructed by the thoughtful self, through their infusion by the world and the autonomous but independent activity of their identity, and so on. More generally, language as a whole is an issue for the teacher or learner because of how it is positioned as a wider phenomenon than the linguistic. Ako insists that language itself be speculated on whilst any linguistic detail is being considered. Language's specialness in this regard is highlighted by Maori writers Browne (2005), Pere (1982) and Raerino (2000), who argue that even a small element such as a word is enduringly influential in more than a cognitive or emotional sense. Language for them is material and is so powerful that an utterance or word continues to exert itself although an individual appears to have moved on from it. A word has an additional component besides its obvious linguistic features; it can envelop the speaker, the listener, the learner and the teacher. For the immediate teacher and learner, in particular, a word is infused with properties that incorporate its usual denotative meaning alongside its draw on the entire world and its things.

A Maori example: Tera te Auahi: an uneasiness of oppositions

My suggestion that an entity is 'this' on the one hand but also all the others, and that these states of being produce a form of language, is one that takes place alongside the interplay of things in the world and with things in the world constituting me as I make that suggestion. In Maori poetic discourse, the self is often seen as being sourced within the very language they are using, even as an explanation of the poem or song tends to place the self 'over there' in relation to what is occurring. The self, of course, has apparently elected to sing or recite (although as I have argued things in the world have oriented the self towards a concern), but they are immediately claimed by that language – or, more correctly, they are reminded that they were never separate from either the language or the things in the world that constitute language. My own claim by things in the world can be seen in the first few lines that compose the lament of an *iwi* (tribe) I belong to; my affiliation to language occurs whilst I appear to *use* language as a separate phenomenon:

> Ko Ngati Taoi i moe ra i te whenua, haere ra e te iwi
> *Lie Ngati Taoi entombed by ash and scoria, farewell to you all*
>
> Ki te po-uriuri ki te po tangotango ki te iwi ki te po
> *(Farewell) to the realm of death, to the darkness, where reside your ancestors*
> (Office of Treaty Settlements, 2008, p.353)

The song refers to the eruption of Mt Tarawera in 1886, in which a number of my people were killed. But there is much more to the song than a one-off event, because the words are materially influential. By 'materially influential', I do not necessarily mean primarily 'emotional'; it is instead the embrace of terms as they constitute the speaker or thinker that is important for this discussion. In the first line, we have entombment, positionality through the use of various linguistic particles, and terms that have a breadth of meaning and sense. There is a mountain that is both remarkable to my own people for its appearance and for the fact that it is so solidly worlded. To begin with: if I am of the Ngati Taoi tribe (as I am) then the apparently past events of the song refer to me in the present sense, despite their reference to past events. Likely, though, the events constitute the reciter of the song even if he or she is not from Ngati Taoi, although the nature of that influence is unknowable.

The phrase 'moe ra i te whenua' alone has vast consequences for things in the world generally because it indicates an 'entombment' that is applicable also to the singer as well as the existence of other realms. Admittedly, the song intends to refer to the victims of the eruption, but as language is its own governing force, it immediately opens onto other experiences that are perhaps not the intention of the composers. Taken as a whole, 'moe ra i te whenua' or 'entombed' seems to be contrastable with a vigorous phenomenon. The stillness alluded to in the phrase is evidently opposed to the vitality of the living world. It is a curious aspect of the Maori language, though, that an opposition always resides within the utterance; however, whatever is not available to the senses may be more influential than whatever is stated and perceived (Mika, 2014). That backdrop of the unstated corresponds with the notion of negativity that a Maori philosophy recounts. If we are to suggest that a group of people has died, then equally as forceful as that statement is the full materiality of those who are living. In other words, I might sing those words, yet they are replete with what is not voiced.

'Moe ra i te whenua' is constituted by the world of the living, and the song immediately references that tacit entity. 'Moe ra i te whenua' is also meant to be a peaceful phrase in itself, but because of its subterranean claim to the more vigorous, it is on its own a thoroughly active set of words as well as serene. Again, we see what I term (cautiously) a paradox: the multiple characteristics of an object that appear for rational thought to be only possible if they occur one after the other or in turn, but which in Maori thought are co-instantaneous.

The tendency of language to disclose much more than what the human world intends is also reflected in the term *whenua* (earth) – it is never unaccompanied. It exists prior to being uttered as an entity determined by the human self and, although we may wish to make a distinction between one object and another (for instance, if I wish to say 'whenua' to demarcate 'earth'), language as an autonomous entity does not necessarily comply. I may *signal* a thing to be discussed but it is forever darkened by the backdrop of all that is unstated. Whenua is an apparently straightforward term but it is something within which we exist. We also exist within the essence of other entities, such as the sky, and this must be recognised whilst the earth is being discussed. To be *entombed* in the earth is to reference the dead and the living as they both actively and peacefully reside within the claim of the earth and all its entities that it claims. In other words, we are all entombed in the earth and we are, in essence, like the dead to the extent that we are always constituted by various states of being. Language is another entity that constitutes whenua, and whenever we speak we are disclosing earth. That material disclosure of earth occurs whether we intend it or not. It should be noted that the human self recites the song, but the invisibility of the non-human world is also unstated within that proposition. Whilst the self appears to recite the song of their own accord, the non-human world allows that to occur in the first instance – or, at least, they occur in conjunction with each other.

We can gain some impetus for further speculation by looking to linguistic particles in a text. They need to be accompanied with that speculation, though, in order to transcend their narrow dictionary definition. One intriguing particle in the song is simply *i*, which forms part of 'moe ra i te whenua'. The composer intends to state that Ngati Taoi reside *within* the earth. As I mentioned earlier, the living reside within the earth, too, in the sense that they are forever claimed by it (Mika, 2014). But the term *i* additionally suggests causation, where one can say that they did something *because of* (i) something. The initial sense of 'withinness' that the word refers to may be no different to that of causation, despite their separate dictionary categories. I suggest here that a certain event or entity is *brought about within* the worldedness of all other entities, not caused by the external, separate influence of something. Here, an entity takes on characteristics that it always had, that are not distinguishable from it due to its always-already relationship with those things. That an entity is forever imbued with the world infers that an aspect could never be caused in relation to it but that the state of being was forever present even when not evident.

An English term for this concept is difficult to find, with one that could suffice being *ingrain*. The 'grained' part of the word, in the context of my theory, implies that a state of constant fulfilment by others occurs to the extent that they are associated, co-constitutive entities. *In* conveys that this graining within an entity occurs at the same time *within* all others. All those others are thence embedded with that one single thing. When thought about as a complete term, a sense of full constitution of a thing by other things whilst being within those things is possible. There are shards of all things within the one, where the one entity is dissipated throughout all those others. The term in the sense that I mean it is less concerned with a force that is brought to bear on a thing than its already-consisted relationship with all others. 'Moe ra i te whenua' in that light would reference that a state of being is 'in-grained' through its thorough entombment in the earth. Recall that the song indicates death as a state of sleeping within the earth. A preferred interpretation, taking into account the above, is that one is imbued with all other things that the earth brings and is thus both asleep and vigorous on the basis of that complete accompaniment. One is in various states of being within the influence of all those things. In the phrase 'moe ra i te whenua' we see an opposition happening, with the word *ra*, which is translated as 'over there'. If thought about in its worlded sense, it is simultaneously nearness. The intention of the phrase is that the dead sleep in a designated space in an ongoing fashion. For our current view of worlded things, however, it is more appropriate that the dead are thought of as among the living. That they are both near and far corresponds with the idea that they are constituting whatever appears to be over there as well as the self.

It should be evident that my thinking is based on/within the fact of the song. It is the speculative ability of a term or a set of words that sets one on a path to thinking; more importantly, it is the material arrangement of the worlded entities of language and its objects within which and because of which I think. In a Heideggerian fashion it can be proposed that "thinking is a certain kind of bringing together, in the sense that man is collected, cognitively and emotionally, towards the mystery of the absent" (Mika, 2014, pp.57–8). The things that the words disclose are fundamentally unknowable, leaving us the creativity to approximate them through freethinking. To use that creative ability to speculate on unstated colonised phenomena within the song may not be common practice but they are there nevertheless. All traditional chants, songs and prayers are themselves together with their other. Not all of these colonised oppositions can be accounted for – they are just as numerous as the worlds within the traditional discourse – but we can at least allude to some of them. Indeed, speculating on colonisation is a creative process, despite its negative connotations. To begin with, there are limitations on the full potential of the Maori terms. That is, they are translated to mean something quite different to the sense they are meant to portray. I discuss this problem more fully in Chapter 5 in light of Derrida's philosophies but some initial remarks can be made about the English terminology for Tera te Auahi. The phrase 'realm of death' does not do its apparent equivalent 'po-uriuri' justice. It works fine as an out-of-register guide or denotative equivalent, for while *po-uriuri* does indeed deal with a sort of mortality, it is not confined to a human state of being. I have argued elsewhere that it indicates the co-creation of uncertainty between the self and a thing, whereby the latter is not fully disclosed to the self. Po-uriuri is indeed a realm, but this realm also exists within the human self; it is not simply an external, transcendent world. It can be likened to 'distress' in a very broad sense, encompassing a tentative vulnerability in the face of a hidden entity. There is a death of sorts in that encounter with the cloaked thing, with one's self-certainty suddenly limited. An entity has decided to withdraw an aspect of itself and throws the self into a state of indeterminacy. In Maori metaphysics this realm is intimately constructed by negativity and its constitutive opposite, positivity, and it is therefore greater than simply a 'realm' of its own making, one that is separate from all those other 'realms' that have apparently preceded it and that follow on from it.

Concrete colonising events have surrounded the entities in the song since before the eruption of the mountain, and these are similarly imbued within the traditional elements. The essence of those that came after the original Tuhourangi inhabitants, and the genealogies that they participate in – including their own lands and landmarks – are ingrained within the utterances. Narrative has it that, at the time of the eruption, Tuhourangi were engaged in a burgeoning tourism trade, rivalling any other in Aotearoa. The act of inserting gold coins into the eyes of one of the local marae (and that of the author), *Hinemihi*, is constitutive of the song. Indeed, attaching the label of 'song' to its more original *waiata* is a colonising act that endures in the song; incidentally, this practice of finding a term for a Maori equivalent that will be understood by a wide audience is not unfamiliar to indigenous writers when they provide a glossary, for instance. The much more recent attempt by scientists to locate Otukapuarangi (Pink Terrace) and Te Tarata (White Terrace) is an entity-act that conjoins with the song, and the scientific approach both to locate them and to regard them as particular chemical constructions is similarly formative. There are thus numerous examples of the ways in which the song and its terms are worlded, themselves taught and then teaching the self although he or she may not be able to perceive that occurring.

Summary

An appropriate way to summarise this chapter is to refer to Maori Marsden's (1985) views on Maori thought. He argues that "abstract rational thought and empirical methods cannot grasp the concrete act of existing [for Māori] which is fragmentary, paradoxical and incomplete" (p.163). By 'incomplete', one can surmise that the self is in a state of constant reconstruction because of his or her response to all things; this description would certainly make sense in the light of the metaphysics of interconnection and animacy that we have discussed. Whatever makes Maori existence 'paradoxical', on the other hand, is uncertain, but the apparent mismatch between the various components of Maori metaphysics may well have been a natural characteristic. It would therefore have been contradictory but reconcilable. Perhaps the biggest paradox revealed by Ako is that one is conditioned by the very world that one speaks of: the self is taught in a bodily sense by the phenomena that are being represented.

Indigenous peoples in general now find themselves confronted by a different sort of enigma than that inherent to their own traditional philosophical values, however. A deeply challenging and even potentially detrimental set of metaphysics exists in the form of 'presence', which dictates that an object is highly positive by virtue of its participation with a static, permanent notion of Being. Consequently, to argue for an indigenous worldedness asks for an immediate assessment of, and speculation on, the nature of presence – how it posits an object, how from an indigenous perspective it therefore depicts the world and the ways in which the self are thoroughly linked to it. These properties of presence all deeply affect indigenous metaphysics and hence ideas around how the self is educated by the world. I now turn to what is undoubtedly unsettling for the indigenous self: the proposition that the metaphysics of presence is beyond sense, and that it augurs a particular regard for the world that typical modes of research cannot fathom. Three key philosophers, who are not indigenous, are called on for some assistance to articulate the crux and the effects of this metaphysics. The paradox, as we shall see, is perhaps more profound than was at first imagined.

References

Abram, D. (1996) *The Spell of the Sensuous.* New York, NY: Vintage Books.

Adorno, T. and Horkheimer, M. (1997) *Dialectic of Enlightenment.* London: Verso.

Andreotti, V., Ahenakew, C. and Cooper, G. (2011) 'Epistemological Pluralism: Ethical and Pedagogical Challenges in Higher Education', *AlterNative* 7(1): 40–50.

Beattie, H. (1990) *Tikao Talks: Ka Taoka O Te Ao Kohatu: Treasures from the Ancient World of the Maori.* Christchurch, New Zealand: Penguin.

Bishop, R. and Glynn, T. (1999) *Culture Counts: Changing Power Relations in Education.* Palmerston North, New Zealand: Dunmore Press.

Brooks, L. (2008) 'Digging at the Roots: Locating an Ethical, Native Criticism', pp. 234–64 in C. Womack, D. Justice and C. Teuton (eds) *Reasoning Together: The Native Critics Collective.* Norman, OK: University of Oklahoma Press.

Browne, M. (2005) *Wairua and the Relationship It Has with Learning Te Reo Māori within Te Ataarangi.* Palmerston North, New Zealand: Massey University.

Dreyfus, H. (2003) 'Being and Power Revisited', pp. 30–54 in A. Milchman and A. Rosenberg (eds) *Foucault and Heidegger: Critical Encounters.* London, UK: University of Minnesota Press.

Eckhart, M. and Schürmann, R. (2001) *Wandering Joy: Meister Eckhart's Mystical Philosophy.* Great Barrington, MA: Lindisfarne Books.

Edwards, S. (2009) *Titiro Whakamuri Kia Marama Ai Te Wao Nei: Whakapapa Epistemologies and Maniapoto Maori Cultural Identities.* Unpublished PhD dissertation, Massey University.

Fromkin, V., Curtiss, S., Hayes, B., et al. (2000) *Linguistics: An Introduction to Linguistic Theory.* Oxford, UK: Blackwell.

Grassi, E. (1980) *Rhetoric as Philosophy: The Humanist Tradition.* Edwardsville, IL: Southern Illinois University Press.

Greenwood, J. and Wilson, A. (2006) *Te Mauri Pakeaka: A Journey into the Third Space*. Auckland, New Zealand: Auckland University Press.

Haig-Brown, C. and Archibald, J. (1996) 'Transforming First Nations Research with Respect and Power', *Qualitative Studies in Education* 9(3): 245–57.

Heidegger, M. (1962) *Being and Time*. Oxford, UK: Blackwell.

Hudson, M., Ahuriri-Driscoll, A., Lea, M., et al. (2007) 'Whakapapa: A Foundation for Genetic Research', *Journal of Bioethical Inquiry* 4(1): 43–9.

Jeffries, R. and Kennedy, N. (2008) *Māori Outcome Evaluation: A Kaupapa Māori Outcomes and Indicators Framework and Methodology*. Hamilton, New Zealand: The University of Waikato.

Kincheloe, J. (2011) 'Critical Ontology and Indigenous Ways of Being', pp. 333–49 in K. Hayes, S. Steinberg and K. Tobin (eds) *Key Works in Critical Pedagogy*. Rotterdam: Sense Publishers.

Marsden, M. (1985) 'God, Man and Universe: A Maori View', pp. 143–64 in M. King (ed) *Te Ao Hurihuri: The World Moves On: Aspects of Maoritanga*. Auckland, New Zealand: Longman Paul Ltd.

Marsden, M. (2003) *The Woven Universe: Selected Writings of Rev. Māori Marsden*. Otaki, New Zealand: Estate of Rev. Māori Marsden.

Mika, C. (2007) 'The Utterance, the Body and the Law: Seeking an Approach to Concretizing the Sacredness of Maori Language', *SITES* 4(2): 181–205.

Mika, C. (2011) 'Unorthodox Assistance: Novalis, Māori, Scientism, and an Uncertain Approach to "Whakapapa"', pp. 89–108 in N. Franke and C. Mika (eds) *In die Natur – Naturphilosophie und Naturpoetik in Interkultureller Perspektive*. Wellington, New Zealand: Goethe Institut.

Mika, C. (2012) 'Overcoming "Being" in Favour of Knowledge: The Fixing Effect of "Mātauranga"', *Educational Philosophy and Theory* 44(10): 1080–92.

Mika, C. (2013a) *Reclaiming Mystery: A Māori Philosophy of Being, in Light of Novalis' Ontology*. Unpublished PhD dissertation, University of Waikato.

Mika, C. (2013b) 'Western "Sentences that Push" as an Indigenous Method for Thinking', pp. 23–6 in A. Engels-Schwarzpaul and M. Peters (eds) *Of Other Thoughts: Non-Traditional Ways to the Doctorate. A Guidebook for Candidates and Supervisors*. Rotterdam, The Netherlands: Sense.

Mika, C. (2014) 'The Enowning of Thought and Whakapapa: Heidegger's Fourfold', *Review of Contemporary Philosophy* 13: 48–60.

Mika, C. (2015a) 'The Co-Existence of Self and Thing through "Ira": A Māori Phenomenology', *Journal of Aesthetics and Phenomenology* 2(1): 93–112.

Mika, C. (2015b) 'Counter-Colonial and Philosophical Claims: An Indigenous Observation of Western Philosophy', *Educational Philosophy and Theory*: 1–7.

Mika, C. (2015c) 'Thereness: Implications for Heidegger's "Presence" for Māori', *AlterNative* 11(1): 3–13.

Mika, C. (2015d) 'The Thing's Revelation: Māori Philosophical Research', *Waikato Journal of Education* 20(2): 61–8.

Mika, C. (2016a) 'The Ontological and Active Possibilities of Papatūānuku: To Nurture or Enframe?', *Knowledge Cultures* 4(3): 58–71.

Mika, C. (2016b) ' "Papatūānuku/Papa": Some Thoughts on the Oppositional Grounds of the Doctoral Experience', *Knowledge Cultures* 4(1): 43–55.

Mika, C. (2016c) 'Worlded Object and Its Presentation: A Māori Philosophy of Language', *AlterNative* 12(2): 165–76.

Mika, C. and Southey, K. (2016) 'Exploring Whakaaro: A Way of Responsive Thinking in Maori Research', *Educational Philosophy and Theory*.

Mika, C. and Stewart, G. (2015) 'Maori in the Kingdom of the Gaze: Subjects or Critics?', *Educational Philosophy and Theory*: 1–13.

Mika, C. and Tiakiwai, S. (2016) 'Tawhiao's Unstated Heteroglossia: Conversations with Bakhtin', *Educational Philosophy and Theory*.

Ministry of Education. (2009) *Ka Hikitia: Managing for Success/Māori Education Strategy – Part One*. Ministry of Education (ed). Wellington, New Zealand: Ministry of Education.

Ngata, A. (1972) *Rauru-Nui-a-Toi*. Wellington, New Zealand: Victoria University.

Office of Treaty Settlements. (2008) *The Affiliate Te Arawa Iwi/Hapu and the Trustees of the Te Pumautanga O Te Arawa Trust and the Sovereign in Right of New Zealand: Schedules to the Deed of Settlement of the Historical Claims of the Affiliate Te Arawa Iwi/Hapu*. Available at http://nz01.terabyte.co.nz/OTS/DocumentLibrary\TePumautangaTrust-DeedofSettlement.pdf.

Otto, R. (1958) *The Idea of the Holy: An Inquiry into the Non-Rational Factor in the Idea of the Divine and Its Relation to the Rational*, 2nd edn. New York, NY: Oxford University Press.

Pere, R. (1982) *Ako: Concepts and Learning in the Māori Tradition*. Hamilton, New Zealand: University of Waikato.

Pihama, L. (2005) 'Asserting Indigenous Theories of Change', pp. 191–209 in J. Barker (ed) *Sovereignty Matters: Locations of Contestation and Possibility in Indigenous Struggles for Self-Determination*. Lincoln, NE: University of Nebraska Press.

Plebuch, D. (2010) *Heidegger's Fourfold*. Unpublished doctoral dissertation, University of Illinois, Urbana IL.

Raerino, H. (2000) *Te Ku O Te Kupu*. Hamilton, New Zealand: University of Waikato.

Reinfeld, M. and Pihama, L. (n.d.) *Matarākau: Ngā Kōrero Mō Ngā Rongoā O Taranaki*. Available at www.kaupapamaori.com.

Royal, T. A. (2008) *Te Ngākau*. Te Whanganui-a-Tara, New Zealand: Mauriora Ki Te Ao Living Universe Ltd.

Royal, T. A. (2009) *Papatūānuku – the Land – Whakapapa and Kaupapa*. Available at *Te Ara – The Encyclopedia of New Zealand*: http://www.TeAra.govt.nz/en/papatuanuku-the-land/8

Schrock, C. (2006) 'From Child to Childlike: The Cycle of Education in Novalis and George Macdonald', *North Wind* 25: 58–76.

Smith, C. (2000) 'Straying Beyond the Boundaries of Belief: Maori Epistemologies Inside the Curriculum', *Educational Philosophy and Theory* 32(1): 43–51.

Smith, G. (2003) *Indigenous Struggle for the Transformation of Education and Schooling*. Available at www.kaupapamaori.com.

Smith, L. (1999) *Decolonizing Methodologies: Research and Indigenous Peoples*. London, UK: Zed Books.

Smith, T. (2000) 'Nga Tini Ahuatanga O Whakapapa Korero', *Educational Philosophy and Theory* 32(1): 53–60.

Storry, M. (2002) *British Cultural Identities*, 2nd ed. London, UK: Routledge.

Sweeney, C. (2015) *Sacramental Presence after Heidegger: Onto-Theology, Sacraments, and the Mother's Smile*. Eugene, OR: Cascade Books.

Tau, T. (2001) 'The Death of Knowledge: Ghosts on the Plains', *New Zealand Journal of History* 35(2): 131–52.

Thrupp, M. and Mika, C. (2012) 'The Politics of Teacher Development for an Indigenous People', pp. 204–13 in C. Day (ed) *The Routledge International Handbook of Teacher and School Development*. London, UK: Routledge.

wa Thiong'o, N. (1986) *Decolonising the Mind: The Politics of Language in African Literature*. Oxford, UK: James Currey Ltd.

Wood, D (Ed.). (2007) *Novalis: Notes for a Romantic Encyclopaedia*. Albany, NY: State University of New York Press.

Chapter 4

An indigenous dialogue with Heidegger

The consequences of presence

At this point I return to my introductory comments about education as world-edness, in particular those that deal with how the self is educated by how entities are perceived. The self is also educated according to how freely he or she can reflect on colonisation: how clearly this self-reflection can occur is also a result of the way things in the world are posited. One then critiques how they are posited, and so on. This continual process is an educational one for the indigenous person, and as I have explained it is underpinned by various incommensurable aspects of things. The several paradoxes at work in indigenous metaphysics and in the educative influence of things in the world are probably irresolvable. Undoubtedly, this complexity sits well with indigenous experience generally, and so it makes sense that indigenous peoples would want the notion of a thing's weddedness to the world to remain unfathomable. One of the key tenets of colonisation, though, is that the indigenous self should be thoroughly knowable and that the indigenous self should perceive things in the world as isolated. The demystification inherent to this problematic view, including the colonial fascination with the 'other' and all the accompanying anxieties of the former, is alluded to in certain postcolonial works (Sardar et al., 1993). What lies at base of that and other manifestations of racism and oppression – overt and otherwise – is a conflict that occurs at an unseen level between that contradictory metaphysics recounted by indigenous literature, on one hand, and another sort that attempts to orient the self towards things in the world so that they 'are as they are'. The metaphysics of presence has smoothed out an object for perception *even before the self has encountered it*, and the indigenous self is educated by the material impact of the leavened entity. As I have suggested, any proposition that a thing could be so permanently itself is not reflected in an indigenous worldedness. The metaphysics of presence, however, engages with a cultural expectation that an object *will* be this or that. Thus, the metaphysics of presence has already served up a thing in its isolation from all others, as a static entity that can be theorised on by a separate self. Perversely, the indigenous self does not just propose the object as alone when colonised but is, in turn, constructed/educated in a way that has consequences for his or her well-being.

It is at this point that I turn to other philosophers to unravel the detailed nature of this other metaphysics, which, due to its determination of an entity, may sound quite foreign to the indigenous self. Martin Heidegger, the first philosopher I refer to, unrelentingly critiqued presence and its various offshoots. It is important to recognise that Heidegger linked presence with other tendencies to supercharge the self so that an entity is oriented towards in a particular way – *as* something disconnected from the rest of the world.

An indigenous approach with Heidegger

It would be unusual indeed for the indigenous writer to work with Heidegger without at least questioning his political and ideological leanings. Heidegger's philosophies, no less than he himself, are controversial. Bowie (1997) states that "Heidegger wrote some really frightful rubbish" (p.139), referring here to those writings of Heidegger's which are complicit with his involvement in Nazism. Heidegger joined other intellectuals, such as Stefan George and Ernst Jünger, who reacted to modernity and to the post–World War I depression being experienced by Germany and joined the Conservative Revolution. Not all members of the Conservative Revolution would turn out to participate in the agenda of the Nazi Party, but Heidegger certainly did, and this fact cannot be controverted or ignored. Whatever the social context, the sinister motives of Nazism are unjustifiable, and Heidegger's involvement would understandably cost him a huge degree of credibility. Indeed, some of his philosophies appear to reflect the fascist regime with which he was linked; his belief that German is (with Greek) a spiritually superior language (Heidegger, 2000) in the absence of any justification, for instance, could only be seen to be motivated by his nationalistic ideologies. Indigenous readers will undoubtedly view this statement of his with a great degree of scepticism, and may understandably refuse to work with him at all.

But for the indigenous reader, the hidden philosopher – the Plato, Aristotle, Descartes and Kant sitting unannounced within first assumptions and thus under the colonised indigenous perception of an object – is just as real and influential as the stated one (Mika, 2014b). With that in mind, if we are going to dispense with Heidegger, then we had better be ready to ignore those philosophers who would drive the brand of anthropology, science, research and law that would prove to be so devastating for indigenous communities, even if those philosophers never had indigenous peoples in their sights. It is here, ironically, that Heidegger is most useful for the indigenous critic, even if we must remember that he is to be approached with caution. Indeed, he is most valuable in his unravelling of presence. After noting Heidegger's chequered reputation, Bowie (1997) continues "he wrote much that was anything but rubbish" (p.139) and so his writings continue to at least raise questions about modernity, even if they might not answer them categorically. His love of questions was often a result of a desire to antagonise the reader into thought, but the questions also sought to work through a complex and difficult historicity which Heidegger saw had been the undoing of modern man. The motivation to provoke thought soon proved to have its desired effect, particularly among the Anglo-American philosophers; critics have variously accused his works of being obscure, weak in advancing arguments and invoking spurious etymologies (Bowie, 1997). Indeed, much of Heidegger's writing can impress the reader as tautologous and unfathomable. But the density of his work is shared by many phenomenologists who do not necessarily wish to articulate in a way similar to that of analytical philosophers. Part of some critics' discomfort with Heidegger's works must revolve, in the first instance, around the fact that he often writes speculatively. And the language he uses is deliberately newly coined because he wishes to leave behind common terms that have become corroded with extreme metaphysical perceptions of Being.

The highly present, isolated thing

In indigenous political gatherings, one quite commonly hears that the West – named in different ways – tends to stress one thing at a time. This complaint is also voiced in various terms, often including the words 'fragmentation', 'unspiritual', 'blinkered' and so on. Yet, an unsettling dilemma rears up at this point for any indigenous critic, with the colonised indigenous person having to now identify this problem among his or her own communities alongside the 'other' West. Here we return to one of my earlier propositions about education as worldedness: that it attends to the notion that one is constructed according to one's ability to reflect on colonisation. In the case of presence, the indigenous critic may be in danger of acknowledging the problem of high appearance, presence and fragmentation in the coloniser in an abstract way but, in asserting his or her own spiritual, holistic and interconnected metaphysics, could assume that the multi-faceted nature of presence has not yet also extended its tendrils into indigenous perception. Or, alternatively, it may be recognised as falling into indigenous lives in the academy and so on but be assumed to fall outside of areas of life such as ceremony, for instance, or be excluded somehow from tangible markers of indigenous cultural capital such as language. None of this is to say that there is not a marked difference in its extent or manifestation between the indigenous person and the non-indigenous self but that it does indeed exert its influence cannot be denied. Just as ominously, a truly holistic view would probably have to concede that what affects a group 'over there' affects the self. Thus, even if indigenous peoples were able to plausibly assert that it is only the West that is burdened with presence, already whilst making that assertion they would have had to reconsider their position.

It remains up to other indigenous authors to argue otherwise, but my own position here is that there is no aspect of indigenous life that presence leaves alone. Included in this worrying state of affairs, incidentally, is my own attempt at dismantling it in favour of an indigenous metaphysics. Both self and thing are moreover affected by presence and not all to the good for the indigenous person. Heidegger's ontological difference – thinking the difference between being and Beings – may therefore have relevance for the indigenous critic of the metaphysics of presence because of its in-depth critique of assumptions. Heidegger places the tendency in Western modernity to think of entities in terms of their properties firmly at the feet of Plato. The overriding assumption is one of forgetting what the real nature of Being is in favour of the beings' unchangeable qualities. Heidegger (1967a) argues that, in the Allegory of the Cave, Plato paved the way for a focus on truth as a set of correct propositions. He stated that the West now believes that an idea is that which illuminates reality the best and is thus ascendant in its provision of truth. The stages of adjustment to the light evident in the Allegory of the Cave are only important to the extent that they explain the idea as appearance "in the sense of the expression 'the sun shines'" (Heidegger, 1967a, p.131). With Idea becoming the visible and the appearance then what matters in the coming-to-presence of Beings is their *what-ness* or their *essential* (as opposed to their *existential*; Richardson, 2003). The clearer things are, the more truthful they are.

Heidegger's proposition that the world is discerned in terms of its solid properties, that this focus confuses Being with beings, and that in total these notions define metaphysics, is thought-provoking from an indigenous perspective. For the indigenous critic also, less emphasis may have been placed on the permanent properties of a thing, simply because of a thing's complete construction by all others. Heidegger (1977) avows that Plato's and Socrates' contribution to the metaphysical notion of essence was such that essence has come to mean "what remains permanently" (p.30). Metaphysics is focused on the way in which a being comes to presence, that is, the properties that make a being possible. Indigenous metaphysics does indeed think about the Being of beings but, as I go on to discuss in the following chapters, this originary way of thinking may be jeopardised by that same tendency that Heidegger laments. An indigenous approach would be to say that a being is simultaneously Being in its grander, ultimately unknowable sense, and that in thinking about beings in a colonised setting we now have to consider Being as a separate issue, whilst ensuring that it is not divorced from beings in general.

Indigenous metaphysics would, however, argue alongside Heidegger that too much emphasis is placed on an entity at the expense of Being, although we may insist that Being is reliant on entities and both transcends and constitutes those things. As with Heidegger, Being for indigenous thought is something that is not controllable as a whole by the human self, and he goes on to argue that the Western Platonic tradition emphasised Being only as equatable with a concept, not as the actual disclosure of the world mystery. In other words, Being has been relegated to the status of idea. The shining forth of the Idea and hence its visible manifestation meant that the Idea became what authentically *is*. The act of seeing, however, was what guaranteed "non-concealment of beings" (Richardson, 2003, p.308). Thus, the Idea is made to configure itself so that it will be viewed and perceived in the sense of knowing. Being is reduced to whatever is correspondent with reason through the ability of the self to see the Idea. Something is made present: "Briefly: non-concealment has become Idea, something seen . . . by a view" (Richardson, 2003, p.307). Colebrook (2006) states that Plato's insistence on the visibility of Being-as-Idea-as-beings flows over into what the word 'idea' means. According to her, words like *theoria* and *eidos* are "tied etymologically to looking" (p.133). In indigenous metaphysics, the idea may well indeed be an entity; however, it is not tied to any one particular means of perception, and it possesses a life force that it is both from itself and afforded by all things in the world. Thus, Colebrook's assertion that words reflecting this focus on sight – terms such as *theoria* and *eidos* – have become self-referential, is compelling, and she further posits that these terms now relate to "the complete and self-present grasp of identical being" (p.133). This kind of 'grasp' turns on a preconceived expectation, in which the equivalence inherent to the 'identical' forces the objectification of that which originally had an enmeshed relationship with the world. The indigenous, worlded object here is matched with an anticipated notion of what it should be, and the self and the object are educated in a disciplinary sense in that act: when a being/idea shines forth, then whether it matches up with an expectation, in other words, its *correctness*, is paramount. Indigenous peoples are hence influenced by a correspondence, an equivalence notion of truth that may not have formerly been their own (Mika, 2015a; Mika & Stewart, 2015). Here I will interject my own response, drawing on a metaphysics that I have argued indigenous peoples share to this idea of truth and its relationship to what Heidegger notes is a forgetting of one's originary thinking:

> Being-as-idea extricates both Being and idea from their constitution by all other things in the world. An idea is now hence posited as something that exists solely within the self. Being must also then be a human phenomenon. Correctness is underpinned by the idea's excommunication from all other things; for a perception to be correct, it must deal with the idea as far as the self has dominion over it.

When viewed from an indigenous worlded perspective, correctness in the sense of truth that is the correspondence between one entity and another is problematic because it assumes that the one entity has not yet interacted with the other. Because of that assumption, an entity is robbed of its relationship with the other – apart from the connection that can be made through an individual's mind. If we take the example of a mountain that the indigenous self has a relationship with through genealogy: with the metaphysics of presence, the mountain only *is* a mountain insofar as it has been equated with the term by the speaker or onlooker. I have made the mountain what it is by virtue of my intervention on it through terminology. I have *correctly* identified it as a mountain because I have managed to connect it to a proper idea of it. The mountain is hence matched with its proper category. In this act, the mountain is capable of being permanently unanchored from its constitution by all other things in the world. Most important, *I* have domain over my representation of the mountain: it (and all other things) has not in any way brought my attention to it in its materiality, but instead it is a cognitive tendency of mine to attend to it. Idea and thing are actually quite separate because ideas exist independently of the thing. Its true form lies elsewhere, but it is up to me to bring the thing in front of me into line with my ability to access that idea.

In the narrower form of education, too, we see a special love of presence and its marriage with the idea of an entity. Elkholy (2008) explains that

> [b]ecause truth is now oriented toward what can be perceived 'as something' through the lens of the idea, education occurs fundamentally with respect to sight. Human nature must subsequently be educated to orient itself toward the outward appearance of things as they may be grasped by the idea lighted by the Idea of the Good.
>
> (p.2)

Education, as Thomas and Thomson (2015) argue in relation to Heidegger's critique, is "quietly" (p.103) led along by presence, resulting in the correct notion of a thing becoming education's most pressing concern. But there is a deeper, even more speculative problem at stake here for indigenous peoples, regardless of whether we are discussing education in its orthodox sense or within its broadest ambit. From an indigenous perspective, as we have seen, the assumptions behind perception and proposition construct entities that have repercussions for well-being. By well-being, I mean the health of entities beyond, but inclusive of, just the human, and beyond what shows up in the self's DNA. There is indeed an indigenous notion of essence that DNA corresponds to in its philosophical sense, as I noted in Chapter 3, but this essence is not able to be studied or conceived of as a 'property' of the entity – it might therefore be *useful* to term this phenomenon 'DNA', but its naming in that way comes at a risk because the term itself, not to mention its entitised nature, carries out a static act on the fluidity of things. In an indigenous conception, it is the world in its entirety that is influenced through the positing of the mountain as correctly corresponding to my idea of it – not simply the mountain or myself. Maori, for instance, might argue that one's orientation to the world through one's spiritual, emotional, mental and physical facets dictates well-being (Durie, 1994); I add here that human propositions about the world also similarly (but invisibly) block the capacity of any thing to culminate in tandem with all others.

The problem with the certain self

It will be recalled that the Maori term *Ako* discloses the fluid nature of the activity of the world within any one thing. It does not just 'mean' this; it actually *reveals* it, works in tandem with it, thereby showing that language is itself actively full with the world. Language for indigenous peoples is beyond the individual's mind, but this belief in the material nature of language is threatened by Descartes's privileging of the self's cognition. Descartes did not *invent* the mind's prominence – Heidegger sees definite strains of Plato in Descartes' thought – but he did intensify it. With the term *Ako* in much New Zealand government literature, we see a Cartesian expectation that both a present-oriented idea of the 'other' and an object to be learned about can be posited before the self. Ako is no more than 'reciprocal teacher and learner' and hence becomes what is manageable in government policy. What is manageable in policy, in turn, is what is allowed to appear as fully present and undisturbed by any other thing. In that process, Ako as a term and concept is reduced to human entities that will be occupied with an equally present correct idea of an object (Mika, 2012). In all respects, a true knowledge of the world is obtained through viewing it as if it were in front of and external to the self. As a participant in the reductionist notion of Ako, I 'throw before' (the etymology of *object*) me what is to be learned, as well as the person from whom I am learning. All truth emanates from me, and hence I have separated myself out from what was one culmination of all things.

It is Descartes in whom Heidegger places this forgetfulness of the ontology of substance. Descartes refers to the divine on the one hand and created entities on the other, as distinctive from each other. The ontology that underlies them is ignored. Because God is ontologically 'perfect', self-sufficient and individual, entities can only exist through intervention. In Cartesian fashion, I continue the message of Plato – against the indigenous perspective – that the mountain is capable of being represented as a shell-like idea. If I continue Plato's thinking in my positing of Ako, then I neatly and tidily assign to each phenomenon – self, other and object to be known – their rightful place. In all respects, I have asserted myself over other things in the world, and I have fragmented things so that they can be easily managed by me. At stake here is not a way of knowing the world but, rather, an initial *turn* towards it, even before the turn as such has happened. A physical entity in indigenous belief, as we have seen, is a fundamentally uncertain one because of its collapse with all facets of time and with other dimensions. But, according to Heidegger, in a Cartesian view the entity is only valid insofar as it is produced and sustained in the widest sense. Here, Heidegger (1962) notes that "[a]ll entities other than God need to be 'produced' in the widest sense and also to be sustained" (p.125), and that one gives *attributes* to make an entity what it is. Its attributes are accessible through its extension, its physical properties which enable it to take up space. The entity, formerly valuable to its own self and to other things in the world (including humans), is now further objectifiable because it is measurable. Heidegger (1962) understands that substances are conceived of through their permanent characteristics which give those substances their ability to take up space, the *"res corporea"* (p.123). The world is defined in accordance with that most basic assumption, where its things are calculated according to "length, breadth, and thickness" (p.123).

Again, it is the intellect that is prioritised as the means through which humanity gets access to the attributes. Mathematical knowing is key here, and Heidegger's view is that Aristotle must accept some of the responsibility for the move from self-presencing nature to nature as involving properties. Heidegger here argues that Aristotle confused nature with artefact (Glazebrook, 2000) and so nature came to be thought of as something which was formed by an artist, rather than as that which came to presence. Thus, nature came to be a *thing*, and it is at this point that we encounter the beginning of the mathematical projection of nature through science. What follows from that interpretation is a projection of nature in terms of a thing's properties (thingness). Thinking in terms of properties is a result of nature being projected so that one understands it as comprising something in advance. In other words, we approach nature already knowing the things that lie in it: here Heidegger refers to the ancient Greek term for 'mathematical' – μαθήματα – and argues that humanity already has already *posit*-ed things in advance. Science is hence *posit*-ivist. Heidegger (1967b) states that

> [t]he . . . [mathematical] are the things insofar as we take cognizance of them as what we already know them to be in advance, the body as the bodily, the plant-like of the plant, the animal-like of the animal, the thing-ness of the thing, and so on.
>
> (p. 73)

Numbers become important because they can describe the thing-ness that is already known. What is crucial is first that the world is approached *as* a predicted ontology and numbers are then assigned because they are the only means of describing that positivity. As Glazebrook (2000) states when she evaluates Heidegger's stance on science, we project nature in an epistemically certain way. This act occurs, however, because we have preordained the world *as* something and have made ourselves certain subjects in that act. Subjectism manifests itself in the subjective reckoning of Being: one can be certain of any other being by bringing it into his sphere of regard. The subject decides what Being is because the subject, in proposing their own selves, proposes beings as objects. Thus, another thing in the world is only that because it has been placed in opposition to the self. Richardson (2003) identifies three consequences of subjectism: first, the world, in being proposed as the object, is cast in opposition to the subject so that the subject can regard it. Second, philosophical anthropology comes into existence, where 'anthropology,' according to Heidegger, throws humanity into subjectism. In line with this second development, after man is proposed as subject, all philosophical analysis rests on explaining man as the ultimate. This is a definitive development for Western humanity, who then, as Richardson states, tries to resurrect a nebulousness through the phrase 'life force' but still encapsulates Being as beings by forcing 'Life force' to fit something palpable. Third, man starts to look for 'values.' By this is meant that as Being becomes lost to immediate appreciation then man compensates by endowing beings with 'value.'

The dominant discourse becomes one of culture. It would seem that this then becomes the domain of philosophical anthropology, linking us back to Richardson's second point.

These more conscious modes of development are not precisely 'presence', but they are sufficiently impactful to be mentioned, and they can be thought of as its progeny or offshoots. It should be obvious that Richardson's reading of Heidegger opens up several possibilities for an indigenous response, fundamentally because subjectism is so widespread. Whilst we may surmise that indigenous peoples have taken on attributes that reflect Heidegger's warning, more important for a discussion of worlding is the *theoretical* consequences of this tendency to throw things in front of the self. Placing the object before the self is the problem of the indigenous scholar, pupil, traditional expert and community in general because it insists that a true grasp of a thing cannot be had until it is distinct from the self. This conceptual rift between self and thing is implicit in most areas of colonisation and it asks for the buy-in of the indigenous self at all times. I have dealt with the first two steps of subjectism earlier, and refer to them again in the next chapter, but it is the third phase that illustrates the problem most concretely. If, as indigenous peoples, we have cast the mountain in front of us to be regarded as an 'out there' phenomenon, we have simultaneously privileged ourselves. We have gained dominion over the mountain (and with presence, dominion is always already gained). But we also make the mountain that much more vulnerable to ourselves in terms of its worth. Indeed, I have acted this very problem out through referring to it fairly consistently as an example, to clarify what *I* want to say. We have then rendered all other things vulnerable due to their constitution with the mountain. Any argument that we have, at worst, only disturbed some quality of the mountain is to revert back to the problem of subjectism, because then we have once again thrown it in front of us as an individual entity. This idea surges out into mainstream social intervention: we try and protect a solitary entity in various ways, whether by legislation or policy, because we have identified that it is the *mountain* that needs protection in this instance. It may become a site of interest, or it could be an object of concern for environmentalists. Similarly, I would be playing into the hands of presence and its subjectism if I simply tried to somehow obscure the *idea of the mountain* in my writing about it (although I do suggest in my conclusion chapter that there is a place for a playful romanticism of a long-held idea, however brief its effect is).

Beyond the senses: metaphysical colonisation

Philosophical colonisation

We have seen that the metaphysics of presence prioritises entities over Being. Moreover, Being in an indigenous sense is separated through presence from the thing before us; the thing is entirely solitary and self-evident as it appears and stays with us in the present. The Being that it *is* informed by is also permanent as a current idea; it is not the Being that indigenous peoples think of as an ever-disclosive entity that itself constitutes that indigenous thinking. The latter instance of Being relies on a collapsed notion of time, in which what is presently before the self is equally past and future. The indigenous self is itself one confluence of all those stages of time. In the metaphysics of what is before us, according to Heidegger, we are prevented from an authentic relationship with the world. We project the world as we want it to appear, without leaving it to show itself on its own account. This "purposeful self-assertion" (Heidegger, 2001, p.114) is an aspect of the self's anthropocentrism, where the self projects itself as highly present, which heralds a break with the fullness of the world. Heidegger is quick to point out that this self-willing nature of man is not a problem of the individual. No one person can claim not to be self-assertive, self-projecting. Nature is represented, and the self is moved towards that idea of nature, not of nature itself. Indeed, the concept of nature is represented by its etymology, according to Heidegger (2005), who provocatively stated that the term refers to what is at base of the properties of a thing. Incorporated into that notion is that nature is given to reproduce, not self-generate in terms of the idea that something *persists*, in the sense of the more original term *phusis*. Vycinas (2008) believes that phusis can nevertheless be nature "as left to be the way it is in itself and not the way it is when faced by an impersonal, scientific subject [natura]" (p.135). In indigenous metaphysics, nature can refer to collapsed time and worlds that are fully infused throughout an entity; it is independent of the self, although the self participates in concert with other things. The presence notion of nature, however, leads to a human delusion that all things are level and unable to be anything but acquiescent. From the vantage point of worldedness, the human self is then capable of ensuring that a thing is forever 'this or that' and passive to the extent that it lacks its own vitality. It is inanimate, unaccompanied by the All that the indigenous worldview looks to. Nature in this respect is reduced to something physical and tangible, nothing to do with imperceptible worlds or concurrent notions of time. Nature is also reduced to concept, and it loses its resonance as a true entity. It will be recalled that an indigenous metaphysics of worldedness acknowledges that even an idea is an entity that is all-constituted. In a metaphysics where nature is laid out flat for humanity (Heidegger, 1977), however, the world is thereby construed *as* this or that. Heidegger (2001) makes a link here between what he calls 'the Open', which in its proper form is the disclosure of the world in all its possibilities, and 'willing', which involves neutralising the world so that it is no longer its former self, depicted by chaos and self-fulfilment. As with Heidegger's admonishment of humanity's tendency to bring things into order if they threaten to present themselves in an unpredictable manner, an indigenous metaphysics would resist suborning the thing, as representative of the world in total, to the isolable.

Underpinning all this is one of the most trenchant criticisms of dominant Western thought – that of Heidegger's essence of technology. Heidegger tracks the notion of technology back to its most essential manifestation and in so doing deliberately makes it a philosophical, not a sociological, issue. In indigenous realities, it is common to see historical descriptions of how schools, health systems, legal processes and so on, oppressed indigenous peoples. Heidegger explicitly removes the problem from these sorts of explanations and forces it into a more abstract realm that is nonetheless important for indigenous thought and well-being. Already we can speculate on this deliberate method from an indigenous perspective, especially if we have at the forefront that ideas are equally worthy of preservation as people. Huffman (2010) has suggested that "American Indian educational scholars have tended to focus more on microlevel issues than they have on macrolevel ones" (p.14). Of course, American Indian scholars are not the only group to which this statement could pertain, and it is interesting that Heidegger and Huffman are both arguing for an emphasis on some deeper problems, with Heidegger's concern being for his own (German) people. But for the indigenous scholar, Huffman's statement is extendable to indigenous peoples generally, and it encourages theorising on some of the reasons for a lack of focus on metaphysical colonisation. To begin with, indigenous peoples are simply too busy to find the time to contemplate deep colonisation. Graham Smith (2003) is sceptical of this busyness, however, suggesting that it has been deliberately introduced by the coloniser to prevent reflection on the possibilities of oppression. Among the plethora of health, legal and political problems that beset indigenous peoples, one is discouraged from speculating and is instead 'consoled' with what is immediately accessible or present. The indigenous self's docility that I anticipate here comes with the proposition of certainty that constantly reassures the indigenous self that he or she should simply rest with what is plainly knowable. An uncritical acceptance of colonisation is therefore the result of colonisation itself. Indigenous writer Waziyatawin (2004) asserts that indigenous minds were infiltrated through "the combined efforts of government institutions and Christian workers" (p.360). It is certainly possible that traditional indigenous community members were wary of assertions of thoroughgoing certainty about things (Mika, 2012), for instance, but the ability and openness to think critically about the nature and sources of those types of utterances would subsequently fall victim to that Western religio-political collaboration. What is important for indigenous peoples here is that a culturally appropriate method of bringing colonial thought into question has been, calculatedly or otherwise, gravely threatened. Regardless of what the colonising agenda has intended, a limited horizon of thinking has been encouraged and has brought about a mere collection of facts – a Freirean 'banking' – to work from, thus maintaining a colonising status quo.

A further explanation that clarifies what appears to be an indigenous engagement with other facets of colonisation but not the metaphysical, may be found in the oftentimes-dire nature of everyday, concrete indigenous existence. I have already mentioned the tendency of colonisation to be thought of as a social event, and the rationale for this may become clearer when we consider that indigenous researchers, commentators and professionals feel that attention to this social deprivation is exigent. This point is somewhat different to the one raised earlier, where sheer distraction is placed in front of the metaphysical problem so that it is not even visible. Ruminations on such abstract matters as metaphysics of presence, seen in this light, are an indulgence that indigenous communities simply cannot afford. Indeed, it may be seen as a problem for the West solely, not one that concerns indigenous communities. Besides being irrelevant, a mode of thought alighting on metaphysics may be considered an undesirable one. This is not to say that other indigenous writers do not address the issue in one form or another but the *sustained* description and theorising around a metaphysics of presence, as the original colonising orientation, still silently calls out to be recognised by the indigenous author. One writer who does indeed maintain a continued discussion of indigenous metaphysics, not as a sole theme but in direct relation to Western metaphysics, is Dolores Calderon. Calderon (2008) argues that there are fundamental differences between the two that manifest as utterly distinct knowledge paradigms. However, her critique of Western metaphysics is described more as its manifestations through fragmentation rather than the even more fundamental issue that flows from representing an object as thoroughly present.

It is, for Heidegger, the essence of technology that blinds the self to an originary thinking about Being. These blockades to de-emphasising the sociological and foregrounding the philosophical, simultaneously or necessarily turn one away from recognising true oppression by making the issue one that does not have to inquire into Being. In relation to indigenous inquiries into colonisation, it seems as if presence has been omitted, but, before continuing that discussion, a further concern needs to be articulated. Whilst it is true that indigenous commentators *appear* to privilege the social aspects of oppression, they may also be dealing with presence in their own way. Presence is not spelt out but it is aimed at through the social lens. I choose here to moderate my former paragraphs because of the worlded nature and the collapse of the imperceptible with the concrete realms that it calls for. Social and metaphysical would not be quite as distinct from each other as I have thus far positioned them. If I depict the mountain as superior to the land around it, or if I tend to make 'Ako' a schooling process, I have acted with social force – but in a way that is no different from presence. Or, rather, presence is present in the social act as much as the concrete act itself. As for Heidegger, we can see that he intends to foreground one tendency over another. He may therefore seem to be too concerned with abstract phenomena. This criticism would sit well with the conservatism that is Heidegger's thinking, where one's wistfulness for the past is buttressed by a cynicism towards what is current in the form of modernity, where it is not the item before us that is the problem so much as its continuing source. As far as we are concerned with Heidegger at this point, the dilemma of presence as a metaphysical, non-social event is certainly emphasised, but, importantly, in the light of its deprivation that threatens humanity on an everyday basis and in terms of its imposition on all domains. In its own way, metaphysics is for Heidegger therefore a thoroughly social event as well, albeit a broad one. He simply has not conducted a sociological inquiry into specific injustices. Indigenous peoples, it is likely, could be dealing with metaphysical colonisation when they are challenging social injustices such as land and language loss, health inequalities and racism, even though this may not be their intention. Although Heidegger and indigenous writers start from different points, each starting point deals with the unstated other.

For indigenous writers, the possibility that presence has been dimly and incidentally targeted through the social phenomenon must nevertheless be considered as not going far enough. What Heidegger has done is switch the emphasis, and with good cause. In doing so, he also re-attunes us to something else again: the self's ability to *question* Being itself in resisting a dominant focus on things as self-evident and present. Is there, then, any benefit to be had in recentring an indigenous notion of Being – re-familiarising our minds to that as a sole issue, rather than incidentally reaching to it through the problem of institutional racism, for instance? Where formerly there may not have been any point in calibrating Being as the essential problem, an indigenous loss of attention to Being means that it now has to be thought of as a separate, urgent issue rather than simply and inadvertently 'there'. There is something profound that is highlighted in that process because suddenly our indigenous response to the social problem is seen in its fully worlded capacity. We would be questioning the largely unfathomable and imperceptible *advance* that has been set up towards things in the world through colonisation, and identifying the deepest motivation of colonisation that we can. Simultaneously, the potential for theorising on the more positive Being of things in the world becomes possible.

This indigenous discussion with Heidegger relates to his rejection of technology as machinery (what I have called the *social* aspect of technology) and his reconnection of technology with its essence, or its enduring call to the human self to establish things in the world as this or that. In its essence, technology blocks an authentic relationship with the world; it is a deeply philosophical impoverishment. He argues that there were distinctive interpretations of the etymology of *technology, technē,* and that these paved the way for certain understandings of the world (Lambeir, 2002). It moved in its sense from practical knowledge in the ancient Greeks to 'factory production' and, thence, according to Lambeir, to the creation of theoretical frameworks that integrate with that earlier emphasis on production and that engage with systems and the meeting of needs. *Technē*, moreover, is linked with 'bringing-forth' or *poiēsis*. Both *technē* and *epistēmē* are related in that they refer to a familiarity with something, to be adept at it (Heidegger, 1977). This form of knowledge is a way of revealing (Mika, 2016b), where something is unconcealed. This, Heidegger continues, is "where *alētheia*, truth, happens" (p.13).

What is this 'mode of revealing' in an indigenous context? In a Maori sense at least, a thing reveals *itself*. Truth, then, could be equated with the ability of a thing to always hold some part of itself hidden whilst presenting itself to my senses; it is the inherent self-constructive nature of the thing, with its full constitution by all else, that I may have a part to play in with that revelation of the entity, but I would not have even considered paving the way for me to focus on it if the world had not configured itself in a certain way or claimed my attention. I may carve its likeness, speak about it in either the Maori or English languages (and hence I appear to express it or give it form), but it is fully *there* whilst holding some aspect of itself to itself – unrevealed as well as disclosed. The Maori term *whaka* that I discussed in Chapter 3 holds some possible similarities with this aspect of a thing showing itself in its own way even though, as I noted, it has taken on a decidedly causative sense. *Whaka* is an extraordinary entity (note, not just a linguistic particle) because it suggests that all things drive against each other so that a thing manifests them all in decidedly different ways. It is active, chaotic but formative.

For Heidegger, there was also in Western history a time when material was brought forth in its own way. Art is one creative mode of bringing something forth; it forms a schism in the world that brings a thing into unconcealment. His well-known explanation of phusis, through the creation and persistence of a temple, asserts what was important for the early Greeks and what is problematic for modernity:

> Standing there, the building holds its ground against the storm raging above it and so first makes the storm itself manifest in its violence. The luster and gleam of the stone, though itself apparently glowing only by the grace of the sun, yet first brings to light the light of the day, the breadth of the sky, the darkness of the night. The steadfastness of the work contrasts with the surge of the surf. . . . Tree and grass, eagle and bull, snake and cricket first enter into their distinctive shapes and thus come to appear as what they are. The Greeks early called this emerging and rising in itself and in all things phusis. It clears and illuminates, also, that on which and in which man bases his dwelling. We call this ground the earth. What this word says is not to be associated with the idea of a mass of matter deposited somewhere, or with the merely astronomical idea of a planet. Earth is that whence the arising brings back and shelters everything that arises without violation. In the things that arise, earth is present as the sheltering agent.
>
> (Heidegger, 2001, p.41)

Highlighted with any one thing, is the emergence and persistence of the world. Earth, rock, tree, snake, eagle, stone, sky, "light of day", surf – all bear a connection through the emergence of the temple but not *because of* the temple. Heidegger does not attempt to exhaust all possibilities through his listing of these things, but insists that they, in turn, are brought into the world through others. The building or temple is only possible through those other things' manifestation, but those other things are only possible through the arising of the building. These phenomena work against and yet with each other (Mika, 2016b), allowing for the possible appearance of all things through the strife they bring to each other. They can only act against each other, though, because they are all implicated together. Heidegger's lengthy description will, I suspect, be familiar to the indigenous reader. He de-emphasises the building whilst starting with it as the main theme. It is not a construction that exists on its own, as a current idea of presence suggests; it actually comes to its true form through its interplay with those other elements he mentions. Although one of his aims is to develop an awareness of humanity's historicity in its relationship with the building – the self's ancient and continuing reliance on presenting material *as* that which is given Being through its thorough association with all else – a relevance for the indigenous reader is that the building is *not* a set of particular qualities. It is not self-sustaining; the stone, sun, light, sky and darkness are not permanently reliable for the purposes of the building; its activity against the rest of the world is its truth, and is only possible because of the fact that the building stands 'there'; and things appear as what they are *partly* because of humanity's intervention but not entirely so.

Heidegger clearly suspects that the building's immersion within its environment indicates a kind of tension between one thing and another. He sets about reflecting this strife in his discussion of the Fourfold, in which sky, earth, mortality and divinities are at odds with each other whilst being inextricably joined. Very little has been written about Heidegger's Fourfold, perhaps because of its association with the esoteric (Plebuch, 2011), but it has several points of entry for indigenous worldedness. It highlights that things in the world do not lie nicely alongside each other, as if they are thoroughly symmetrical. Indigenous peoples are well aware that things are interconnected, but how one thing positions itself alongside another whilst they construct each other deserves more thought. For Heidegger, earth is at one with all other three but moves against them, the sky does the same, divinities are inseparable and at odds with the other three and one's eventual demise is 'crunched' within the perpetual reach of those other things with the human self. An indigenous worldedness could respond that one's death is the constant drive towards the earth that is at once in tension with the sky. And what of those first beings that indigenous people often refer to in their creation narratives – the 'divinities', as Heidegger calls them? In the Maori tradition at least, they represent both "the finite, temporalizing Being-process which is the very condition of the possibility of the presencing of the gods'" (Capobianco, 1988, p.185) and the gods themselves that participate as entities along with other things. They are composed of those other entities and cannot be thought of as independent, but they are also responsible – as much as other things – for disclosing other entities (Mika, 2014a). Their dual status as entity and constitutive force suggests that the "powerful beauty and brilliance of mythical names" (Capobianco, 1988, p.185) is only possible because of their influence from whatever resides outside of (yet as part of) them. Thus, the idea of Maori 'gods as natural phenomena' is only partly correct because it ignores the fact that Being, the totality of the world that includes those gods, allows those gods and their names to manifest at all. Heidegger similarly believed that any preconceived formation of religion, in which humanity incidentally *created* the place of gods, hindered a truly phenomenological approach to religion. Crowe (2007) maintains that Heidegger advocates considering the experience of the Greeks, before approaching 'religion' in an assumed way: "[Heidegger] warns against simply taking over the common conception of the Greek gods as 'personifications' of natural forces and of abstract concepts like 'justice' or 'truth'" (p.229). For Maori, the 'divinities' are activity and entity, and are intimately connected with all other things.

But if we recall Heidegger as indigenous critics, we may be struck by his excitingly critical approach to the notion of earth. Earth is foremost *not* a solid entity, taking up space or important for having its extension (Mika, 2014a). Such a view of earth runs completely counter to an indigenous understanding, which presents the earth as a multidimensional entity that shares in, and enfolds with, the history, practices and philosophies of indigenous people. In an indigenous colonised experience, presence has reduced earth in its scope to mean exactly what Heidegger warns against. Presence obliterates all other orientations towards it so that it will only ever appear as a solid, constrained entity. Heidegger calls this very first approach to a thing 'enframing'. The German original, *Gestell*, has a direct relationship to the practice of 'gathering' so that things are put in restraint or set in disciplined order. Earth is a poignant object of enframing for indigenous people in general because it does indeed constitute the apparently solid phenomenon of *land* that forms the basis of a great deal of debate within law, for instance, which has the "power . . . to organize our awareness of phenomena before they reach the level of consciousness" (Banner, 1999, p.807). Earth in legal forums, and also in usual and everyday perception, is put in order not just through any particular conscious act – it can be set aside in what Heidegger terms 'standing reserve' – but also through one's deepest expectation of how things in the world are generally meant to manifest. Enframing is primarily a metaphysical demand that cannot be sensed in any way; it simply *is*, without having any special form. Earth falls victim to the gathering of all things to enframing because it is proposed as one of several highly present entities. Park (2006) hints at the dissimilar meanings between land, on one hand, and a Maori notion of earth, on the other, when he states that "losses that Māori have suffered since the treaty, while sited in the solid surface of the Earth that we call 'land', have been much more than the loss of ground" (p.242). Land is posited as solid ground and very little else (Mika, 2015b).

Earth's reduction to its *usable* qualities as land is part of what Heidegger calls 'standing reserve'. While 'enframing' is the orientation towards the world such that it will appear as ordered, standing reserve is the stockpiling of things. It is not the initial metaphysics of presence but a subsequent act. Where an enframing view would have already expected entities to have formed a present idea, standing reserve would find voice in Ako, for instance, in its relegation of knowledge, the human selves (teacher and learner), and curricula, to the side for a later date, ready to be called on and used when required. But to achieve that step, enframing has to have taken place – although 'taken place' is a misnomer, as enframing has always-already occurred. It never has not occurred. Heidegger suggests that we have always already been constrained by a continual perception of things, without realising it. An assertive voice has been established that insists on the proper and productive place for things.

An indigenous interpretation might be that, at some stage, things in the world were set up to resonate in a particular way and they hence are established to always show themselves in only one way to the human self. The human self, incidentally, has also been attuned in that way. Heidegger laments the fact that there is now no longer any god that puts humanity in the realm of deep mystery, and suggests that the blinkered orientation to the world that enframing insists on is so close to the self that, like a god, it seems hidden (Mika, 2016b). In fact, the modern essence of technology reveals itself so completely and is so present that it is taken for granted. As Bonnett (2002) has identified, "we 'enframe' things by turning them into *instances*" (p.234), indeed by having turned towards them *as* instances, meaning that things have become suddenly, consciously part of the perpetual Being of presence. One of these things, earth (or *whenua* in Maori), was always bound to become the removed thing – land. It would thereafter mean no more than land in policy and law, which are themselves examples of enframing.

The relationship of metaphysics of presence to language

If language is as straightforward as an outcome of an idea – I think such and such, and transmit a likeness of that through speech (either because I have directly experienced an entity or because I have something in mind) – then there are no problems to deal with. If, however, language is truly more precious than that, having a spiritual component as Abrams (1996) has maintained it does, then an enormous dilemma awaits us, still to be confronted. It certainly seems that language is especially difficult to handle in a discussion because it is the very means of conveying thought *whilst* originating from the full interplay of the world. It is thus tempting to treat it in terms of its linguistic features. and so we are moved away from addressing language and distracted by the problem of specific terms. I maintain that the latter focus is valid, but it only helps us in a limited fashion to answer our inquiry into what language is in its essence. Certain terms in one's native language may provide signposts to a discussion about the essence of language, but they must be incorporated into a much bigger intention of considering the nature of language in its entirety.

If language for indigenous worldedness is one means of expressing the All of the world, as I have suggested earlier, then its nature exceeds a description of 'spiritual' because it is simultaneously material. One aspect of presence, though, is its continued representation as having the static property of 'otherworldly', removing it into a much more rarefied realm. Language itself is then better off conceived as 'thiswordly' according to presence. By 'thisworldly', though, I have something specific in mind: that indigenous thought is trained to focus on the current dimension of perception as all that exists. We have seen that an indigenous worldedness does not privilege such a view, as dimensions instead may be collapsed. 'Thisworldly' would not otherwise pose a problem for our metaphysics, but it does if other realms are excluded from our thought. Language is unconfined in interconnection; like all other things, it resonates with the world so that it is itself 'worlded'. However, in presence, language becomes a human attribute that is moreover positioned so that it seeks the accuracy of the self's ideas.

Central to the influence of presence that singles one thing out from another in advance, 'de-collapses' it so that things are separated from one entity (if we think of the problem in indigenous terms), is a representation through the bedrock of an idea about a thing. Language is crucial in this pursuit. Paradoxically, as I noted in earlier chapters, language itself may well be another thing in the world within which we exist, even as we now talk about it. It then gives us the impression, if we are not careful, that it emanates solely from us, but it is not a human attribute so much as a thing constructed by all things in the world. The effects of a metaphysical view of Being as beings, and the pervasion of a technological worldview in which objects are proposed before the human subject and then considered as raw materials, reveal themselves in instrumentalist views of language. We are not concerned simply with wrongly translated terms here (although inadequate and reductive translations are an offshoot of presence); we are also worried about what language is *in itself* (Mika, 2015b). The effects of a metaphysical view of Being as beings, and the pervasion of a technological worldview in which objects are proposed before the human subject and then considered as raw materials, reveal themselves in instrumentalist views of language as a phenomenon in its own right. Heidegger (1971) thus noted that "[s]peech is challenged to correspond to the ubiquitous orderability of what is present" (p.420). Returning to the vernacular of technology, we can see that Heidegger was evaluating the dominant belief that language itself was made to come forth at our whim, waiting to be discovered as material, ready for construction. Language in that view is then a standing reserve and is no different from any other aspect of modern human life. In that respect language may be said to have become instrumental. Obviously that view of language sits well with capitalist language which identifies and names objects in terms of their value. Terms such as *human resources, human capital* and even *expenditure* are clear examples of that sort of language by which, Heidegger might say, the self-showing of language is instead suborned to fit a view of the world that has already decided what it wants to see – a permanent and reliable normality of wealth creation. His predecessor Novalis resisted the normalisation of the world into figures and numbers; Heidegger explores in as much detail the pathology of that process.

There are various approaches to language that Heidegger wants to bring to our attention, but one of the most central is that which aligns directly with the enframing of the world through our preordained orientation to it (Mika, 2016b) – the idea that that language is there to express a cognitive state of the self. The idea that language is available for human creation, to express a logical story, is evident in the structuralist school of thought, whose main linguistic theoretician was Ferdinand de Saussure. Saussure's work, titled *Course in General Linguistics*, would soon be heralded as a major revolution in linguistic theory and is worthy of mention here. Briefly, Saussure's *language* is concerned with the ways in which language functions at a precise moment by considering "how the elements fit together" (Johnston, 2006, p.187). The relationship between a 'sound-image' (signifier), which is essentially psychological and not an audible sound, and the concept (signified) is arbitrary. Heidegger argues against the signification model of language because it forms an abstraction that consists in the divorce from the Being inherent to the spoken. It is the very realm of the spoken that is important to Heidegger (David Smith, 2003). An indigenous response here may be that not only is the separation from Being innate to Saussure's approach detrimental to an indigenous view of language, but that it is also problematic for a relationship with the world's things. The thing is lost in favour of the word assigned to it. An indigenous worlded view of language is far more expansive than that allowed by Saussure's, as it rests outside the domains of human thought and emotion. Additionally, an important difference resides in the view of the thing to be named. In dominant approaches to language, the thing is always there to be named, and thus, it is ever present. The subject is always able to name the thing, and indeed, it must be named so that we can grasp its reality.

Language has its own way of interacting with and constituting the self, and the opposing view that language is a human product, devoid of anything of its own making, does not sit well with an indigenous worlded perspective. Browne (2005) discusses the principle of *wairua* (spirit) to explain language's essentially non-human derivation: "Wairua, a spiritual phenomenon . . . enters the learning environment through a variety of means, which can then be utilised within the teaching and learning process" (p.6). Wairua is connected with the body and sound, and language is therefore an entity that cannot be reduced to the human sphere. There is a relationship between the external world and the self with language, where the profound elements of the Maori language are indeed the natural world (Jeffries & Kennedy, 2008). Another's utterances are material and abide with the self. In all cases, it is language that deals with the human self first. Similarly, language for Heidegger is our master: it is the world of language "that things first come into being and are" (2000, p.15). The danger of hardened terms that try to block the intrusion of other things in the world arises in translation but also in a much more primordial intention to discipline those things in the first instance (Mika, 2016a; 2016b).

Again, an example from a Maori context illuminates this scenario. There are several Maori terms that are liberally drawn on in policy and law; these terms have become no different to their English counterparts, to such an extent that one is left wondering what the point is of the translation. It will be recalled that I referred to the term *whakapapa* and its coalescing nature, with things in the world contained within the world itself whilst it alludes to that worlded phenomenon with other things. In policy, however, it will be recounted that it is nearly always translated as 'genealogy'. Not only is its meaning reduced; as Novalis (2005) put it, it engages with "the mere breadth and system of knowledge" (p.115), resulting in the loss of forcefulness to the word. It becomes something overused and tamed. The term *whakapapa* may well be one of the most-used terms in policy (*whanau*, equated with 'family', is another one). Other terms, such as *ako, whanau, mana* (status/pride) and so on, are often used in conjunction with *whakapapa* to refer to something apparently different to their English equivalents. More than simply window-dressing, though, the practice of peppering Maori terms throughout a strictly presence-oriented text such as policy makes the entities within the term adhere to one desired outcome. The things are governed by the text as a whole more than they are by the English equivalent, but perhaps the latter is particularly influential on the Maori term and its phenomena.

These Maori terms are forced to conform quite deeply to the presence nature of the text and they become its emissary. In a worlded indigenous view, presence devitalises the full interplay of things with one thing, resulting in that one thing – and thereafter a representation of it as an idea – becoming the most important aspect. Indigenous focuses on language often emphasise that it should be protected; presumably, the various facets of integrity of even a term need to be retained. Alongside its pure meaning, a term's deep sense and orientation to other things are to be guarded. A term is capable of being subverted to reflect the subtlety of its context – it could well be that indigenous writers have this in mind when they use their languages – and it ends up becoming presence-oriented. This prospect is deeply disturbing for indigenous groups because language is perhaps seen as at once extremely precious and yet vulnerable to colonisation. Indigenous languages in these instances are tools of presence, in that they add to the presence of the text but with an indigenous exterior. In this context, language is merely a set of sounds that convey an idea of the emptiness of the term; thus, the indigenous term in the text carries out the aim of presence without any threat to it.

In his book *Phenomenology of Perception*, Maurice Merleau-Ponty (2003) summarises two philosophies of language that he saw as dominant. Firstly, he describes the empiricist model, whereby the word is "called[ed] . . . up in accordance with the laws of neurological mechanics or those of association" (p.205) and which then empowers the person to speak. The second model is the result of what he terms 'intellectualism,' which is essentially another name for a rationalistic process of language. In that process language is the result of thought. Both consider that language is primarily there for communication where importantly the world is separated from the human subject apart from the latter's ability to represent things. In the case of the empiricist model, the object is the external world which provides sensations. In both cases, language itself is the result of either thought or sensation and hence may be viewed as the object of a human process. Kockelmans (1972) states that Aristotle "presumes . . . that the written letters and words of a language signify sounds, that the sounds, in turn, are signs of the thoughts of the soul, and that the latter, finally, signify the relevant things or state of affairs" (p.4). Heidegger was of two minds about Aristotle, finding vestiges of pre-Socratic Being in the latter's *Physics* (Glazebrook, 2000) but disagreeing with Aristotle's assertions that "logos as discourse" (Heidegger, 2000, p.136) is its truth or otherwise. Heidegger disagrees that language is a product of 'thereness' that exists for someone to convey a correct idea. He is not averse to language being thought of to promote an idea, just that this does not show an authentic relationship of self to language. Just as indigenous peoples argue for language's autonomy, Heidegger (2001) states that "Language speaks" (p.191). With their emphasis on all things within the one, indigenous peoples are likely to add to that by saying that things speak as a whole, and language integrates with them as they speak. Things work together with language and are presented as a whole but always with some aspect of themselves hidden: here Heidegger states in relation to poetry – which for him is an authentic language – that a kind of shift in the presencing of the world occurs. This poetic calling allows us to invoke something so that it remains at a distance (Mika, 2007) and keeps to itself its own integrity. The word itself has an energetic expression quite apart from its meaning so that it will disclose itself with things and withdraw with them. But words are not brought into total nearness, as the metaphysics of presence advocates; such a view belongs to the essence of technology that is paired with that metaphysics. The word *nature*, for instance, seems innocent enough but because of its location in the metaphysics of presence it bears little ontological resemblance to its earlier *physis* (Wolcher, 2004). Translations that draw equivalences between indigenous terms and colonised ones, or propositions of that illuminate language so that it merely conveys ideas, are part and parcel of that overall drive to make things highly present.

In this dominant view of language, one is placed outside of language, and we are proposed to be its masters. Indigenous worlded philosophy, although allowing for one's agency with language, would argue here that the self is deprived of a true relationship with things in the world by positing in advance where they should be placed through language. Language itself is divorced as an autonomous phenomenon that is nevertheless constructed by everything from the self, which is one entity that composes language. In presence, language becomes something that we alight on as separate rather than work with as *amongst* it. We can then use it precisely to clarify or point out an entity rather than leave it in its context. It is something we *have*; it will no longer claim us in any way. Sometimes – and perversely – language as a whole is given the language of precedence over other things. In other words, language is considered to be the most privileged aspect of cultural capital, and it may even be given that title in policy and law. In Aotearoa, for instance, language is considered to be a *taonga* (treasure). Maori who vest in language that sovereign status are not necessarily saying that language is a separate event, but, because it is labelled in that way, it threatens to be treated separately from other things. Similarly, as an envelope of meaning, it becomes an instrument of precision, able to elucidate a thing in the world at the whim of its user.

Summary

In presence, the ground of indigenous existence is one that now privileges the final idea of a thing by making it 'what it is'. Presence threatens an earlier notion of the ground within which one was immersed, as part of all other things in the world. Heidegger has the capacity to provoke indigenous thought on the nature of presence, and it is no exaggeration to suggest that he saw presence as the very foundation of a particular kind of colonisation that he saw emerging in Western modernity. Indigenous peoples are not immune from that same form of colonisation, although it may manifest itself differently for them. Whether it can be dealt with by recapturing a sovereign concept of Being, as Heidegger argues, is uncertain. The philosophies of both Novalis and Derrida, which I turn to now with the concern of worldedness, would suggest that while we can identify that there is a resplendent idea of Being and also one of presence, it is impossible to escape the structure presence imposes on thought. Both Novalis and Derrida can be thought of as expanding on aspects of Heidegger's presence, while keeping in mind that it cannot be dispensed with. They also bring our attention to the more pragmatic (but still abstract) versions of worldedness that I propose also correspond with education. That is, Novalis brings the certainty of the Maori self into question; he makes that bringing-into-question itself a question, and a Maori conversation with Derrida, in particular, highlights how the Maori scholar is forever forced to engage with presence even as he or she appears to act against it.

Bibliography

Abrams, D. (1996) *The Spell of the Sensuous.* New York, NY: Vintage Books.
Banner, S. (1999) 'Two Properties, One Land: Law and Space in Nineteenth-Century New Zealand', *Law & Social Inquiry* 24(4): 807–52.
Bonnett, M. (2002) 'Education as a Form of the Poetic: A Heideggerian Approach to Learning and the Teacher-Pupil Relationship', pp. 229–43 in M. Peters (ed) *Heidegger, Education and Modernity.* Oxford, UK: Rowman & Littlefield Publishers.
Bowie, A. (1997) *From Romanticism to Critical Theory: The Philosophy of German Literary Theory.* New York, NY: Routledge.
Browne, M. (2005) *Wairua and the Relationship It Has with Learning Te Reo Māori within Te Ataarangi.* Unpublished Master of Educational Administration thesis, Massey University.

Calderon, D. (2008) *Indigenous Metaphysics: Challenging Western Knowledge Organization in Social Studies Curriculum*. Doctoral dissertation, The University of California, Los Angeles.

Capobianco, R. (1988) 'Heidegger and the Gods: On the Appropriation of a Religious Tradition', *Proceedings of the American Catholic Philosophical Association* 62: 183–8.

Colebrook, C. (2006) 'Martin Heidegger 1889–1976', pp. 125–35 in J. Wolfreys (ed) *Modern European Criticism and Theory: A Critical Guide*. Edinburgh, Scotland: Edinburgh University Press.

Crowe, B. (2007) 'Heidegger's Gods', *International Journal of Philosophical Studies* 15(2): 225–45.

Durie, M. (1994) *Whaiora: Māori Health Development*. Auckland, New Zealand: Oxford University Press.

Elkholy, S. (2008) *Heidegger and a Metaphysics of Feeling: Angst and the Finitude of Being*. London, UK: Continuum International Publishing Group.

Glazebrook, T. (2000) *Heidegger's Philosophy of Science*. New York, NY: Fordham University Press.

Heidegger, M. (1962) *Being and Time*. Oxford, UK: Blackwell.

Heidegger, M. (1967a) *Wegmarken*. Frankfurt am Main, Germany: Klostermann.

Heidegger, M. (1967b) *What Is a Thing?* Chicago: Henry Regnery Company.

Heidegger, M. (1971) *On the Way to Language*. New York, NY: Harper & Row.

Heidegger, M. (1977) *The Question Concerning Technology and Other Essays*. New York, NY: Harper

Heidegger, M. (2000) *Introduction to Metaphysics*. London, UK: Yale University Press.

Heidegger, M. (2001) *Poetry, Language, Thought*. New York, NY: Perennial Classics.

Heidegger, M. (2005) *Die Grundprobleme der Phänomenologie*, 2nd edn. Frankfurt am Main, Germany: Vittorio Klostermann.

Huffman, T. (2010) *Theoretical Perspectives on American Indian Education: Taking a New Look at Academic Success and the Achievement Gap*. Lanham, MD: AltaMira Press.

Jeffries, R. and Kennedy, N. (2008) *Māori Outcome Evaluation: A Kaupapa Māori Outcomes and Indicators Framework and Methodology*. Hamilton, New Zealand: The University of Waikato.

Johnston, D. (2006) *A Brief History of Philosophy: From Socrates to Derrida*. London, UK: Continuum.

Kockelmans, J. (1972) 'Language, Meaning, and Ek-Sistence', pp. 3–32 in J. Kockelmans (ed) *On Heidegger and Language*. Evanston, IL: Northwestern University Press.

Lambeir, B. (2002) 'Comfortably Numb in the Digital Era: Man's Being as Standing-Reserve or Dwelling Silently', pp. 103–21 in M. Peters (ed) *Heidegger, Education, and Modernity*. Oxford, UK: Rowman & Littlefield.

Mautner, T. (1997) *Dictionary of Philosophy*. London, UK: Penguin Reference.

Merleau-Ponty, M. (2003) *Phenomenology of Perception*. New York, NY: Routledge Classics.

Mika, C. (2007) 'The Utterance, the Body and the Law: Seeking an Approach to Concretizing the Sacredness of Maori Language', *SITES* 4(2): 181–205.

Mika, C. (2011) 'Unorthodox Assistance: Novalis, Māori, Scientism, and an Uncertain Approach to "Whakapapa"', pp. 89–108 in N. Franke and C. Mika (eds) *In die Natur – Naturphilosophie und Naturpoetik in Interkultureller Perspektive*. Wellington, New Zealand: Goethe Institut.

Mika, C. (2012) 'Overcoming "Being" in Favour of Knowledge: The Fixing Effect of "Mātauranga"', *Educational Philosophy and Theory* 44(10): 1080–92.

Mika, C. (2014a) 'The Enowning of Thought and Whakapapa: Heidegger's Fourfold', *Review of Contemporary Philosophy* 13: 48–60.

Mika, C. (2014b) 'Maori Thinking with a Dead White Male: Philosophizing in the Realm of Novalis', *Knowledge Cultures* 2(1): 23–39.

Mika, C. (2015a) 'Counter-Colonial and Philosophical Claims: An Indigenous Observation of Western Philosophy', *Educational Philosophy and Theory*: 1–7.

Mika, C. (2015b) 'Thereness: Implications for Heidegger's "Presence" for Māori', *AlterNative* 11(1): 3–13.

Mika, C. (2016a) 'Worlded Object and Its Presentation: A Māori Philosophy of Language', *AlterNative* 12(2): 165–76.

Mika, C. (2016b) 'The Ontological and Active Possibilities of Papatūānuku: To Nurture or Enframe?', *Knowledge Cultures* 4(3): 58–71.

Mika, C. and Stewart, G. (2015) 'Maori in the Kingdom of the Gaze: Subjects or Critics?', *Educational Philosophy and Theory*: 1–13.

Novalis. (2005) *The Novices of Sais.* New York, NY: Archipelago Books.

Park, G. (2006) *Theatre Country: Essays on Landscape and Whenua.* Wellington, New Zealand: Victoria University Press.

Plebuch, D. (2011) *Heidegger's Fourfold.* Unpublished doctoral dissertation, University of Illinois, Urbana, IL.

Polt, R. (1999) *Heidegger: An Introduction.* Ithaca, NY: Cornell University Press.

Richardson, W. (2003) *Heidegger: Through Phenomenology to Thought*, 4th edn. New York, NY: Fordham University Press.

Sardar, Z., Nandy, A. and Davies, M. (1993) *Barbaric Others: A Manifesto on Western Racism.* Colorado, CO: Pluto Press.

Smith, D. (2003) *Sounding/Silence: Martin Heidegger at the Limits of Poetics.* New York, NY: Fordham University Press.

Smith, G. (2003) *Indigenous Struggle for the Transformation of Education and Schooling.* Available at www.kaupapamaori.com.

Thomas, C. and Thomson, I. (2015) 'Heidegger's Contributions to Education (from Thinking)', *Chiasma: A Site For Thought* 2(Article 9): 96–108.

Vycinas, V. (2008) *Earth and Gods: An Introduction to the Philosophy of Martin Heidegger.* The Hague, The Netherlands: Martinus Nijhoff.

Waziyatawin, A. (2004) 'Indigenous Knowledge Recovery Is Indigenous Empowerment', *American Indian Quarterly* 28(3 & 4): 359–72.

Wolcher, L. (2004) 'Nature and Freedom', *The Independent Review* 9(2): 263–70.

Chapter 5

Presence, the Maori student and writer/critic, and Ako

Novalis and Derrida

The full extent of presence is impossible to describe, but some of its likely manifestations can be identified in a more culturally specific context. Here, I return to the Maori concept of Ako and ask the reader to recall that it prefigures a non-foundational ground that is itself worlded. Ako indicates that any one thing is attended by all others, and it also calls for the self to be able to express a thing in that way. It encourages the Maori self to reflect on that expression and to consider whatever obstructs it. The task of speculating on all of these themes is that of both the Maori student and the Maori critic/writer. Ako extends beyond these two instances, of course, and I would quickly note that, as Pere (1982) argued, Ako is a phenomenon that one is forever engaged with at all points of one's life. However, my aim here is to revisit Ako with the student and critic in mind, as they quite clearly reveal how one participates with both a worlded view of Ako and its more orthodox, educational mode. This chapter will therefore be of interest to the educationalist, particularly as it addresses schooling for the Maori student but also because it encompasses what the Maori critic – and here we could be including the Maori researcher, postgraduate student and so on – must encounter when attempting to represent worldedness within the horizon of thought imposed by presence.

This chapter aims to give examples, from a Maori perspective, of the broad nature of presence identified by the dialogue between Heidegger and indigenous worldedness in the previous chapter. It continues the dialogue more specifically by referring to the matter of presence to two additional non-Maori philosophers – Novalis and Derrida – who, like Heidegger, do not limit my engagement with the topic. Their views on presence are useful for enhancing two aspects that Heidegger identified in the previous chapter: in my discussion of the Maori student, I refer to Novalis's arguments against the strong ontological self; and where the Maori critic or writer is undermined by the presence of terms and concepts (and yet supported by the unstated absence that immediately attends them), I consult some of the main ideas of Derrida. I draw on their philosophies that are most likely to represent their broad views, and thus, this chapter is not meant to give a full treatment of them as such but rather to refer to them in order to signpost the issues of presence for the Maori student and critic/writer.

The schooled Maori self: the ultimate ground of perception

It should be acknowledged that several writers have shown deep interest in holism, and it is discussed widely in the literature with varying degrees of the sense of worldedness that I outlined in earlier chapters. Hall (2014) notes that holism can mean several things, and she refers back to a good deal of the literature, some of which I now summarise. Miller (2006) advocates that holism revives meaningfulness for one's existence; traditional modes of educating have detrimentally affected the potential for a fuller life. Miller et al. (1990) explore the connectedness aspect of holism; ideally, education strips away the "artificial barriers" (p.66), when appropriate, to make sure holism ensues. Mahmoudi et al. (2012) also explore interconnectedness, citing the example of indigenous thought which seeks to drive an understanding of the world away from fragmenting its things, and Uhl and Stuchul (2011), who note that learning must take place in a full learning environment, where there exists a relationship between the self as a total entity and the external world. In New Zealand, environmental education is seen as promoting holism, with indigenous worldviews as a central concern (Eames & Barker, 2011; Eames et al., 2008). As Tulloch (2015) warns, though, the human/nature divide that exists in the West is not reparable through science and technology, which are themselves shaped by a prior ontology. Steiner education is similarly sceptical of thoroughgoing scientific explanations of existence, although science can be used as a measured means of self-formation.

Despite these valiant attempts at regaining holism, though, there remain two chief problems. First, according to Miller (2007), these holistic endeavours have been weakened by an overwhelming assumption that one needs to be educated in certain ways; the focus is on "testing and preparing students to function in today's global economy" (Hall, 2014, p.48). For Miller (2007), it seems that "the emphasis on linear, analytic thinking" that leads us to "become plodding in our approach and lose spontaneity in dealing with problems" (p.95) is not yet over and is even regaining its former momentum. Undoubtedly, the unmitigated discourse of globalism that sees one being trained in particularly linear ways of thinking carries with it seductive echoes of progress and unity across borders. Holism's progress, then, may depend on countering various optimistic utterances that propose a way forward for all. Like Miller, well-known critic Ken Robinson (2011) repudiates the dominant focus of education on the grounds that it is too heavily based on intellectual capacity and does not allow for other modes of thinking. Gardner (1983) also tries to emphasise other forms of intelligence because of the dominance of logic (interestingly, one of these intelligences, *existential*, is for Gardner only half an intelligence because it cannot be located anywhere in the brain: his preference for a neurological explanation for intelligence may thence privilege the empiricism that lies at the basis of logic).

However, the second problem that occurs is to do with the fact that worlded-ness has not comprised much of the corpus of holistic literature. The authors of holistic education are still too human-derived and, alongside that, advocate too strongly that a thing is individually *there*. In that, it reflects the metaphys-ics of presence. Rarely does one encounter in the literature a philosophy that is premised on thinking as deriving from, and constituted by, all things. Nor is the student or the teacher encouraged to think of him or herself as constituting, or being constituted by, the external world. Relatedly, one's ideas remain self-derived and adequate for referencing another thing in the world and all its constituent things. In an attempt to be holistic, for example, the Te Whariki early childhood curriculum document (Ministry of Education, 1996) incorporates a number of 'approaches' that ensure bicultural learning and teaching with Maori, and even includes a list of Maori metaphysical terms with translations that can be drawn on to ensure that culturally appropriate learning occurs. As White and Mika (2013) note, though, the document does not propose how the thinking process of the Maori child entirely corresponds with the worlded object. Furthermore, well-meaning declarations around curriculum principles that "put students at the centre of teaching and learning" (Ministry of Education, 2007, p.9) are ultimately anthropocentric because the non-human derivative of thinking is neglected.

Introducing Novalis

The strong self was indeed a central concern of the early German romantic poets and philosophers in general. Alongside that problem lies its nemesis, mystery. Mystery has to be accounted for in every act for the early German romantics, and the threat of presence in one's anthropocentrism and in how the world is fragmented even before any particular is encountered, thus figures prominently. Novalis was a key member of this movement, and although he did not name the metaphysical expectation of the self as ultimate ground 'presence' as such, he remarked at some length on its manifestations. He is useful for the Maori critic because he highlights the problem of the unmysterious *self* at some length. In this section, I am interested in referring to him so that the quandary faced by the Maori student (in the conventional sense) can be discussed. He is not the authority in my discussion, however, and indeed, Novalis was directly opposed to the idea that his philosophies be taken as gospel. We see a circular return to his arguments against the self-as-ground in his resistance when we identify that he does not wish to be claimed as authority: in other words, he sets out a method that one can use to refer to him so that he is *not* the final arbiter of the writer's scenario. In the indigenous context, he would most likely want the writer to brush up against his ideas, and to that extent he is no different to either Heidegger or Derrida. He lays out a description of teaching and learning that attempts to sidestep presence by introducing the unknown in multiple ways. Deep within the mystery that he presents as an educational force for student and teacher is the possibility of the other – the banal self and object.

Novalis clearly prefigures Heidegger in key ways. It is not the aim of this book to clarify all of these crossovers but some preliminary comments can be made. Greaves (2010) notes that Novalis was an important contributor to Heidegger; indeed, Heidegger would have read Novalis "a number of times" (p.xiv). Holland (2006) observes that there are marked similarities between the two. With that fact of correspondence between them in mind, we could most definitely have stayed with Heidegger for the Maori-centred discussion that follows, and to some extent this might have been more fruitful, especially as Heidegger's critique of modernity is more *explicitly* radical than Novalis's. Despite Heidegger's mammoth popularity, though, there is an enchantment about the lesser-known earlier philosopher's works. Chief among these is that Novalis is directly and sustainedly concerned with presuppositions about the self's identity with the self. Novalis drills into this problem with a poetic obscurity that is also used immediately in relation to a student's learning and a teacher's teaching. He addresses education in its orthodox senses and renders it an act of mystery, but in that act he critiques any idea that the self is central to the self and any other object as he or she learns or teaches.

Novalis's presence in Anglo-American philosophy is faint but it seems he is becoming increasingly popular as his works have been translated into English – perhaps also because his writings are decidedly romantic in the non-cloying sense. They hark back to a past of a golden age, when rational thought was not so pervasive. There is a peculiar irony at work with Novalis, though, which may interest the indigenous reader. While acknowledging the wealth of philosophy the other had, he also had a tendency to naively idealise the other, with his fascination for the ancient 'Morgenländer', or Oriental, for instance (Mika, 2015c). One needs only read his novel *Heinrich von Ofterdingen* to observe that he looks to other cultures to provide a poeticising of the world. This reliance on the other for the survival of his belief system may well strike an uneasy chord with indigenous groups, many of whom have been exoticised themselves. It is with these writings of his that he could be accused of being too romantic about the other, with the other becoming a symbol for a greater good (and hence potentially losing their personhood). It is true that not all of his works display this heavy reliance on the other's magical ability to poeticise and release the Western self from the burden that a lack of mystery brings but that there is this tendency at all is worrying for indigenous thought.

Novalis's attribution of childlike qualities to the other is coupled with a belief that those same characteristics are to be esteemed, not spurned. In fact, here we meet one of Novalis's central philosophies that he shared with Kant (to whom he was in other respects completely opposed): a thing cannot be fully known. The other can therefore not be fully comprehended and nor, importantly, can the self. According to Novalis, we are all childlike in the sense that all things lie beyond our grasp, but it is the other that is aware of that fact. When we are concerned with ourselves, we suffer from a lack of knowledge; thus, upon extension we cannot make assertions of certainty about any particular thing. Coming to realise that we possess the qualities of the other is a gradual process, but this realisation takes on a deeper hue as we are constantly confronted by the fact of those qualities' elusiveness. Put simply, we find some sense of the others' qualities in ourselves, but the true nature of those qualities escape description. Novalis was never trying to *know* the other.

The Ako of certainty

It is with Novalis's elusiveness of a thing in mind that we can turn to consider some general concerns that education poses for a Maori student. Maori have a difficult relationship with the schooling aspect of education, but even more perturbing for the worlded perspective are the assumptions underpinning mainstream education in Aotearoa. As early as 1982, Dr Rangimarie Rose Pere was questioning those colonising assumptions whilst proposing various Maori antidotes, mainly voiced through her own experience as having been raised in a traditional way and learning through being immersed in a Maori community. She identified that the so-called spiritual world has a profound place in Maori teaching and learning and that the opposite of that belief tends to reign in mainstream formalised education. I would further suggest that presence lies at base of the educational thought that the self is the final ground of thinking and knowing. We can call this final ground of the self, 'self-assuredness' or 'self-certainty'. It should be noted that this sort of assuredness is not meant to include the states of mind of Maori students, who for various reasons feel daunted in the face of colonising institutions; instead, I mean to indicate that there is an unrelenting but subtle push for Maori students to understand thought and perception as emanating from themselves (Mika, 2012). The 'self-certainty' or selfhood that I talk about here is ontological, in that it cannot be sensed. A template of selfhood is instead the point of Novalis's critique, and he is particularly keen to attack the assumption of the grounded self, along with any suggestion that epistemic certainty is supreme. Novalis also encourages one to think about one's finite ability to know an object. This self-reflective exercise is itself valuable and emphasises that one is within the world rather than above it, detached. Presence may not overtly discourage the self from this sort of reflection, but it certainly does not promote it as either a mode of thinking or a discipline in its own right.

Much focus on Maori underachievement is centred on the mismatch of learning material with Maori experience or else on the pedagogical problems that mainstream schools or universities pose for the students. The influence of presence structures the mismatch and the teaching methods in the first instance, and it makes more sense, then, to consider that much more fundamental problem than its manifestations. It is quite likely that any Maori student in a conventional learning setting, regardless of the level, is caught up in a dilemma of not really being able to articulate what is wrong with the mainstream learning process. My speculation here is supported by the fact that presence is invisible. Thus, a student may describe the problem as one that revolves around language – that the material to be learnt is not delivered in the Maori language, for instance – only to discover that a sort of disquiet remains when the lesson is in the Maori language. Similarly, their mode of learning might be understood as resting on kaupapa Maori (Maori critical bases) or matauranga Maori (Maori knowledge methods and theories), but students may not be able to feel the difference between that apparently Maori-centred way of learning and what they have experienced elsewhere. Their inability to discern the difference is because there may well be *in essence* no difference between the mainstream approach (that is underpinned by presence) and the stated Maori one (that presence also informs in some measure). The experience of the Maori student, as we shall see, is similar to that of the Maori writer as he or she writes in opposition to presence: the curriculum is not necessarily one that reflects worldedness simply through the use of certain Maori terms and concepts – especially when these adorn the curriculum but do not especially inform its ontology.

It will be remembered that presence offers both the self and the object as simply 'there', with the object comprising the properties that make it what it is. The thing is separated out from the rest of the world and is characterised by its stillness. The self is similarly calm because he or she is unconsciously posited as self-certain, undaunted by any possible chaos posed by the thing and its full worldedness. Hence, the only link between the self and thing is that which starts with the self. For Maori, such a possibility is likely untenable, but it is actioned on a continual basis for the Maori student. In his *Fichte Studies*, Novalis highlighted in relation to the certain 'I' that one has to step outside of oneself to say with certainty that the 'I' is indeed the 'I', and thus the I is no longer the I. Indeed, "we abandon the identical in order to represent it" (Kneller, 2003, p.3). The 'I' is always constituted by the unknown of what he calls Being or the Absolute: the 'I' can never identify itself with the full expectation that the German Idealist Fichte had for it. The sovereign self is always already constituted by, and dependent on, the mysterious totality of the world. Novalis refers to Being as the excess on which we depend and states that

> [a]ll aspects of Being, Being above all is simply being free – *hovering* between extremes that are both necessarily unifying and divisive. From this point of light of hovering all reality flows – in it is contained everything – object and subject are there because of it, it is not there because of them.
>
> (Kneller, 2003, p.266)

Although geographically worlds apart, Novalis has the potential here to highlight for the Maori student that the certainty of the self's judgments and perceptions is misleading. Mainstream education insists that the Maori self posit him- or herself so that the 'I' is understood to be at the basis of learning, although this self-positing is unconscious. Jones (2001) highlights that there is likely to be no beneficial outcome for teaching in its dominant form for indigenous students as there is a massive gulf between indigenous epistemologies and Western pedagogy, with the latter engaged with the tacit belief that there will be a "linear and cumulative increase in knowing" (p.288). She places the problem here in knowledge but preceding it is the certainty of the self. Durie (2004) observes that "[p]eople are the land and the land is the people . . . we are the river, the river is us" (p.1139) with good reason, because the question of the self is not immediately answerable. Meyer (2008) continues with that thinking when she asks who the self is. For her, and for indigenous peoples, it is dependent on its very construction on the thoroughgoing enmeshed nature of the external world with the self. In discussing alternative pedagogies of education, Ahenakew et al. (2014) argue against the self as "universal, self-sufficient and autonomous" (p.225). In these cases, indigenous writers and their advocates see in education the ultimate privileging of an ontology of the self – the immediate and unassailable phenomenon of the self *as* self.

Novalis was equally sceptical of the suggestion that an object is the 'not-I' because one could not fully say that the I was, in fact, the I to begin with: "[t]he essence of identity can only be presented in an *illusory* proposition" (Kneller, 2003, p.3). Thus, the object was always immediately constituted by Being and can never be understood as fully self-constituting. Of course, Novalis's reactions were to Fichte, who was nowhere near as influential as Kant (Fichte's mentor), but they are not confined to Fichte and they deal also with the most basic idea, stemming from the Renaissance (Robinson, 2011), that the self is ultimately the ground of his or her thinking. Whilst the Maori student does not have to contend with the offshoots of Fichte *per se*, he or she is confronted with the reality of a cultural norm in which all things are interconnected and one, *against* the very strong tradition of teaching and learning being aimed at the self and the self being solely responsible for perception and thought (of which Fichte was part). The Maori student is asked to place an object *over there* even before he or she comes to the object – as we have seen, this predetermined stance against the object is key to the metaphysics of presence. He or she is subtly encouraged to confidently approach the object so that it remains at a distance. As may be expected, education plays out on the field of presence in various ways here. In the modernist concept of 'curriculum', which is basic to the process of mainstream teaching and learning even if it is not mentioned, an object is ordered so that it can produce an outcome for the Maori student (see, for instance, Hodge, 2015). This outcome is likely knowledge of the object or some aspect of it that leads to a particular type of progress of the Maori individual. A thing and its constitutive world in that act are covered over with the term 'knowledge', but what is presupposed here is that there is a certain way for an object to be approached. In 'curriculum', knowledge appears to be stratified, but it is in fact the world that is put in its rightful place.

None of this is to say that there is no such thing as the 'I'. Novalis, and his own brand of worldedness, do not do away with the self, but he simply argues that the self and an object are underpinned by the Absolute, and thus, the 'I=I' proposition is untenable. Due to the Maori self not being entirely self-constitutive, any proposition about identical selfhood with the self's (apparent) ground is untenable. It becomes even more so when we remember that, in a Maori worldedness, the thing over there is constituted by the self (among all other things). The Maori notion of whakapapa generally does away with any suggestion that what lies at a distance is not constituted by the self, although the self may be noting its separate form. In past times, a Maori student may well have been encouraged to perceive of the object as inseparable from him- or herself, and he or she would then be 'over there' *as* the object, whilst considering it from afar. Mainstream schooling does not overtly place the object so that it is separate from the Maori self, but then it does not explicitly encourage him or her to perceive the object as completely constitutive of the self, either. It could be argued that schooling is neutral in this regard, but I suggest that it simply does not need to push the agenda of presence – schooling is purely an outcome of the prioritised self, and it naturally reflects the representative notions of language, thinking and even selfhood that presence advocates.

The proposition that the self is indeed the self, and is the ultimate ground of everything else that conceptually proceeds, is reflected also in various facets of language use in curricula. There are arguments in favour of thinking that schooling becomes progressively inclined to reflect presence as one moves through its ranks. The early years of education are then more open to the worldedness that I have discussed. Or, perhaps more insidiously, the agenda of presence has not been made so visible at that stage. It will be recalled that a worlded view of language argues for terms themselves to have force. In the early years *Te Whariki* handbook, we still see the bedrock of presence through the translation of certain metaphysical Maori terms. *Te Whariki* is a seminal document that engages with early years teaching. It literally means 'the mat' and is meant to refer to a place for all to feel secure on. The translations in *Te Whariki* are thought to be sufficient to reflect the meaning of the Maori terms, but they are either scientific or overly hardened (White & Mika, 2013). Novalis (1960b) might have repeated his view of scientised nature here that it is a hardened entity, and the toddler would be implicated in the terms themselves – they are not just for the teacher to draw on. *Whakangaromanga Ao* is given the gloss 'black hole', *whakamātau* is identified with 'assess', *whakaputanga* with outcomes and so on (White & Mika, 2013). As to the first of these, the recession (*whakangaromanga*) of the world (*Ao*) that is hinted at is not merely a scientific discourse but is also a phenomenon that refers to the self – child and teacher. It may instead carry with it a sense of the following: the becoming of world absencing. In other words, the self is always undercut with the withdrawal of other things in the world, and other things, being constituted by the self, are worlded by the self's disappearance. *Whakamātau* does indeed mean 'assess' but is more deeply textured with the intuitiveness of *mātau*, where the latter refers to a feel for the deep mystery of a thing even as one sets out to reveal its nature through cognitive awareness. *Whakaputanga*, when subject to the language of enframing, can be equated with outcomes, but it more intrinsically and quite clearly claims a thing as appearing.

In the last example I have referred to an ability of language to actively set about doing something quite independently of our ability to perceive it. *Whakaputanga* carries with it a force of 'bringing things to the fore', where they are becoming (*whaka*) apparent (*puta*). It is hard to imagine that precolonial Maori would ever have equated the sense of *whakamātau* with 'assess', either: it is too imbued with a force of 'gradual movement' and is similar to the continuing claim that *whakaputanga* has on the self. *Whakangaromanga Ao*, when thought of as an actively constitutive potency, is not simply an *idea* of the recession of the world but reinforces the idea that language in a Maori worldview has a productive, material effect on the self and the self's world.

What all this means for the early years is that, while the child is not yet evolved to be self-certain, the Maori terms to which they are meant to be subject are blunted to meet the descriptors of presence. The language that would have once constructed the child as avowedly self-mysterious and constitutive of/ with other things is now brought forward so that it specifies both itself and the child as certain objects. The child is thus constructed and potentially constructs him- or herself as certain. We have seen that how one is named or discussed through language is materially important because language is more than a shell of conceptual meaning. White and Mika (2013) note here that the terms themselves in the document need to forcefully represent and reflect the child as an unknowable and formidable phenomenon. However, it is difficult to see how a document could deal with the problem of presence and the overly certain self. It is unlikely that the child could indeed be "reflected in and through the document as an unfamiliar, yet powerful, presence" (p.107) because presence immediately configures the self so that he or she is talked *about*, not as materially *part of*, the document. The object can be talked about as if not part of the self because, from a Maori viewpoint, the Maori student is governed by a force that repudiates the notion of 'becoming' that is unique to the term *ira*, discussed in Chapter 3. It will be recalled that with *ira* an object is 'over there', which in the sense of *ira* is meant to identify that the self is continuously constituted by the deep mystery of the thing (and this mystery is hence what is intrinsic to the self; Mika, 2015a). In self-certainty, though, the thing over there is indeed distant from the self, separated by qualities and space, and is quite different from the self. The mainstream schooling experience does not encourage the self to reflect at length on the fact that a thing is not knowable and, moreover, to celebrate this lack of knowledge about a thing. Contemplation about the limits of knowledge, then, is much less privileged than is knowledge about a thing. The primary aim of the school is to set about demystifying a thing.

Perhaps this knowledge focus of schooling reaches its zenith for the Maori student in universities, for here, more vehemently than anywhere else, the problem of feeling and emotion is put to rest. The self-assured individual "feels that he is lord of the universe, his self soars all-powerful over this abyss" (Novalis, 2005, p.49). In his *Novices of Sais*, which offers us a complete glimpse into Novalis's notion of formative education, we see a group of students discussing nature. It becomes abundantly clear that any aspect of nature is beyond them and any rational explanation; moreover, they are all placed within nature and its things as they discuss it. Novalis deliberately names the natural forms that come to bear on the students as they talk about it, thereby further emphasising students' dependence on those forms whilst trying to make sense of them. But despite the vulnerability that accompanies the ongoing speculation, there is, for Novalis, a joy that one's thought, for instance, takes place within the world. To show this indebtedness to all things, he "starts with nature at times and radiates his discussion outwards to its speakers" (Mika, 2015c, p.7). He deliberately alternates between the voice or display of nature and the language of the human world. This continual reminder of the external world for the Maori student is absent from the assumptions of tertiary education, though, with the result that the profound sense of Ako is forgotten in favour of its teaching and learning focus. Ako for the Maori student is promulgated as simply teaching and learning in both the way it is described and in practice. This version of Ako "has been rendered to mean an activity that almost exclusively involves human beings" (Mika, 2012, p.7): in relation to that predicament, Novalis (1990) might have said that it has become the means of all access to all creatures.

The Maori student's reflection on limits of knowledge

Both kaupapa Maori theory and research and matauranga Maori have made certain political and social gains, and on the face of it have endorsed placing the self within his or her own writing; however, seldom is the non-foundationalism of the self reflected on. This is unusual, given that the concept of ground is so central to kaupapa Maori in particular (Mika, 2014a; 2016a; 2016b). In research, kaupapa Maori is overwhelmingly strived for as a human-centred approach, where the Maori student is encouraged to conduct research as an autonomous, individual entity – self-reliant, grounded, and the ultimate arbiter of how one writes and thinks. How a thing displays itself to the student and the student then acts on that display, is not commonly considered a cause for thought in its own right. It is true that kaupapa Maori theory and matauranga Maori do reflect on the wider social group and the spiritual beings and phenomena that are at work in the world, but very rarely does "being . . . precondition not only the subject/object distinction, but also the subject's consciousness of itself" (Stone, 2008, p.145). It seems that schooling reflects presence by not opening up the possibility for the Maori student to consider that seemingly exterior forces are directly responsible for the constituted, writing self. One notable exception is Te Ahukaramu Charles Royal, who is arguably the first proponent of the term *matauranga Maori* as it is referred to as a discipline. He suggests that the world brings humanity to an understanding of things through its display (Royal, 2008); this observation is made within his overall context of the world and the self being one. Matauranga Maori (in some forms) is meant to be an accessible discipline to all, and the idea that one's vulnerability, or lack of complete certainty, about both the self and things in the world, should similarly be one that is available to the Maori student.

The creative power of the Maori student to reflect on his or her lack of groundedness – his or her vulnerability in not being identical with the self and not knowing the full nature of the thing yonder – is an important aspect of well-being. In deliberately and typically poetic language, Novalis (2005) highlights the importance of uncertainty, excitement, darkness, and inarticulateness, when he surmises the well-being of the student:

> 'Whose heart does not leap with joy,' cried the youth with glittering eye, 'when the innermost life of nature invades him in all its fullness! When the overpowering emotion for which language has no other name than love, expands within him like an all-dissolving vapor and, trembling with sweet fear, he sinks into the dark'.
>
> (p.103)

Novalis speaks poetically to capture something of the inadequacy yet jubilation that the self feels when he or she is made aware of a non-foundational ground of thought. His language here is clearly more uncertain than it was when he was dealing with Fichte. Even how we pose our uncertainty, then, needs to be thought about, not least of all by the student. Both the Maori students' deliberate reflection on their limits of knowledge as well as the language they can draw on to express it is incredibly important because they are a reminder of the self's small part in the nature of things. They also reinstate the self's integral, balanced aspect with what is assumed to be the external world. Thinking is a form of being within the rest of the world – a particular interpretation of *whakaaro* (Mika, 2014a) – and is important as a directive of how other things are placed in relation to the self and in relation to each other. Deloria's suspicion that there is a rupture between the existence of the indigenous student's thinking and their more authentic existence could extend to the current dilemma where this self-reflective discipline is not made particularly possible. A holistic attitude to well-being advocates speculation. In the context of thinking about one's own inherent inability to fully grasp a thing, it can be interpreted as follows: I reflect on the limits of my knowing, which ensures that my family (all things in the world) are kept away from any pretence at being 'mine'; I am constituted by all things and how I depict that possibility – preferably through a sense of mystery – has consequences for the physical well-being of those things and myself; and thinking is, among other things, a mental faculty that is nevertheless constructed by the world as a whole. Thus, we return to each individual aspect of health. Even in making the assertions I just have, I am in a state of unknowing: I am reflecting on their possibilities and am considering my own limits in relation to them. This act of reflection is constantly destabilised but could be central to the well-being of the Maori student.

Taken together, these aspects of self-reflection are not simply exercises that fortify a particular intellectual faculty; additionally, they herald consequences for

one's well-being in a political sense. To contemplate one's metaphysical colonisation, for instance, is a huge step away from being taught to *know* one's metaphysical colonisation. Speculating on the potential mystery of colonisation as
it impacts on one's self-perception, and on one's ability to express the fullness
of things, is a never-ending process that does not have a scientifically fruitful
outcome. It is thus not overly useful from the point of view of 'outcomes' that
frequently steers the process of schooling. It is also potentially too critically
oriented for current and dominant modes of schooling, insofar as it asks the
student to disdain any proposition that one should only focus on what can be
proven. Alongside that it sits well with a Maori notion of well-being, it also
subtly undermines a repetitive overture that insists it is somehow pointless to
spend much time reflecting on the self's limits in relation to other things in the
world. It is as *transformative* because it asks the Maori student to consider the
validity of what is often proposed to be unhelpful.

It is perhaps that very issue of well-being – where the self is free to use his
or her faculties as a worlded subject to consider the limits of knowledge – that
Novalis had in mind when he considered the role of the teacher. Novalis is well
known for attempting to make the widely understood, mysterious. In his *Novices
of Sais*, he was more intent on demonstrating that one's continual thought after
what was basically unobtainable was the most important facet of education.
Moreover, the teacher is constituted by all things and is preferably able to reflect
on that basically unknowable phenomenon:

> When [the teacher] grew older, he roamed the earth, saw distant lands and
> seas, new skies, strange stars, unknown plants, beasts, men, went down into
> caverns, saw how the earth was built in shelves and multicoloured layers,
> and pressed clay into strange rock forms. Everywhere he found the familiar,
> only strangely mixed and coupled, and thus strange things often ordered
> themselves within him.
>
> (Novalis, 2005, p.7)

Novalis has an implicit warning for the teacher here. The teacher is asked to
guard against the belief that the world is simply external, only important as a
source of sensory information, and that is then made into a knowledge form
ready for transmission. The teacher is deluded, in other words, if he or she
assumes that the world does not constitute him or her. One role of the teacher,
then, is to render what is banal, fundamentally unknowable, even if just for a
while. In the Maori context, the student should be able to fulfil his or her own
right as self-reflective in a finite sense; the teacher should be both responsible
for "bringing forth knowledge and ignorance" (Wood, 2007 p.109). If a teacher
is just focused on 'bringing forth knowledge', however, an imbalance results
and the student (and indeed the teacher) is no longer understood as a fragile,
overwhelmed entity that is central to Ako. It is within what Novalis has called
'ignorance' that the full extent of such terms as *whakapapa* can make itself be

felt, because the obscurity of a thing and the self's lack of grasp is brought to the fore as itself a topic of merit.

What does all this herald for the notion of worldedness and, more specifically, the worlded concept of Ako? The student is tacitly encouraged to turn to the world as if it is made up of separate entities that he or she is distant from because he or she is the ground of decision on the appearance of those entities. He or she has always already conceived of the over-thereness of the entity well before it is encountered. The self is hence conceptually distanced from the self, taught to understand the entity as not really enmeshed within the daily act of thinking, writing, singing and so on. Equally, the self is conceptually dispatched from the entity by the self-governing nature of thinking and knowing that presence has established. The full force of Ako − its ability to call the self to ponder the mystery of a thing as it constitutes him or her − is blunted, much as the *Te Whariki* terms I noted were formerly forceful but are now perceived as economical entities that match up with the meaning attributed to them by a preordained template.

Dealing directly with presence: the Maori writer

The divorce of the self from the thing is not just confined to the Maori student who learns in the classroom. It extends to the plight of the Maori writer who is trying to address colonisation − even if he or she wants to describe how presence blocks the worldedness of thought. Despite its enormous influence and apparent success in colonising the Maori mind, there is an increasing Maori awareness of presence, although perhaps not in those terms. It may not have been widely and sustainedly addressed in academic work, but suspicion is growing that something not entirely our own lurks beneath our statements, arranges and structures them in advance even before they are made. Furthermore, Maori critics of presence argue that it is the self as a whole that engages with the world, not just the intellect. For them, the most trenchant and revolutionary counters to precision stem in their most fundamental sense from the premise that the Maori author is both *within* the argument to begin with whilst paradoxically talking *about* the problem. Referring to Schelling, Grant (2006) would therefore state that "[t]he philosophical exposition of the unconditioned, or Absolute, is not like the analysis of a concept or state of affairs, rather, the exposition of the Absolute occurs within the Absolute, as the medium of its own exposition" (p.1). Heidegger (1998) also identified as much in his *Was ist Metaphysik* and went so far as to say that the question of metaphysics could indeed only be asked if the questioner was inseparably part of the question. Hegel's 'inverted world' illuminated the unusual event of asking about something while residing among that something (Flay, 1970). From the outset, the illusory practice of standing outside of the question is put paid to for Maori and non-Maori authors alike. Indigenous writers Ahenakew et al. (2014) − Cooper and Hireme are Maori − clarify that we are not above or outside things in the world even though colonisation suggests we are. A critique is in order as far as they are concerned, as it is for Mika (2012) when he states that we cannot speak *of* things as precise entities. Although the Enlightenment has tried to cool things down by trying to console the writer that he or she is outside of his or her work, the heat under the collars of many driving the critique is not to be so readily extinguished. The critics themselves are, it seems, not about to disappear from their assertions.

Not only is published material on the matter slowly becoming more common, but anecdotally speaking it seems that Maori forums are more consciously starting to theorise on the limits of the self's knowledge of a thing and, indeed, on the fact that our theorising is located on the field of that 'something that lurks'. Alongside the growth in speculative thought here, cynicism is mounting at any suggestion that our statements about Maori epistemology or existence are not somehow structured by that colonising metaphysical field to begin with. In Maori graduate research settings, for example, straightforward assertions about a Maori worldview, or a highly agentic self that can do whatever he or she wants, are rarely sufficient. These sorts of utterances do arise, and they are eagerly seized on by those who cannot stomach the thought that colonisation is so thorough. The advocates of the view that we can say whatever we want, free from the restrictions imposed by whatever conditions the writing in the first place, may find the general theme of colonisation uncomfortable – and there can be various and deep reasons for that discomfort – but the more pragmatic in the Maori audience are inclined to disregard those arguments as simply mistaken. It is increasingly evident that the quiet self-assuredness presence teaches us, and its insistence that we are at the base of our own thoughts, does not simply vanish because we make a statement against it, seemingly directed in the opposite direction.

In the previous chapter, in conjunction with Heidegger's philosophies, I discussed presence from the perspective of the worlded nature of things in the world. Presence renders an entity so thoroughly *itself* that there is no room left for a view of it as being constituted by all other things in the world. In presence this is the fate of the term *Ako*, and we have to return to it in order to consider how its more expansive thought has been reduced to fit the mores of presence. Here, we are considering how the world that Ako formerly may have disclosed has now been reduced, and correspondingly how the term itself has become a very narrow discourse. Sheilagh Walker (1996) has identified that colonisation has added a particularly negative set of thoughts to Maori perception. Quite often, references to colonisation have privileged the *loss* of cultural capital, such as land and language, with a loss of well-being acknowledged by such writers as Levien (2007), and Reid and Robson (2006). But the implantation of a different set of perceptions as a theme often slips under the radar. There is both loss and substitution occurring in this situation. We can liken this newly inserted perception that characterises presence to a forgetting of mystery, within which things in the world would normally have been allowed to coalesce within any one entity. What is most interesting is Walker's likening of the detrimental mindset to an illness. For her,

> [it] is also a spiritual disease; it attacks the hinengaro [minds] of Maori. The name of this spiritual disease – 'internalisation of colonisation'. Here the disease is most potent. . . . [The] causes are hard to see. They came in latent form, in the crevices of the minds, in the processes of thought, in the guise of World Views that sought to appropriate, dominate and negate other World Views that it found in its path.
>
> (p. 122)

Ako, it will be recalled, is actively constitutive of all things, it has to it a sense of the self's vulnerability as he or she recounts how colonised views are held and replicated; it indicates that this reflective exercise on self, thing, tradition and colonisation is continuous; and it acknowledges the non-foundational ground of thought as itself a phenomenon that constitutes the self and all other things. The metaphysics of presence, however, forces the self to engage with things as if Ako is a constrained and restrictive idea. First, it proposes that Ako is now about the idea that a thing and the self are separate – and this can occur through the suggestion that Ako is translatable and implementable as 'teaching and learning'. It is less to do with a deep sense of collapse of self and world – and even less still about a reflection on that event, with colonisation as a key facet of that contemplative act – and is now much more compact and tidy. Ako, as a Maori rendition of 'teaching and learning', is hence economical and predictable; it is simply there with its given meaning. Moreover, it corresponds with similarly present attitudes about the things that evolve as knowledge: a present view of Ako is commensurate with the absence of things themselves in what the self knows.

As I have suggested elsewhere, it may be that other indigenous peoples have seen their traditional concepts reduced to other meanings that do not, in any way, represent what indigenous people intend by those terms. As we have seen from the previous chapter, presence sits uneasily with indigenous notions of well-being through worldedness, and, for Maori, presence conveys itself through equivalent translations of equivalence (for instance, 'Ako = teaching and learning') even if those linguistic signposts are simply symptoms of presence. It posits real, material entities as thoroughly there, suggesting they are singular and inanimate. One is inclined in presence to represent the thing because it is capable of being isolated. Presence with Ako, I shall suggest, therefore has repercussions for Maori well-being as one is perceiving the object in ways that do not synchronise with interconnection and animacy. Although there may be Maori who do not subscribe to a holistic view, nevertheless indigenous literature (and that of Maori, in general) is quite clear that such thought is the most foundational of all beliefs and perception. Worldedness – whether the object is acknowledged as 'world' or not – then infuses a Maori notion of health.

Introducing Derrida

Just as care must be taken when referencing Heidegger or Novalis, the indigenous writer may be immediately sceptical of Derrida when he argues for writing to be prioritised over speech. Derrida has his reasons for this position. An incomplete focus might insist that Being works solely within speech because indigenous peoples typically privilege orality, but a metaphysics of worldedness does not support that view because both are influenced by all things in the world. And in a more general sense, according to Peters (2009), Derrida is critical of the view that "writing is dead and abstract. The written word loses its spiritual connection to the self and the written word, untethered from the speaking subject, is cast adrift from personality and intentionality" (p.3). Thus, written text encloses us as well, and while we may have different ways of explaining that process, we are nevertheless brought to understand writing as an utterance of all things, although this holism is betrothed to the very presence that we seek to undermine. Moreover, Derrida himself noted that "[i]f writing is no longer understood in the narrow sense of linear and phonetic notation, it should be possible to say that all societies capable of producing, that is to say of obliterating, their proper names, and of bringing classificatory difference into play, practice writing in general" (Derrida, 1997, p.109). The writing that Derrida does privilege is what he terms 'arche-writing', which refers to the infinite act of writing within which both speech and writing (in its orthodox sense) operate.

Derrida drew heavily on Heidegger's work on presence and would also blame the West for the corrosion at work in its thought. Like Heidegger, he asserts that "[w]ithout a doubt, Aristotle thinks time on the basis of *ousia* as *parousia*, on the basis of the now, the point, etc" (Derrida, 1982, p.61). Derrida proposed that there are no self-sufficient identities; they all involve their other, which are absent. The metaphysics of presence is built on the premise that a thing can be conceived of as if it is total or complete (Biesta, 2010), ensuring that even a critique of presence, through a conception and its language, draws on a notion of self-sufficiency and "*always amounts* . . . to reconstituting, according to another configuration, the *same* system [of Being of presence]" (Derrida, 1982, p.60). Presence, that great Western unconscious preoccupation, does not acknowledge its absent partner, although for Derrida the absent is most certainly constitutive of the present. Things are ineluctably related to their differences, with the result that things constantly comprise *différance* or an original ontological reality (Sweetman, 1997). Thus, speech for Derrida has become ascendant because it is able to draw without any consciousness on the honour that presence can bestow on an idea. Speech is thoroughly present because it is so closely linked with definite moments in human existence. As speech occurs, it occurs immediately: writing, on the other hand, engages with a delay between thought and its representation and is therefore less able to resort to the presence of a representation.

Note, however, that writing is bound to privilege the idea that a true representation of an entity – its self-sufficient presence – is valid if it is conceived of as merely an extension of speech. I have argued elsewhere from a Maori viewpoint that both the Maori and Western philosopher remain materially within any outcome of their invention (Mika, 2014b) regardless of whether they are named or not. From that worlded perspective, they have not ceased to exist simply when they are no longer mentioned; they still personally insist on a particular ordering of the article or thesis. In this process, the indigenous writer still has to contend with the antithetic Western philosopher: "Maori theorizing is forced to engage with [a] hidden colonizing presence even when it remains hidden within writing" (Mika, 2014b, p.34). Along with any other writer, Western philosophers actually exist in the writing; to describe it in a Maori way, their *mauri* permeates the literature although they appear to have withdrawn. Any Maori student or writer thus immediately restates the metaphysics of presence, especially when he or she tries to address it directly. The continuation of an initial prompt is also visible in the works of the early German romantics, who devised the fragment in light of that premise that things continue. In a more optimistic note than I have thus far intended in my own description of the pervasiveness of unannounced presence, Novalis, for instance, notes of the fragment that it processes an "ongoing dialogue that is going on [in him]. . . . First poesy – then politics, then physics en masse" (Novalis, 1960a, pp.241–2). Novalis likens this initial and continuous growth of thought to 'shoots', as in the origin of a seed that remains throughout time. His love of poetry means that it is original musicality of thought that provides the impetus for subsequent analysis (and we should remind ourselves here that he was a mathematician, but his version of mathematics and science is premised on poetry). The point to be made is that in various strains of thought, including those of Maori, there is a strong precedent for the belief that a dominant arrangement of text, including what someone may say against presence, exists despite its invisibility.

We can see a certain to-ing and fro-ing of the argument here, for if the metaphysics of presence is inherent to a piece of writing, then its counter, absence, must also be. Thus, we could equally argue that if those architects of presence are themselves present, along with the self-sufficiency of presence, then something completely other must also construct the Maori self's writing. All things in the world therefore attend an apparently present-oriented assertion or term. Let us turn at this point to the futility of arguing directly against the metaphysics of presence.

Writing academic text – obstructing Maori worldedness

Perhaps serendipitously for this book, Trinh Minh-ha brought together thought about Derrida with the collapsed time of Maori – in a different example to what I have outlined in the previous paragraph but still addressing the problem of teleological time nevertheless. It is often said of the greatest thinkers of Western philosophy that one cannot even speak of them until one has looked at other, preceding Western greats. In Trinh Minh-ha's (1999) book titled

Cinema-Interval, Pohatu asked the author about her interest in Maori culture when she arrived in New Zealand and pointed out to her that a Maori idea of time brings together past, present and future. Trinh Minh-ha responded – with some vigour, it seems – that such a proposition of time was very interesting for her, and that it can be distinguished from "Western education . . . [in which] the process of learning and of transmitting knowledge is very much based on a linear notion of time" (p.188). She relates that inscribed idea to reading Derrida, where "I have been told that one cannot teach Derrida without also teaching the classical texts of Kant and Heidegger. . . . when this linear approach is legitimized as the only valid way to teach or to learn, then we are again dealing with cultural authority and established power relationships" (p.188). Instead, she asked, "[W]hy not explore . . . how Derrida's theories . . . intersect with certain trends in contemporary performance arts[?] . . . Why follow only the vertical and its hierarchies when the oblique and the horizontal in their multiplicities are no less relevant and no less fascinating for the quest of truth and knowledge?" Although Kant and Heidegger are hugely important for a variety of reasons – and Minh-ha does indicate that if one wants to refer to them, then that is perfectly fine – as Maori critics we should be able to understand Derrida in relation to our current contexts. It seems that switching between the concepts of named experts in Western philosophy is to merely understand their theories and not to particularly transcend them, so that this approach becomes too dependent on names and their personal concepts (Mika, 2015b). My point here is that the discussion between an indigenous/Maori critic and a philosopher should not be reduced to simply the recall of names and their genealogies but instead should involve "the [indigenous] writer bringing together the spheres of lived experience, intellect, and the unknown" (Mika, 2015b, p.5). This takes place within the present but only as a direct relationship with past and future.

A key aspect of this chapter is to discuss the sense of Ako that deals with the Maori self's in/ability to portray worldedness, its historicity and its materiality, in his or her academic writing. The question arises: What resources in academic language do Maori have to immediately depict worldedness – to show the life of each term, to convincingly propose something other than presence (and hence be free of it themselves) and so on? We can start this discussion by stating upfront that writing for Derrida is not itself free of presence, because for him the problem of presence is evident in all text (which includes "almost any . . . combination of objects" (Sweetman, 1997, p.236). Instead, "[h]is proposition that writing is [ontologically] prior to speech is simply part of his . . . tactic of exposing the weakness of a position by turning its own strategems against itself" (Coward, 1991, p.142). The ambivalence even Maori academics may feel towards what can be assumed as their craft – writing – is informed by the colonising nature of writing: writing is unrivalled for its colonised representation. In public forums, the Maori academic writer is charged with revealing ideas to his or her community in a manner as accessible as possible and not replicating colonising ideas, so frequently the theoretical and methodological framework of kaupapa Maori is called on to deal with filtering out them out. However, whilst kaupapa Maori can act as a sorting mechanism for what lies *on* the page, it cannot destabilise the presence that exists beyond the page but is yet Derrida's 'text' – at least, not in its common form.

An example is called for to show what occurs with presence and academic writing in a Maori context, and here I speak anecdotally. It is quite common for a Maori writer to argue that, if a non-Maori source is being used, the Maori voice must precede it in a published article (Mika, 2016c). The main reason for this stance is that the Maori voice must be highly visible and more important than the other. The assumption, it may be obvious, is that the Maori description is lesser than the other because it follows on from the colonised one: what is first is most important. I have little argument with the proposition that a Maori voice must be more privileged than any other – especially in an indigenous or Maori publication – but whether it occurs before or after either a non-Maori discussion or, indeed, the name of a non-Maori theorist does not in itself constitute a solution. In our current example of debates around the physical priority of Maori content, a teleological approach to time is resorted to in order to categorise things and their importance: the "present-now" as Derrida (1973) calls it is grasped as "*evidence* itself" (p.62). It conflicts with the oft-cited metaphysical Maori notion that time is collapsed, and it also creates some logistical problems for that argument because, then, what comes last has the final and conclusive say. To be sure, the Maori content could conclude as well, but then we are left with the dilemma that, at some point, the non-Maori material is sovereign if even for a brief while. But the non-Maori material is not contained by being designated somewhere because the briefest time is enough for it to spread throughout the writing. It simply appears to have been allocated, but from a worlded perspective it must be thought of as spilling over to all corners of every page.

The worldedness of the invisible – in the context of the above, the continued existence of the non-Maori voice within writing – does illustrate that what is absent is influential throughout the words. However, the *placement* of the voice reveals something further that goes to the heart of presence. It is a tendency that all academic writers appear to have to wrestle with. Where those arguing for the first Maori voice appear to be concerned with the most visibly and politically savvy location of the Maori content, I am more interested here in how the notion of sequence reveals something more complex. The link between Being and its things is incidentally one that we have to express logically and sequentially. This responsibility is the sort that academic convention calls for, and its logic shows that the writer has understood the worlded thing's connections to all things to be governed by a chain of causality, in which Being *makes certain things happen*. I have thus fallen into a trap of the 'normal teaching' I have discussed thus far: I am expressing the infinite with a language (not necessarily just English) that insists on depicting the world and its things as finite. As a Maori critic of presence, for instance, I have to make my work as comprehensible to an audience as much as possible, and that includes describing Being as an original source of all else. This message is reiterated despite the fact that I might insist that Being is at once original and is yet composed by all other things. It *is* reiterated because I can only ever talk about one thing at once; I cannot immediately present Being as utterly constructed by the all because I have to deal with it on its own as I write. Similarly, any discussion about worldedness is compromised by the fact that I must encounter it in terms of its own, discrete properties. Once I have dealt with it by defining it, I can then move on to any subsequent elements that are related to it. Again, I am not able to present things in the world through text but have to announce them individually.

Maori terms to deal with presence

Central to the influence of presence that singles one thing out from another in advance, 'de-collapses' it so that things are separated from one entity (if we think of the problem in indigenous terms), is language. Paradoxically, as I noted in earlier chapters, language itself may well be another thing in the world within which we exist, even as we now talk about it. It then gives us the impression, if we are not careful, that it emanates solely from us, but it is not a human attribute so much as a thing constructed by all things in the world (and also constructs those things). The effects of a metaphysical view of Being as beings, and the pervasion of a technological worldview in which objects are proposed before the human subject and then considered as raw materials, reveal themselves in instrumentalist views of language. We are not concerned simply with wrongly translated terms here (although I do move to some Maori terms that have been reduced in their sense, as one example of enframing and presence); we are also worried about what language is *in itself*.

It should be recalled that language is derived from both the human and non-human worlds. I further emphasise, however, that language in a Maori worlded sense is not first a linguistic phenomenon. If we think about language in its *conventional* sense, then we become aware that it is insufficient for a Maori worldedness. We might therefore be tempted in thinking about language (in that orthodox way) as what we cannot escape. Derrida himself notes here that

> there have been several misinterpretations of what I and other deconstructionists are trying to do. It is totally false to suggest that deconstruction is a suspension of reference. Deconstruction is always deeply concerned with the *other* of language. . . . The critique of logocentrism is above all the search for the *other* and the *other of language*.
>
> (Kearney, 2004, p.154)

From a Maori worlded viewpoint, one is always contingent on things in the world (and things in the world are themselves language in a Maori worldedness, to the extent that they are both constituted by/constitute language, and arrange themselves so that the self gives expression to the world in particular ways).

Language, or *reo*, is simultaneously the 'other' that Derrida identifies and language as a conventional mode of communication. To that extent, Derrida's ideas are useful because they highlight that one is claimed by the other *as* constitutive of the self. It is not primarily language as a referential system that claims the Maori critic; it is the language as the amplification of all things in the world that one is dependent on. Thus, while academic critique cannot on its own destabilise the presence of terms and names, Derrida consoles us – at least partially – that presence is always constructed by absence. The linguistic signs of the Maori critic are thus undermined and rendered absent by what lies beyond the words.

Again, an example from a Maori context illuminates this scenario. There are several Maori terms that are liberally drawn on in policy and law; these terms have become no different to their English counterparts, to such an extent that one is left wondering what the point is of the translation. Stewart (2016) identifies that there are problems with "the loss of meaning when these words are extracted from their original philosophical context" (p.96). I surmise that there is a greater loss than that of meaning in this scenario, however. It will be recalled that I referred to the term *whakapapa* in Chapter 3 and its coalescing nature, with things in the world contained within the world itself whilst it alludes to that worlded phenomenon with other things. In policy, however, it will be recalled that it is nearly always translated as 'genealogy'. Not only is its meaning reduced; as Novalis (2005) put it, it engages with "the mere breadth and system of knowledge . . . the gift of relating this knowledge easily and purely to familiar concepts and experience and of exchanging the peculiar, strange-sounding words for common expressions" (p.115). It becomes something tamed. The term *whakapapa* may well be one of the most used terms in policy (*whanau*, equated with 'family', is another one). Other terms, such as *ako, whanau, mana* (status/pride) and so on, are often used in conjunction with whakapapa to refer to something apparently different to their English equivalents. More than simply window-dressing, though, the practice of peppering Maori terms throughout a strictly presence-oriented text such as policy makes the entities within the term adhere to one desired outcome. The things are governed by the text as a whole more than they are by the English equivalent, but perhaps the latter is particularly influential on the Maori term and its phenomena.

Derrida's (2004) talk of 'text' is the entire, referring field within which we operate. It is for him "forever imperceptible. Its law and its rules are not, however, harboured in the inaccessibility of a secret; it is simply that they can never be booked, in the *present*, into anything that could rigorously be called a perception" (p.69). In a Maori worlded context, Maori Marsden's (2003) observation that there is an element that lies "beyond expanse" (p.22) – a 'text' of sorts – amplifies that one's experience does not limit the full capacity of Papatuanuku. In other words, *experience* is an inadequate term to describe the self's claim by 'ground'. Indeed, the term *ground* is fraught. Derrida (2003) notes of terms like these that "all the names related to fundamentals . . . have always designated an invariable presence – *eidos, arche, telos, energeia, ousia* (essence, existence, substance, subject), *aletheia*, transcendality, consciousness, God, man, and so forth" (p.355). Ground is a term that is not capable of describing the nature of Maori world-edness because it suggests too strongly that there is an ultimate phenomenon that is not itself dependent on all other phenomena. This problem consists in the fact that Western philosophical terms are largely inadequate in this role and that Maori philosophy is cordoned off by the terms at the writer's disposal. Another problem thus confronts the academic Maori self: not only does Papa relate to an idea – and therefore we have to admit in our philosophising that Papa claims us in terms of both that idea and a physical entity – but we also have to accept that this representation may be impossible. In universities, where rational language is highly privileged, the full representation of Papa – and this is just one Maori term among many! – is simply not that easy to make (Mika, 2016a). This difficulty is unsurprising: as I argued in the previous chapter, such a full exploration has not been encouraged from the early years at school, where Papa is often simply and economically referred to as 'Earth Mother', comprises one of the elements in the stories about creation (and, incidentally, is the main object of the inevitable triumph of man), and is something that, according to the *Te Whariki* early childhood curriculum document, should earn 'respect'. It makes sense, then, that the highly regulated nature of text itself in universities would be especially vigilant against the kind of language that would need to be used in Maori thought.

The problem here might appear to be one to do with language, and certainly language shares in it, but just as implicit is philosophical imperialism. Any talk about 'Papa' is necessarily counter-colonial, or at least involves a discussion about colonisation. We are therefore urged to recognise Derrida's argument that the absent constitutes the present. For a Maori writer, the proposition that Papa is a living entity should stand on its own, and any suggestion that the proposition occurs because of colonisation may be rankling. But in a much broader sense, any discussion about a Maori metaphysics has arisen only because it has been made an issue by its dominantly colonising counterpart. As I discuss the fact that Papa is a living entity, for instance, I am unconsciously (but always) drawing on a key idea proposed by Western colonisation – that Papa is not one complete, living entity. This negative, hidden participant is equally as important as my assertion that Papa is animate because it forced me to raise it as an issue to begin with. I would never have written it to begin with if the other had not existed: it merely remains unspoken in the visible assertion I've made. This highly inter-woven 'metaphysics-as-countercolonialism' is present at all points of discussion about Papa, reflecting Deleuze's notion that difference implicates phenomena (Bell, 2015) – in this case, Maori metaphysics and colonisation – that are in and of themselves unstable. They do not remain constant, and neither do the categories we impose on them to describe them. Affected by each other at all nodes of conversation, Maori assertions about Papa and colonisation are co-constitutive and cannot be discussed as if separate from each other (Mika, 2016a). In a most basic sense, one reaches over and touches (and reforms) the other. To return to our earlier point about 'experience', its inadequacy is perhaps so tangible that it usefully highlights for us other aspects to Papa that we could describe, albeit in a limited fashion. If we experience something in its conventional sense we somehow feel it, but in our present discussion we could be referring to the limitless possibilities of a ground that far exceeds our experience.

Maori terms are forced to conform quite deeply to the presence nature of the text and become its emissary. In a worlded indigenous view, presence devitalises the full interplay of things with one thing, resulting in that one thing – and thereafter a representation of it as an idea – becoming the most important aspect. Indigenous focuses on language often emphasise that it should be protected; presumably, the various facets of integrity of even a term need to be retained. Alongside its pure meaning, a term's deep sense and orientation to other things are to be guarded. A term is capable of being subverted to reflect the subtlety of its context – it could well be that indigenous writers have this in mind when they use their languages – and it ends up becoming presence-oriented. This prospect is deeply disturbing for indigenous groups because language is perhaps seen as at once extremely precious and yet vulnerable to colonisation. Indigenous languages in these instances are tools of presence, in that they add to the presence of the text but with an indigenous shell. There is the prospect that language is merely a set of sounds that convey an idea of the emptiness of the term; thus, the indigenous term in the text carries out the aim of presence without any threat to it.

A key ground to this problem is that academic language lacks terminology to adequately describe indigenous metaphysics (Mika, 2014b; 2015d; 2016a; 2016d; Mika & Stewart, 2015). This signals that rational text is not just expert at aiming to be precise but is additionally another tool for corralling objectivity from irrational thought. It therefore naturally forecloses any other possible metaphysics. In academic text, there are several terms that approximate the oneness of all things but for the indigenous scholar I suspect they never quite suffice: they run up against a wall of resistance that rational thought has erected to oust its opposite number. Included here are oneness, interconnection, unity, co-instantaneity, sublime, totality. They are solely abstract and do not display in the everyday or concrete realm. 'Interconnection' is a possible description of what indigenous peoples have argued is at the heart of their metaphysics, with Fixico (2003) indicating that "seeing is visualizing the connection between two or more entities or beings, and trying to understand the full context of things identified within a culturally based system" (p.2). However, the term also falls short because it emphasises links between separate entities rather than their immediate immersion or collapse within each other. The intricate relationships between entities is indeed important to acknowledge, along with the belief that they are somehow associated with each other through genealogy, but at the same time they are not separate at all.

What is that?

Derrida (1976) asked the following about language and philosophy: "if we consider the history of philosophy as a great and discursive chain, does it not dip into a reserve of language . . . [i]s it not henceforth limited by the resources and the organization of that reserve?" (p.527). He would turn the assumption of language's priority on its head when acknowledging the role of philosophy in bringing language about. A possible version of worldedness is that a view of language does not simply pop up; instead, it comes about as a result of a particular philosophy. Yet, the Maori thinker has to apprehend language as also a thing that always already existed. It is the pre-existence of the ground of thinking that gives rise to one of the smallest yet most frequently used terms – *is* – that Derrida is taking to task in the above quote, not language itself. The Maori critic might say that both are immediately addressed, for language is entitially composed of that ground and vice versa. Moreover, it is the problem of an entity – the 'is' – being inserted into Maori thought and expression, even where it previously did not exist in Maori concepts, that must be concerning for the Maori critic (Mika, 2016a; 2016d). The 'is' is so completely present as to be absent from our critique: we use it daily in our conceptual reach for an object. With its omnipresence in mind, Hart (2013) argues that "[a]mong the claims for radical differences between languages, the absence of the copula has seemed to be the most concrete and the most significant, for the copula has seemed to be the most plausibly connected with philosophically important consequences" (p.59).

Benveniste, as Derrida points out, has alluded that the copula ('to be') has always already presupposed a much more primordial notion of Being than the copula's lexical appearance (Hart, 2013). The 'is' in its form of presence here is predicated on what is not necessarily grammatical; it is a fixing unit, the liberation from which is the domain of "thought and poetic creation" (Heidegger, 1999, p.218). In the case of Maori worlded thinking, a problem is evidenced by the fact that, while language may not have given rise to the copula as Derrida states, it is nevertheless an emissary of a fixed Being that endures in presence (but that is also, admittedly, incorporated by absence). From a worlded perspective, Derrida is correct when he notes that statements about a linguistic problem are always already sourced in a philosophy. We could not have made such a statement at all if it were not for philosophy – which from a Maori worlded view is an entity. Language from a worlded perspective must at once account for the philosophy of presence. Said (1994) therefore remarked on the 'is':

> Rather than listing all the figures of speech associated with the Orient – its strangeness, its difference, its exotic sensuousness, and so forth – we can generalize about them as they were handed down through the Renaissance. They are all declarative and self-evident; the tense they employ is the timeless eternal; they convey an impression of repetition and strength. . . . For all these function it is frequently enough to use the simple copula *is*.
>
> (p.72)

The Maori critic also inherits a similar mechanism. He or she is forced to use the 'is' throughout writing. It can occur in both describing a traditional worldview – 'Worldedness *is* connected to the idea of things in the world and their interconnection' – and counteracting presence – 'a Maori worldview is more expansive than one preordained by presence'. In both cases, the Maori writer has reiterated presence, at least, through the determination of what worldness *is* and what a Maori worldview *is* in relation to its other. What is perhaps most striking for the Maori critic is how much he or she is a product of language, which, it seems, is a product of philosophy but which really is coexistent with the latter. Presence claims us as much as worlding, as I noted earlier, now as a result of its correspondence with the language we need to use to adhere to academic convention.

Even as I try to designate a place for something I am forced to use such terms as *is*. I also use *is*, as Said has suggested, to make things comply with what I would have them *be*. As I critique, I therefore am caught in a conflict between, on one hand, the 'is-ness' of the is and the idea that the thing I am identifying was constituted before all things in the world before I even identified it or claimed it in my writing, on the other. The nature of a critique, it seems, relies on clarifying the individual thing so that it falls away from its relations. Any judgment is reliant on the Maori self's constitution of all things, as I have noted, and while there may then be a judgment of sorts taking place, it is a judgment that is not of my own entirely. One term in Maori for judgment (usually used in relation to formal judgment but also relatable to the most basic act of discerning one thing from another), *whakawā*, does indeed allow the critic to see one thing, but the term carries with it a sense of both the self's and the thing's (and that of the world within it) temporalising. In other words, if I say in the Maori language that I am making a judgment about what a thing will be, I am really stating how both I and the object become situated in time and place – importantly, by all other things in the world (Mika, 2013). Judgment from a worlded perspective, then, is thoroughly constructed by the world. Unfortunately for me, I am undermined in my attempt to articulate that process by the words and conventions of academic language. To begin with, I have to say that "a judgment is being made": I cannot say all at once that "things in the world converge on my ability to perceive the object and then I speak them". Incidentally, it is not just the 'is' that is at fault here; it is also the very layout of argument that prevents the all-at-once worldedness of a statement and its (and my) constitution by all things (Mika, 2016d). The much more complex continually signified nature of a thing is equally as challenging (and, indeed, the 'is' is merely one example of this problem, because 'is' is not really a linguistic idiosyncrasy). As Derrida notes, however, the 'is' is not a finality, even though it acts as if it is. Instead, it is consistently undermined by absence. So is any other entity: this idea fits quite nicely with worldedness. But as I have suggested earlier, things themselves are constitutive of any utterance I make, and even if I could avoid the 'is' or any other logical form of speech and writing, I would have to account for the colonised entity and its aspect within any discussion. This emphasises the problem of resorting to one's native language to try and subvert presence, for the present in its infinite forms already exists as a colonising counterpart to any absence that my language proposes. Derrida (1997) himself stated that "writing is not a sign of a sign, except if one says it of all signs, which would be more profoundly true" (p.43), and the thing that I am giving form to within my writing is already an enmeshed one, referring endlessly to other entities.

Asking what something is, participates in trying to ascertain what the identity of something is to another entity. In the Maori language, 'what is' is glossed as 'he aha'. The Maori version, however, takes a completely different path than the what-ness that 'what is' expects. *He aha* asks after what is not audible or visible. It is a call into the depths of voidness that Maori have long cherished; it inquires after the dark backdrop to what is apparently the subject of discussion, such that the subject is not really expected to be a subject any longer. The present thing is therefore as immediately constructed by its unspoken, invisible counterpart to the extent that it is not a 'counterpart' so much as counter-constitutive. 'He aha' also evinces the moment of the fact that something *is* in its lack of presence. Thus, 'what is', with its admittedly stunning attempt at bringing an entity forward in its shininess, is not equipped with the almost overwhelming ability of 'he aha' to bringing to the fore the void of silence that comes with and surrounds an entity.

Inquiring after silence and voidness with 'he aha', though, does something different: asking after silence with 'he aha' is curious because 'he aha' is itself a bringing to the fore of silence and nothingness. In that respect it is a silent inquiry. 'He aha' in that context, although voiced, is characterised by what is not present, and this absence of things is evident in the voice of the inquirer. Hence, the inquirer is placed under a thrall of nothingness even as he or she asks after nothingness. This incomplete, void or silent inquiry shows itself in the uncertainty of the inquirer in a complete sense. Another way of imagining this permeation of the self by nothingness is in the following: I ask after nothingness with 'he aha' and am immediately destabilised by the withdrawal of things, or their own reticence. Innate to the voidness of the voiced 'he aha' is the mystery of the world. Thus, instead of translatable as 'what is', 'he aha' could less economically (and in a less Aristotelean fashion) be thought of as 'in what fashion does the All, in its withdrawal, incline itself towards us and show itself as constituting us through the nothingness of the thing we are inquiring after?'

Summary

It will be recalled that there is more at stake here than simply a philosophical issue: as we have already seen Deloria indicate, the apparently conceptual difficulty corresponds immediately with one's thoroughgoing well-being. Derrida also identified that one is deprived by presence, even if such presence is constituted by absence. Sartre bluntly explained it in the following way, and we can surmise that he meant presence in a more postcolonial way when he noted that

> [t]he European elite undertook to manufacture a native elite. They picked out promising adolescents; they branded them, as with a red hot iron, with the principles of Western culture; they stuffed their mouths full with high-sounding phrases, grand glutinous words that stuck to the teeth. After a short stay in the mother country they were sent home, whitewashed.
>
> (Fanon, 1963, p.7)

The problem is a deep one for the indigenous and Maori thinker, as he or she must be aware of his or her immersion within a colonised field even while try-ing to undo it. One is also caught between the proposition that a thing irrupts through writing, on one hand, and that a thing is merely an idea, on the other. In critiquing presence, for instance, I have been encouraged to talk about 'the proposition' of a thing rather than help bring a thing itself to the surface. The irruptive nature of a thing from a worlded view (again, we see 'view' here, con-noting a critical distance) is tamed through the thing's logical representation, by my having to explain it as nothing other than a concept. Where *whakaaro* meant an amplitude of the thing as it constructed my thinking (and hence it is greater than an 'idea'), now it is constructed and disciplined. My ability to argue against that reductionism is itself constrained.

I reiterate here Derrida's view that, notwithstanding the logocentrism of aca-demic language that the Maori critic is forced to act within, absence always pervades the highly positive representation. As a Maori critic of presence, I am therefore fairly optimistic as I recount the above present-oriented terms and concepts in relation to an incomplete aspect of their absent *other* (my expres-sion of which is always-already incomplete). While it appears that the absent other follows the colon, in fact, the absent other is also always already defined by presence:

The idea of things: the logical explanation of them through worldedness
Genealogical and temporal sequence through worldedness: Collapse of time and things through worldedness
Collapse through worldedness: always-already one (whakapapa)
Always-already one: nothingness
Nothingness: inarticulateness
Inarticulateness: attempts to clarify (through an idea of that which cannot be explained) – and so on *ad infinitum.*

We will remember that one key aspect of Ako is the ability or freedom to explain the worldedness of a thing – to *deliberately* try to encounter absence in our terminology and concepts. Additionally, Ako comprises the ability or freedom to explore how one is constrained or disciplined to *not* explain the worldedness of a thing. This process is infinite, and the critic who is engaged in it must be aware that things are conducting that thinking in the first instance. That thing-constituted thinking is – not incidentally – key to contemplating Ako. But how can the seemingly insurmountable problems of this and the last chapter be mediated? What can the philosophies of worldedness suggest that would allow us, the indigenous student and critic, to regain some lost ground? Preferably, that 'ground' would be non-foundational, but can that ground possibly be regained? The forthcoming conclusion chapter considers how, if at all, the indigenous self in the colonised/worldedness realm can approach any proposition about a thing so that it retains the fullness of the world to it.

Bibliography

Ahenakew, C., Andreotti, V., Cooper, G., et al. (2014) 'Beyond Epistemic Provincialism: De-Provincializing Indigenous Resistance', *AlterNative* 10(3): 216–31.

Bell, J. (2015) 'Infinite Pragmatism: Deleuze, Peirce, and the Habits of Things', pp. 21–37 in S. Bignall, S. Bowden and P. Patton (eds) *Deleuze and Pragmatism*. London, UK: Routledge.

Biesta, G. (2010) 'Witnessing Deconstruction in Education: Why Quasi-Transcendentalism Matters', pp. 73–86 in C. Ruitenberg (ed) *What Do Philosophers of Education Do? (and How Do They Do It?)*. West Sussex, UK: Blackwell Publishing.

Coward, H. (1991) 'Speech Versus Writing' in Derrida and Bharthari', *Philosophy East and West* 41(2): 141–62.

Derrida, J. (1973) *Speech and Phenomena, and Other Essays on Husserl's Theory of Signs*. Evanston, IL: Northwestern University Press.

Derrida, J. (1976) 'The Supplement of Copula: Philosophy Before Linguistics', *The Georgia Review* 30(3): 527–64.

Derrida, J. (1982) 'Ousia and Grammē', pp. 29–67 *Margins of Philosophy*. Chicago, IL: University of Chicago.

Derrida, J. (1997) *Of Grammatology*, 2nd edn. London, UK: The John Hopkins University Press.

Derrida, J. (2003) 'Structure, Sign and Play in the Discourses of the Human Sciences', pp. 354–63 in G. Delanty and P. Strydom (eds) *Philosophies of Social Science: The Classic and Contemporary Readings*. Berkshire, UK: Open University Press.

Derrida, J. (2004) *Dissemination*. London, UK: Continuum.

Durie, M. (2004) 'Understanding Health and Illness: Research at the Interface between Science and Indigenous Knowledge', *International Journal of Epidemiology* 33(5): 1138–43.

Eames, C. and Barker, M. (2011) 'Understanding Student Learning in Environmental Education in Aotearoa New Zealand', *Australian Journal of Environmental Education* 27(1): 186–91.

Eames, C., Cowie, B. and Bolstad, R. (2008) 'An Evaluation of Characteristics of Environmental Education Practice in New Zealand Schools', *Environmental Education Research* 14(1): 35–51.

Fanon, F. (1963) *The Wretched of the Earth*. New York, NY: Grove Weidenfeld.

Fixico, D. (2003) *The American Indian Mind in a Linear World*. New York, NY: Routledge.

Flay, J. (1970) 'Hegel's "Inverted World"', *The Review of Metaphysics* 23(4): 662–78.

Gardner, H. (1983) *Frames of Mind: The Theory of Multiple Intelligences*. New York, NY: Basic Books.

Grant, I. (2006) *Philosophies of Nature after Schelling*. New York, NY: Continuum International Publishing Group.

Greaves, T. (2010) *Starting with Heidegger*. London, UK: Continuum International Publishing Group.

Hall, S. (2014) *Holistic Education: A Vision for 21st Century New Zealand Primary School Classrooms*. Unpublished masters thesis, The University of Waikato, New Zealand.

Hart, R. (2013) *Imagined Civilizations: China, the West, and their First Encounter*. Baltimore, MD: John Hopkins University Press.

Heidegger, M. (1998) *Was ist Metaphysik?* Frankfurt am Main, Germany: Vittorio Klostermann GmbH.

Heidegger, M. (1999) 'Letter on "Humanism"', pp. 239–76 in W. McNeill (ed) *Pathmarks*. Cambridge, UK: Cambridge University Press.

Hodge, S. (2015) *Martin Heidegger: Challenge to Education*. London, UK: Springer.

Holland, J. (2006) 'From Romantic Tools to Technics: Heideggerean Questions in Novalis' Anthropology', *Configurations* 18(3): 291–307.

Jones, A. (2001) 'Cross-Cultural Pedagogy and the Passion for Ignorance', *Feminism and Psychology* 11: 279–92.

Kearney, R. (2004) *Debates in Continental Philosophy: Conversations with Contemporary Thinkers*. New York, NY: Fordham University Press.

Kneller, J (Ed.). (2003) *Novalis: Fichte Studies*. Cambridge, UK: Cambridge University Press.

Levien, J. (2007) 'Maori Health: One Area of Risk', *Nursing Journal Northland Polytechnic* 11: 17–21.

Mahmoudi, S., Jafari, E., Nasrabadi, H., et al. (2012) 'Holistic Education: An Approach for 21 Century', *International Education Studies* 5(2): 178–86.

Marsden, M. (2003) *The Woven Universe: Selected Writings of Rev. Māori Marsden*. Otaki, New Zealand: Estate of Rev. Māori Marsden.

Meyer, M. (2008) 'Indigenous and Authentic: Hawaiian Epistemology and the Triangulation of Meaning', pp. 217–32 in N. Denzin, Y. Lincoln and L. Smith (eds) *Handbook of Critical and Indigenous Methodologies*. London, UK: Sage.

Mika, C. (2012) 'Overcoming "Being" in Favour of Knowledge: The Fixing Effect of "Mātauranga"', *Educational Philosophy and Theory* 44(10): 1080–92.

Mika, C. (2013) *Reclaiming Mystery: A Māori Philosophy of Being, in Light of Novalis' Ontology*. Unpublished PhD dissertation, University of Waikato.

Mika, C. (2014a) 'The Enowning of Thought and Whakapapa: Heidegger's Fourfold', *Review of Contemporary Philosophy* 13: 48–60.

Mika, C. (2014b) 'Maori Thinking with a Dead White Male: Philosophizing in the Realm of Novalis', *Knowledge Cultures* 2(1): 23–39.

Mika, C. (2015a) 'The Co-Existence of Self and Thing through "Ira": A Māori Phenomenology', *Journal of Aesthetics and Phenomenology* 2(1): 93–112.

Mika, C. (2015b) 'Counter-Colonial and Philosophical Claims: An Indigenous Observation of Western Philosophy', *Educational Philosophy and Theory*: 1–7.

Mika, C. (2015c) 'Novalis' Poetic Uncertainty: A Bildung with the Absolute', *Educational Philosophy and Theory*.

Mika, C. (2015d) 'Thereness: Implications for Heidegger's "Presence" for Māori', *AlterNative* 11(1): 3–13.

Mika, C. (2016a) ' "Papatūānuku/Papa": Some Thoughts on the Oppositional Grounds of the Doctoral Experience', *Knowledge Cultures* 4(1): 43–55.

Mika, C. (2016b) 'The Ontological and Active Possibilities of Papatūānuku: To Nurture or Enframe?', *Knowledge Cultures* 4(3): 58–71.

Mika, C. (2016c) 'What Is Intellectual Freedom Today? A Māori Perspective', *Continental Thought & Theory: A journal of intellectual freedom* 1(1): 47–8.

Mika, C. (2016d) 'Worlded Object and Its Presentation: A Māori Philosophy of Language', *AlterNative* 12(2): 165–76.

Mika, C. and Stewart, G. (2015) 'Maori in the Kingdom of the Gaze: Subjects or Critics?', *Educational Philosophy and Theory*: 1–13.

Miller, J. (2007) *The Holistic Curriculum*. London, UK: University of Toronto.

Miller, J., Bruce Cassie, J. and Drake, S. (1990) *Holistic Learning: A Teacher's Guide to Integrated Studies*. Ontario, Canada: OISE Press.

Miller, R. (2006) 'Making Connections to the World: Some Thoughts on Holistic Curriculum', *Encounter* 19(4): 19–24.

Minh-ha, T. (1999) *Cinema-Interval*. London, UK: Routledge.

Ministry of Education. (1996) *Te Whāriki: He Whāriki Mātauranga Mō Ngā Mokopuna O Aotearoa*. Wellington, New Zealand: Learning Media.

Ministry of Education. (2007) *The New Zealand Curriculum: For English-Medium Teaching and Learning in Years 1–13*. Wellington, New Zealand: Learning Media Ltd.

Novalis. (1960a). 'Briefe von Novalis', in P. Kluckhohn & R. Samuel (Eds.), *Schriften: Lebensdokumente* (Vol. 4, pp. 63–344). Stuttgart, Germany: W. Kohlhammer.

Novalis. (1960b). 'Fragmente und Studien 1799–1800', pp. 527–693 in P. Kluckhohn and R. Samuel (eds) *Schriften: Das philosophische Werk II*, Vol. 3. Stuttgart, Germany: W. Kohlhammer.

Novalis. (1990) *Henry von Ofterdingen*. Long Grove IL: Waveland Press Inc.

Novalis. (2005) *The Novices of Sais*. New York, NY: Archipelago Books.

Pere, R. (1982) *Ako: Concepts and Learning in the Māori Tradition*. Hamilton, New Zealand: University of Waikato.

Peters, M. (2009) 'Academic Writing, Genres and Philosophy', pp. 1–13 in M. Peters (ed) *Academic Writing, Genres and Philosophy*. West Sussex, UK: Wiley-Blackwell.

Pihama, L. (2001) *Tihei Mauri Ora: Honouring Our Voices: Mana Wahine as a Kaupapa Māori Theoretical Framework*. Unpublished doctoral dissertation, The University of Auckland, New Zealand.

Reid, P. and Robson, B. (2006) 'The State of Māori Health', pp. 17–31 in M. Mulholland (ed) *State of the Māori Nation: Twenty-First-Century Issues in Aotearoa*. Auckland, New Zealand: Reed.

Robinson, K. (2011) *Out of Our Minds: Learning to Be Creative*, 2nd edn. West Sussex, UK: Capstone Publishing Ltd.

Royal, T. A. (2008) *Te Ngākau*. Te Whanganui-a-Tara, NZ: Mauriora Ki Te Ao Living Universe Ltd.

Said, E. (1994) *Culture and Imperialism*. London: Vintage.

Smith, L. (1999) *Decolonizing Methodologies: Research and Indigenous Peoples*. London, UK: Zed Books.

Stewart, G. (2016) 'Indigenous Knowledge and Education Policy for Teachers of Māori Learners', *Knowledge Cultures* 4(3): 84–98.

Stone, A. (2008) 'Being, Knowledge and Nature in Novalis', *Journal of the History of Philosophy* 46(1): 141–64.

Sweetman, B. (1997) 'The Deconstruction of Western Metaphysics', pp. 230–47 in R. Ciapalo (ed) *Postmodernism and Christian Philosophy*. Washington, DC: The Catholic University of America Press.

Tulloch, L. (2015) 'Is Emile in the Garden of Eden? Western Ideologies of Nature', *Policy Futures in Education* 13(1): 20–41.

Uhl, C. and Stuchul, D. (2011) *The Promise of a New Education Culture.* Baltimore, MD: The Johns Hopkins University Press.

Walker, S. (1996) *Kia Tau Te Rangamarie. Kaupapa Maori Theory as a Resistance against the Construction of Maori as the Other.* Unpublished masters thesis, The University of Auckland, New Zealand.

White, J. and Mika, C. (2013) 'Coming of Age? Infants and Toddlers in Curriculum', in J. Nuttall (ed) *Weaving Te Whāriki.* Wellington, New Zealand: NZCER.

Wood, D. (Ed.). (2007) *Novalis: Notes for a Romantic Encyclopaedia.* Albany, NY: State University of New York Press.

Chapter 6

Cause for optimism?

Worldedness and presence continue despite what we say or do, making any discussion convoluted. I have theorised that indigenous peoples have always had a fraught relationship with presence and that now our thought about worldedness must be similarly and deliberately complicated. Throughout my discussion of worldedness in Chapters 2 and 3, I have hinted at the 'presence of presence', or the loitering of something within our thinking that is not originally part of our worldview. It is this fully incorporated, colonised thing that undermines our ability to learn from the world as one constituted by all other, absent worlds, and it is this same thing that restricts our thinking and thereby our language. Paradoxically, presence also opens up possibilities for further thinking. It is vulnerable to our thinking because it draws us on to speculate on the absence of a thing or idea. It is itself an entity with its own worlded constitution – including, importantly, the absence that it seeks to stifle. It is therefore futile to try and convey presence and worldedness as separate phenomena because they construct each other. The All is defined in terms of its components, in a sequential manner, but the sequential discussion is so thoroughly unworlded that it demonstrates its immediate correspondence with the All. Presence is destabilised by absence at every step, and it gives us cause for optimism because it always reveals the possibility of all worlds within any one, apparently present, thing. All of worldedness and presence compose a possible indigenous view of education.

If the West cannot be completely dislodged from its metaphysical inheritance, as Derrida has argued, then it is likely we are also tied to it. This gloomy reality, however, does not preclude us from identifying ways of thinking which aim to reiterate a stance against it, and in fact we are not so much intent on doing away with presence as bringing it to the fore, identifying it. We might also want to obscure an idea or thing so that the self-certainty of presence is made less certain, at least temporarily. Most fundamentally, this chapter concludes by reflecting on the tools at the indigenous self's disposal that can disrupt the surface of presence and lend themselves to creative thought. Speculative thinking is a type that is not so intent on finding a solid foundation of truth. It is more of an imaginative enterprise than an epistemically certain one. As I discussed in the previous chapter, indigenous peoples have been denied the freedom to speculate on their own existence. This existential and creative theorising is most certainly not meant to be fettered by colonised assumptions (as far as that is possible) and is particularly forceful in assertions of sovereignty, by which indigenous populations seek to pursue aspects of importance in line with what they deem to be appropriate. How indigenous peoples educate their own, for example, is a problem that intersects directly with indigenous notions of creativity, and the management of ethics, research, legal systems and health also signals a possible, innovative divergence from practices established by Western institutions. In current contexts, the need for creative reflection on these political facets – which, it must be reiterated, are also deeply rooted in philosophy – is especially urgent. Indigenous peoples are constantly described by statistics that depict their ill health, lack of education, or lawlessness. These numbers paint a bleak picture in research reports and government documents, but they brush economically and lightly over the feelings of despair that accompany the experiences they refer to. An indigenous method of dealing with these extraordinarily negative experiences involves creativity. Creative speculation is hence culturally centred: it is a phenomenon that accords directly with both current experience and the possibility of individual and collective ethical expression and practice.

The creativity I allude to, though, is philosophical and abstract. We have seen that colonising metaphysics has privileged the presentation of an object so that it is smooth and seamless. With the object thus anticipated, indigenous peoples are not meant to unsettle the surface of the object with mythical thinking or with propositions about their own metaphysical regard of the object. But one role of indigenous thinkers is to fulfil precisely that duty and to take to task that deep colonial assumption about how the world is expected to present itself in the very first instance – even if they find themselves replicating it. Quite what this determined yet tentative thinking is, is open to creative interpretation. The writings of philosophers such as Deloria (2001) and Pere (1982), who broadly state that the world is thoroughly interconnected, are quite basic to indigenous belief, but that they are apparently so easily written or uttered should not lead the reader to confuse them with anything simplistic. Those authors intend to direct the reader not just to a general metaphysics but also to a mode of thought that has to attend to it, and this maxim makes their assertions all the more complex. It would be far more painless and straightforward indeed to read their philosophies as merely abstract fragments that do not have much relevance for current life. The common practice of placing indigenous metaphysics into the realm of 'creation stories', so common in dominant teaching and learning settings, for instance, may fuel that sort of interpretation. Those statements of holism, though, disclose indigenous views on language (including the nature of the words that those authors chose to use), the relationship of the self, academic or otherwise, to verbal, creative and scholastic expression and to the nature of colonisation itself – how it regulates our lives, closes off possibilities for thinking that is opposed or at least antidotal to the highly present object, and how it even constitutes our utterances about the world.

The true reach of those highly abstract utterances clearly calls for creative and free thought. We cannot really be certain of the way in which the utterance 'a thing is worlded' truly plays out as I, for instance, choose to speak to a colleague or drive my car; yet this is precisely where the remark aims. What is left to us is a form of theorising that attempts to retain the core of that utterance *whilst* addressing the everyday context. This philosophical act is a creative one but, as we have seen, the insidiousness of a single term and concept lies in its potential to constrain in advance what indigenous peoples are allowed to think (and is thus itself an impediment to placing the holistic statement into the everyday context!). Martin (2014) emphasises that current constructions of creativity may be as discursively prescriptive as any other colonial mechanism. In that warning we can see that even terms, and the abstract or concrete phenomena they refer to, need to be reinterpreted or possibly discarded in favour of others less influenced by practices that indigenous peoples decide do not belong. But in order to achieve this fairly ambitious outcome, an indigenous frame of thinking needs to be brought to bear on the problems that hide in the recesses of the colonised mind, as well as provide signposts to ways that destabilise those problems. Creativity is at once a political and a philosophical concern, not just an aesthetic one (although it may include that form of expression).

Returning to indigenous speculation

Indigenous peoples have various names for the particular method of critique that I have just outlined. This sceptical approach interprets the ontological consequences of both dominant Western and indigenous uncritical thinking. One term that I have proposed is *counter-colonialism*, where one draws on the possibilities offered by colonisation to oppose it (Mika, 2015a; Mika, 2016a; Mika & Stewart, 2015). In that critical way of perceiving how an object is commonly given to us as indigenous peoples, we have to account for the totality of the world both in that object and in the phenomena that give rise to our critique even as we critique. One similarity of indigenous counter-colonialism with Heidegger's *Destruktion* lies in the liberation stemming from a paradox that arises: that the problem immediately exposes its potential for thought. Central to this task for both Heidegger and the indigenous self is the *question* of Being:

> If the question of Being is to have its own history made transparent, then this hardened tradition must be loosened up, and the concealments which it has brought about must be dissolved. We understand this task as one in which by taking *the question of Being as our clue*, we are to *destroy* the traditional content of ancient ontology until we arrive at those primordial experiences in which we achieved our first ways of determining the nature of Being – the ways which have guided us ever since.
>
> (Heidegger, 1962, p.44)

This act of loosening up a 'hardened tradition' or 'ancient ontology' (for Heidegger, originating in both Plato and Aristotle) is one that depends on the external world for indigenous peoples. It therefore makes sense that the question of Being raises an ongoing, infinite process which in the indigenous realm is itself dependent on Being as a worlding event. In counter-colonialism, the question of Being arises in direct respect of its other – the complacent belief that beings just manifest on their own account with no interruption from all other beings. With that, it is not sufficient to simply make an assertion based on traditional belief as such a statement might itself belong to that fixity. Instead, counter-colonialism might meld both those precolonially based utterances whilst staring directly at what is thought of as the problem. Heidegger uses the term *destroy*, but the destruction of hardened discourses is not meant here *to get rid of*. Instead, one suspends them for a time by referring them to the deepest cause of the problem that can be identified.

Creative speculation that takes into account colonisation is important even if indigenous communities do still have access to a pure, unaffected strain of traditional knowledge. All debates aside about whether any claim to any unadulterated knowledge is valid, we are left with the need to think creatively to understand presence rather than resort solely to traditional knowledge. Unfortunately, as I suggested earlier, creative thinking as a theme appears to have received diminished press in most academic text, taking an inferior position to knowing. Heidegger (1966) lamented the fact that what he called 'meditative thinking' is forever endangered by its opposite, calculative thinking, which is an inevitable outcome of viewing the world in terms of its highly present attributes. Indigenous writers such as Calderon (2008), Deloria (2001), Royal (2008) and Smith (1999), among others, emphasise a way of comporting oneself to the world that is not entirely defined by seeking to know how that world is organised. Thinking can still be as fixed as its counterpart, knowledge, but in its capacity to draw and expand on the endless possibilities of a phenomenon, it surpasses the latter. Where knowledge strives to set an entity in a fixed position, speculative thinking withholds certainty from its gaze, and hence places the thing in a shadowy interconnection with other things. For indigenous writers such as those I have just noted, it is important that a kind of immersion *within* the world, and hence the thing that is the topic of discussion, is maintained, and that the gaze does not attempt to unproblematically distance the thing from the self, despite the colonial pressure to transcend it and gain detachment from it.

The problem is not just one to do with knowledge. In parts of this book I have described worlding as a 'metaphysics'. Some Maori writers might rightly say that the term is a Western one and that it deserves our cynicism or perhaps even our disregard, yet freely use the term 'knowledge'. What is notable in these instances is that some terms are taken to be neutral simply because of their popularity. They have become so imbued throughout discussion as to be acceptable. We have apparently distanced them from something in the first ('metaphysics') while remaining close to the utility of the second ('knowledge'). Yet, in the same ways both are problematic from a worlded perspective that has a presence in mind because they indicate an immediate withdrawal from the worlded nature of the thing. To paraphrase Adorno (2001) here, to be a valid discipline, metaphysics must involve a theorising; entities themselves are not 'metaphysics'. The distancing of thought from entity, of concept from thing, is also notably reflected in Cassirer's and Bakhtin's works. Cassirer (1953) insisted that a more sophisticated mode of thought lay in creating a critical interval between the entity and one's terminology but that it was typical of pre-scientific groups to connect the object with the term referring to it. These groups, according to Cassirer, are forever bound to appearances (Friedman, 2011). Tau (2001) also thinks that Maori did not possess true knowledge because of this lack of critical distance. Bakhtin saw poetic discourse as too monolithic – too impenetrable because it was "under the power of images [which] fetter the free movement of its intentions" (Bakhtin, 1981, p.369). *Knowledge*, as embedded in the term through a dominant belief in escaping the world of appearances, is now linked with the sense of 'standing upon' innate to the term *epistemology* that I noted earlier: to reiterate, *episteme* means "to stand or something on which we stand, certainty and knowledge" (Connaway & Powell, 2010, p.33). *Knowledge*, then, has the same impact on one's thinking and on one's orientation towards the world as 'metaphysics': both presuppose that one is distinctly a thinking being and that the world is there to be conceived of.

It should be noted that indigenous peoples have always had 'knowledge' just as any other group have. Smith et al. (2016), for instance, give a broad description of how indigenous knowledge is multifaceted. It is strongly focused on how to interact with the natural world, and it attempts to traverse several realities at once. This latter facet resonates especially with our discussions about the worldedness of a thing, and thus, there appears to be no problem with the currently dominant discourse of knowledge (indigenous knowledge, or IK as it is acronymised). But there are concerns, some of which revolve around the assumption that the term *knowledge* is the best one to deal with worldedness. Much more probable is that *knowledge* is far too anthropocentric in its general use to deal with the complexity of worldedness and, in turn, its call to speculation. Here, the concern lies both with the term itself and its associated assumptions and its dominance in much literature. With the first of these two concerns, we have to consider, from an indigenous worlded perspective, that a term is itself constituted by both its current use – what it seems to be conditioned towards or what it is preordained to carve out from the world – and by its historical associations. Heidegger's own love of etymology, the deepest origins of words, is useful because it allows us to consider both at once. The etymological origins of the term *knowledge* appear to be quite straightforward, but its association with *episteme* from an indigenous worlded perspective detracts from the complete interconnection and animacy of thing, thought and self.

These sorts of critiques, while useful, are only partially helpful. I emphasise that none of what I say pretends to undo presence: I am merely emphasising that it needs to be identified and that the limits of the indigenous self need to be recognised in order to try and propose anything about it at all. In that respect, whilst Heidegger has been extremely useful in identifying the broad machinations of presence, trying to identify an unadulterated Being is pointless. Derrida noted this, and I agree with him, although I do understand Being to be a central theme in any discussion about destabilising presence. We have to think about the total sum of all things in order to highlight its antithesis. If all things have a life force, and this energetic principle is to be held in our minds with the integrity it deserves, then Being must be thought about in its colonised sense as well, for this colonising entity both undermines and constitutes the idea of the spiritual. Whilst indigenous peoples undoubtedly do honour the interconnectedness of the world, it has become increasingly necessary to both retain that concept *and* cautiously make some determination about it that accounts for colonisation and traditional ways of thinking. The key word there is *cautiously*, and indigenous writers have invoked various strategies, at times highly resourceful, to manage the remoteness from the material. Some will keep themselves 'here, in the matter' by reciting chants or prayers at the beginning of their presentations or texts; others will deliberately position themselves in the text by alluding to their backgrounds and thus forcefully personalise their writing. Other writers, who wish to retain a high degree of academic logic in their work but yet briefly step back from and dilute that very attribute, will clash unexpected sources of thought with that conventional discourse. This intentionally political act, in which rational text is disrupted for an instant, takes place through creative-led practice, particularly dominant in artistic research and scholarship in which the artist steps outside of the expectations of academic text. It can also occur in politically charged pieces of writing where an audience's complacency with the matter and text – nurtured by years of being accustomed to academic discourse – is undermined by, for instance, indigenous poetry or metaphor.

The ethics of playfulness

For indigenous text, a similar innovation reveals itself when the writer intends to purposely transform the concept of the world by starting with the kind of voice he or she uses. Here, as with those Western counter-colonialists, the way in which something is represented is equally as influential on the well-being of a community as any social or political phenomenon. Being continuously critical and addressing colonisation but proposing a way forward, by writing through diverse sources, destabilises the rational field on which that author is forced to write and exposes for the readers a chink in its armour. These disparate registers, incidentally, may not at first accord with indigenous thought – indeed, they might be inimical to them – but the indigenous person can cautiously and ethically subvert their normal meanings in that poetic exercise. We may think of this act as *playful* because it brings together what does not seemingly correspond. The indigenous person may therefore recognise points where presence crops up most obviously and then set about deliberately clashing them against whatever does not sit well with them in a logical sense. This act is a determined one; it has the self-certainty of terms and ideas directly in its sight and seeks to undermine the authority of presence through those smaller items.

In all these acts that are mindful of colonisation, and especially of its grand suggestions of truth, orthodoxy and normalcy, unhindered creativity may step over the boundaries of conservative indigenous thought. Individuals in these scenarios practice creatively but occasionally tread on the toes of their own. This occurs especially widely in contexts where gender boundaries are deliberately transgressed – where indigenous critics, dissatisfied with the status quo of (predominantly) male-oriented events, aim to expose its limitations with their own novel approaches. This may take the form of the individual practising an art form that is conventionally held to be the domain of the other gender, or, if a woman, speaking in forums where only the male is allowed to speak. In instances where sexuality is an issue, although pressure is on the homosexual individual to conform to the heteronormativity of their communities (Driskill et al., 2011), the opportunity instead arises for the self to deal with the hegemonic situation through various 'rebellious' acts. Similarly, the indigenous academic who is disgruntled with other indigenous arguments because they adhere too closely to traditionalism, rationalism or essentialism may appear to be iconoclastic in his or her own propositions or, more importantly, in the novel sources they draw on to place forward their views.

For the indigenous self, the challenge here must lie in re-emphasising the mysterious and its attendant reflection of the totality of the world, whilst recognising that to do so is to always re-emphasise presence. The first question must then be, is it enough to think of ourselves as *worlded* selves, even as we propose something? In other words, is it enough to remind ourselves that we are constituted by all things in the world – does this reminder then bring out the mystery of a thing on its own? Most likely, this initial act is an important one, as it could destabilise the deep-rooted self-presence that is a hallmark of presence. Following on from the possibility of the worlded reminder, it would be tempting for us to think of schooling as being able to incorporate a version of education that did not privilege such a strong selfhood. It is certainly possible for curricula to try to incorporate a move away from the ontological ground of the self, but whether this has the effect of referring the self to the entire world is debatable. Education in its dominant sense is already enframed; it is too inclined to posit the world in advance as knowable, certain, and present. Incorporated within it are views of language, selfhood and thing that simply do not sit well with the co-instantaneity we have been discussing. Caught in the presence of education is the indigenous student, who is governed by the enframing language of policy, for instance, as an entity. Words do not simply exist inertly on the policy document; they structure the student and have repercussions for his or her well-being. To explain this aspect of language again in a negative sense: the indigenous student's well-being is not simply dependent on how those words are implemented by officials either – rather, they constitute and either support the indigenous student or, as is the case with the language of presence, they rob the student of something vital.

The freedom of the indigenous student to reflect, speculate and think about the limits of knowledge is key to reminding him- or herself of the world's interconnection. It is not enough to merely keep asserting that a thing is worlded without even critically thinking about the nature of that very statement. Here, we encounter the boundaries of our certainty about a thing. If an indigenous student states that a thing is worlded, what corresponds with that thinking is the following: How is the *self* and his or her assertions constituted by all things? Novalis's version of education, where a student's role is to reflect on the self's lack of certainty in relation to another thing, is meant to simultaneously approximate the full interchangeability of things in the world. How we think is therefore correspondent with the world itself. For the indigenous student, the freedom to be able to simply understand a thing as worlded whilst speculating on the barrier that he or she encounters when trying to grasp that thing is necessary for bringing into practice the worlded self. Of course, we can only achieve an idea of ourselves as worlded by acknowledging what impedes us – presence – and we will consistently be drawing on the tools of presence to remind ourselves. This dilemma repeats the one told in the previous chapters: the exchange of presence with the thoroughgoing world. But the impetus of presence in the indigenous student's thinking is simultaneously likely to provide opportunities to critique ideas of knowing and certainty.

I suggested in Chapter 5 that 'curriculum' as a concept was too tightly arranged by presence to be anything other than highly present. Related to its presence is its pursuit of measurability. It would be a mammoth task indeed to organise an entire way of teaching and learning around this self-reflective process because it does not seem to produce anything tangible. There is no measure of its success – 'success' as a concept would need to be rethought – and the language of instrumentality, or the 'aims', 'objectives' and 'outcomes' would need to be de-emphasised. For the indigenous student, the consequences of self-reflection are enormous because he or she is suspended in favour of the influence of whatever is being considered. While the focus is on his or her lack of ability to fully grasp an idea or thing, it is the thing's ultimate obscurity that is responsible for that thinking. It seems like a particularly depressing encounter because the indigenous student is finally led to understand that he or she is limited in relation to the thing; however, a teacher can provide signposts to further thinking about the mystery of the thing as it relates to all sorts of matters. It ends up being a playful, rather than depressing, exercise because the student is led by the idea or thing towards it but without alighting on it; posed properly, the object becomes one that the student is constitutionally engaged with rather than just conceptually adjusted towards. The full possibilities of the idea or thing become important, not just its logical or scientific representation or its contribution. In that sense, language that approximates must be understood to be more significant than its counterpart, the sort that encourages the grasp of a phenomenon as if knowable.

As Freire (1970) noted, a vital component of any educational endeavour is to encourage the participants to reflect on their own oppression. In the context of worldedness and presence, the indigenous student would be urged to speculate on the ways in which presence infiltrates particular terms and other forms of representation. This originary thought is linked to the cultural mode of thinking of that individual. It should be indeterminate in nature so that the student or the teacher can continue speculating rather than believing that they have arrived at a final answer. The student here contemplates what prevents them from being true to the idea that a thing is more than an idea, materially impactful on the self, not governed by linear notions of time and so on. A mountain, for instance, becomes very difficult, if not impossible, to describe authentically outside of the bounds of presence. As we cannot really identify the true nature of that combative idea, we then contemplate what hinders us, and so on. In a deliberate teaching context, a teacher may offer a student an outright provocative or even convivial statement and encourage the student to represent it in the worlded sense. This could be through art or language. When the student falls short of describing it adequately, the exercise then turns to him or her contemplating the nature of presence. Presence is then subjected to its own regress, in that it similarly cannot be felt or touched. And so the opportunity for teaching and learning continues. The teacher may respond to the student and join in to theorise alongside him or her.

Signs of disagreement

A key aspect of any such educational approach is to offer concrete strategies to emphasise, even if just for an instant, the idea that a thing is thoroughly intermeshed with the rest of the world. Revisiting language may be a vital starting place for the indigenous student in the curriculum of worldedness because it is the main mode of representation. The same applies here for the indigenous critic or writer, who is at a loss to 'get around' presence to properly present the worlded object. It is likely that the self is disrupted through constantly referring to the world as thoroughly and continuously co-constituting. Here, the indigenous writer would be asked to consider the possibilities of an object through language, as well as offer a critique of its common position as an unworlded, highly present entity. This exercise is a particularly creative one, and the cynics among us would say it is unlikely to be implemented as it does not have any measurable outcomes. It is a process on its own, an unseen engagement with a thing and the various ways in which it comes to bear on the self or on any other entity. Crucial to this educational commitment is an act very similar to Derrida's double reading, where the self conducts a reading of a text and then seeks "a problematic attitude, a double reading that is both critique and complicity, a way to move beyond inside and outside" (Lather, 2007, p.14). The indigenous writer/critic is already part of the text, of course, and he or she is the product of things whilst making propositions about the elements of the text, but it is important that he or she keep this fact in mind whilst uncovering the vulnerability of the text. The language he or she chooses to reconfigure – it could be a small term in indigenous writer's/student's own language, for instance, or it could equally be a term that comes from the colonising language – is visited in light of its colonising qualities to begin with. I referred to 'is' and its issues of presence in Chapter 5. The indigenous critic or student could then refer it to its 'other', so that it ends up being shaded by its 'isn't-ness', which as we have seen may well be a central facet of indigenous worldedness. Heidegger and Derrida carried out this technique of erasure, with different specific aspirations, but generally so that a term's necessity would not be given overwhelming presence. For the indigenous critic and student, an entire piece of work or speech could be textured with this 'isn't-ness' that reverberates within the use of the 'is'. It could also be crowded out, to a certain extent at least, with other terms from the student's or critic's own language. These terms could be placed alongside the 'is' so that its effect is blunted.

Similarly, the antithesis as a linguistic tool could be particularly relevant for indigenous thought. The 'isn't-ness' of a proposition may be reclaimed by placing a contrasting idea against the usual one. This forces the already apparent to the fore – brings it up into a sort of 'hyperpresence' whilst colouring it with what offsets it. In the Maori language, we could call this process *whakakore*, or 'making void' (or, indeed, *erasure*), where the metaphysics of nothingness is foreshadowed in the linguistic strategy. Creative writers will have their own strategies here, but for the indigenous academic writer these signposts of nothingness include *but, nevertheless, yet, however*, and so on. An example (with key terms bolded) is the following:

> I can say quite clearly that indigenous peoples have been divested of their language, **but** it is somewhat more difficult to articulate the thoroughgoing aspect of Being within language. I am trying to step outside of language to conceive of it in its totality, **but** I cannot because I always try to utilise language to achieve that. From an indigenous standpoint, that limitation could be said to arise because we act *within* the constraints of language, as much as we act within power and place. **Or**, more probably, we act *within* language as a whole, not just its constraints. **Yet** it does place constraints on us, because talking definitively about that power of language proves to be impossible.

Although we cannot be too certain about the effect of signs of disagreement, we could surmise here that the highly apparent thing is made so apparent as to expose its other, more oppositional, facet. Whatever was highly present is made more so, quite deliberately, by introducing the *yet, but*, or similar term. Thus, simply saying, "I am trying to step outside of language to conceive of it," is simply alluding to presence; quite possibly, following that statement with "**but** I cannot because I always try to utilise language to achieve that" forces presence to shine even more vibrantly through the initial statement. Presence is set up to fall, in a sense, because of the introduction of the other. For the indigenous worlded commentator, things in the world are given some space to show themselves not simply by the antithetic idea that comes after the *but* but also by the fact that we have set presence up in such a way that it has no choice but to *immediately* expose its otherness. Things in the world attend the obscurity that comes with that otherness. Heidegger's (1977) *saving power* similarly attributes an ability to think against enframing by virtue of enframing itself and shows that the self can think meditatively and straight away within the very problem that arises. The *immediately* is crucial here, because it foregrounds the problem of time that presence poses for an indigenous worlded philosophy. Whilst we have not managed to thwart the sequential nature of an assertion, as indigenous writers we would have managed to force presence to shine, thus also forcing it to display the fact that it is constituted by other, invisible entities at almost the same time. We could have tried to deal with sequential notions of time by arguing directly against it in the following way:

> *Time* is in fact both entity and concept that collapses apparent linearity, and we can therefore assert that time is not the teleological template that is dominantly posed.

But to repeat earlier thinking, even in doing so we have abstracted time so that it is purely idea. We have not managed to resist sequential time at all. This separation of time's concept from its form then has consequences for how we posit anything at all, and although we can try and entitise a concept (or, more precisely, reiterate the entity nature of something that is already an entity), our efforts soon end with disappointment. By not directly addressing the problem of logocentric time, by offering an oppositional thought, though, we may have managed to force it to outdo itself. We also manage to introduce more directly the oppositional idea after the antithetic term, which could comprise the worlded statement (for example, from the earlier antithetically related quote: "**but** it is somewhat more difficult to articulate the thoroughgoing aspect of Being within language").

Not only is the dual sway of opposition in indigenous worldedness important, but so, too, is the overspill into something more significant that presence simply cannot deal with. The limits in presence for indigenous worldedness can be catered for in writing by signalling this surplus of meaning. The indigenous writer, as we have seen, immediately incorporates presence but then can add something on to that colonising expectation, by simultaneously identifying and diminishing presence – pointing out its horizon of thought – and then indicating what it misses. This direct reference to presence is really only a nod to its symptoms, of course, but identifying presence through its linguistic and conceptual units is useful as a start to destabilising presence. Pointing out the banality of certain ways of speaking and writing so that it is duly noted and circumscribed, and then moving on from its influence towards what the indigenous writer on worldedness really wants to say, requires the writer to consciously subvert the banal statement by indicating what is expected by presence. Thus, if we return to a recent statement of mine,

> [f]or the indigenous worlded commentator, things in the world are given some space to show themselves **not simply** by the antithetic idea that comes after the *but*, **but** also by the fact that we have set presence up in such a way that it has no choice but to *immediately* expose its otherness.

I suggest that if we left the sentence at "things in the world are given some space to show themselves by the antithetic idea that comes after the *but*", we are limiting the means by which things can have some space. In other words, we are limiting things themselves: the statement rests as one of presence. By opening up the possibilities to an act with presence itself by stating "not simply . . . **but** also by the fact that we have set presence up in such a way that it has no choice", we have signalled an incompleteness of that initial statement and started on a path towards gesturing to the further possibilities that are always available. Often, these add-ons may also take the form of contradictory logics, where I would state something like "Presence is **not simply** the presence of an object **but also** the display of that fact that it is worlded". I have contradicted myself by saying that presence is indeed worlded. Again, as with the previous example, if we were to restate the observation so that "presence is the presence of an object", we have simply stated the *is-ness* of presence, and thus replicated the demands of presence. The indigenous writer or student, too, is made to feel vulnerable in the face of its possibilities, particularly where it is carried out consciously and continuously. If I always correct the initial assumption in my writing – always by identifying it and then by either disagreeing with it or by adding to it, noting its limits – then I am made aware that this process does not itself have any limits.

Importantly, too, I am acknowledging that any one idea and thing always has its negative or surplus other to it. The signs of disagreement I advocate here remind us of the entities that are infused throughout our expressions. I am thus honouring their complexity in a way that complies with the metaphysics of indigenous worldedness. I am not just leaving the statement as a complete one that deals with its things; I have complicated things, by attempting to present them as uncontainable.

Thinking 'in the wake of'

The problem that presence challenges us with surges into tertiary education as much as other levels. It is overwhelmingly common for Maori postgraduate students, for instance, to complete doctoral research by 'doing data'. Interviews most frequently are undertaken, the language and the views of the interviewee are collected, and then the material is transcribed and thematically analysed. Of course, this thematic analysis can be conducted in a number of ways and with several forms through the Maori language, but basically they amount to an arrangement of the material so that it arrives at a clean, seamless outcome. Due to the dominance of this approach, a particular kind of knowledge is amassed that is external to the self. The Maori student may be responsible for seeing what emerges from the data – and to that extent the data are mysterious up to a certain point – but he or she does so in a way that transcends the materiality of things both within and without the data. Whilst this approach has its merits, it results in a self that is divorced from things in the world because it arranges them logically as distinctive phenomena. The Maori student may be emotionally involved with the data, but the approach to, and treatment of, the interviewee's language is as a separate self. In these cases, the focus is much more likely to be on the technical analysis that finds links between existing scenarios rather than on thinking about each utterance opens up further possibilities for speculation, how they stand alone as provocations for ongoing thinking, and so on. The Maori student is contained, as it were, by the self-sufficiency of the data.

We cannot get at the ontology of data by using data themselves, but it is possible to start with the banal and branch out towards mystery. Here, a term that has become overly used, or one that occurs in a banal context, is deliberately embellished so that it perhaps no longer even resembles its intended use. It is both serious and playful, because it acknowledges the problem of philosophical deprivation yet calls for a great deal of creativity. The early German romantics identified a device additional to those above that would reflect the natural fluidity of the world and at the same time remain critical of any imposed structural dominance: Beiser (2003) states that "the most essential feature of any Romantic work is 'its becoming,' the fact that it is never complete but that it destroys itself only to create itself forever anew" (p.17). Poeticising and romanticising, terms commonly used by that movement's poets/philosophers, are both creatively critical and reconstructive. This strain of creativity does not seek to adhere to dominant and hegemonic thought because no particular mode of expression, practice or existence is unassailable. Instead, creativity in a poetic vein is necessarily sceptical of grand truths and claims, and aims to expose and counter those metanarratives. Thinking with a certain degree of hesitancy in the background is key to this dialectic, retaining some level of uncertainty about the very essence of the topic being addressed. Thus, text, as one highly dominant method of representation, is one phenomenon that draws the critic to it.

For the early German romantic metaphysicians, creative discussions and propositions, usually manifest in fragments, provoke an emotional reaction from the audience to keep both the writer and the recipient 'here'. Novalis extended the irrationality of the fragment to the fact that it could never be systematic – it could never wind up thinking for good. Nor, importantly, should it have a central beginning: "[w]hy do we need a *beginning* at all? This unphilosophical – or semiphilosophical goal is the source of all error" (Wood, 2007, p.115). Thinking for the indigenous person is similarly as expansive as the world is interrelated. Novalis similarly identified that the fragment's job was merely to reveal an aspect of this fact; it both adumbrated the immensity of these connections as well as the limitations of one's ability to pierce the world and know it in its totality. A fragment could indeed be a piece of data that is not particularly remarkable on its own (apart from divulging a new form of the continually same ontological knowledge). For the indigenous researcher, student or critic, the aim is to listen to the knowledgeable other but then to take the utterance in another direction altogether than would normally be expected by academic convention (Mika & Southey, 2016). The researcher in these scenarios might think of any number of random associations that skyrocket away from the intended meaning. Thus, if I am treating one of my elders as knowledgeable other, they can derail my assumption by throwing me a curve ball: they themselves can respond to my research question in their own, unrelated way by ignoring it, laughing at it, responding with an unrelated answer, or responding with a much more fulsome answer than I expected. As Linda Smith (1999) has suggested, "indigenous elders can do wonderful things with an interview. They tell stories, tease, question, think, observe, tell riddles, test and give trick answers. Conversely, they can also expect that an indigenous researcher will do the same back to them" (p.136). In all these cases, the elder has provided room for other things in the world to enter the utterance or the silence. In all of these scenarios, the expectation of language's presence has been thwarted.

But then – and at this juncture those of us who carry out this next step could be accused of being disrespectful! – I might take those knowledgeable responses and work *them* so that they do not accord with what they were originally meant to be (Mika, 2013b; 2014). Presence reassembles itself constantly, as I have reiterated, so our task as indigenous researchers, students, teachers and critics is to refer the data (if we are collecting them) back to their unintended use – to disrupt their seamlessness and symmetry. Incidentally, I have been using data collection research as an example here, but we can equally relate this process to writing itself: when we encounter the obviously overused term or concept, we can explode it outwards so that it momentarily loses its banality and opens space for other things that constitute that term or concept to emerge. Essentially, we are thinking in the wake of another's utterance here, and we are treating another's thinking not as a final ground but as an impetus for our own (Mika, 2015b; 2016b; Mika & Tiakiwai, 2016). Moreover, our own thinking is neither final nor authoritative and is open to the same sort of 'play' that we ourselves indulged in. With the reactive self, things in the world are less constrained, because they are allowed to configure themselves as they see fit. We have stopped ourselves from 'fore-thinking' (Mika, 2013a) the entities that allowed us to think in the first instance.

Ethics and postgraduate committees could respond to my use of data with some wariness, primarily because the researcher or scholar is deliberately subverting the response of the participant or ignoring the core meaning of the participant's statements. Interestingly, if a committee is uncomfortable with that method, it indicates a huge divide between indigenous and mainstream ethics, because the creative use of another's utterance – from an indigenous ethical stance – may well be preferable to simply reiterating what was stated. To reiterate and recount is to render banal the essence of the interviewee's language. To respond in indigenous belief is not necessarily to respond neatly and tidily, and the disconnected answer starts with the interviewee at times. Thus, if I do conduct interviews, I might ask a question but not get the desired response that connects neatly with what I want. Indeed, indigenous interviewees will often respond either with silence, with a tangential remark, or with an answer that *appears* to be completely unrelated – all of which are prompts and provocations for the interviewer. While this freedom to respond is one that appears to be solely that of the interviewee's, the indigenous interviewer is also invited to approach what the interviewee stated with the same kind of creativity. Yet, the interviewee has ignited my response, and moreover, his or her utterance rests materially throughout my entire response. I would be wrong in assuming that my subsequent material was entirely my own, even though it appears not to be related to the interviewee's utterance. As I have argued throughout the book, whenever the individual speaks he is presenting whatever lies beyond the obvious. When we misread someone else's statements deliberately in order to think creatively, we nevertheless re-present that person's statements, although we might not be recounting them.

An indigenous ethics – preferably specific sets of ethics that sit with discrete indigenous groups – does need to be argued, and it may even take the form of resisting conventional approaches that we take for granted as being ethical. For example, an indigenous ethics might note that a thematic analysis of an interview is completely or partially untenable, because such a method undermines the self's speculative thinking, disciplines the interviewee's language or utterance, and casts the interviewee in advance as knowledgeable other. To return to our indigenous worlded notion of 'ground': it presupposes that the other, his or her language (and indeed that of the interviewer's), and the things that are presented in that interviewee are utterly *there* and that they participate in a ground upon which they act – one that helps them with the certainty of things – not within which they are situated.

The funniness of presence

That discussion about the explosion of thought leads nicely into one about the potential for humour because one is caught up in the thrill of the uncertain. It is probably a truism that a writer finds out his or her limits as more distance is covered. It was earlier on that I found myself wanting to include a discussion on humour as a quick antidote to presence. I made the terrible mistake of giving presence an actual face that, despite itself, crumples with laughter at the tickle of its opponent, worldedness. I had written it for the conclusion and then deleted it on the grounds that it was so horribly florid it throbbed of its own accord. I hadn't written it deliberately as a nice, stylish conclusion but actually meant what I wrote. Eventually, if nothing else, I thought, it would make for a fine example of how an author can be inadvertently hilarious while they think they are onto something – the *occasional* Florence Foster Jenkins of penmanship. It reads thus:

> Granite-faced presence in these cases is fleetingly irritated by this absent other, forced to fold in on itself as it submits to the absent other's prickling touch.

There is no doubt that my attempts to personify presence in that purple way are risible. The gasp of the 'aha' moment, when I thought that it could not possibly be included in an academic text and is the sort of thing that you tell others to 'diarise', ended up giving way to its inclusion as an example of what language can do to the serious self and to presence. Inadvertently, I had made fun of presence by virtue of the playfulness of language that worldedness asks us to respect. For me, as an indigenous writer, the silliness of language – or, more appropriately, the silliness that emerges from one's attempt to grasp language – became an issue rather than an idea that it is a tool at my disposal. In short, I got carried away.

But in a certain way, language did serve my purpose even though it set me up to say something that I initially thought was rather tidy. I thought I would be able to write about presence as if it were nicely containable; I had become overly serious about it but then found a splinter of humour within it. So far, we have dealt with presence as if it is a serious business. It is indeed serious, to the extent that it involves indigenous people's well-being of psychology and perception. But there is an additional side to presence that gives us the lovely gift of incongruity. Either we could stand whatever is present (and itself completely rational and serious) next to another incongruous object or we can simply see the funny side of that present idea or object because it seems to take itself too seriously. Suddenly, we see the dark side of presence, its side that it wants to hide, the mischievous interplay of things in the world as they crowd out the solemnity of presence. James Beattie argued that humour "seems to arise from the view of things incongruous united in the same assemblage" (Beattie, 1778, p.344). Classically thought of as the preserve of those who are malicious (Morreall, 1983), humour in philosophy is capable of momentarily dispersing the idea as conceptual and giving the entity (and its constituent entities) its true interruptive force. It thus may remind us that the idea is entity. If we recall Linda Smith's quote about research and elders, we become aware that humour is important for indigenous peoples. It is vital not only because it helps us cope with our colonised realities but because it also puts the too-serious in its place. Whilst the overly serious person bears the brunt here of humour in indigenous communities, we could equally direct the potential of laughter at the seemingly staid proposition or idea. As indigenous scholars, teachers and students, "our understanding of 'how things are supposed to be'" (Morreall, 1989, p.243) is put to rest for just a while.

It may be obvious that one can create humour by bringing together contradictions, but what is it to automatically perceive the absurd or at least something askew, in a single term, for instance, without actually having done anything? Of course, terms in their own right are often hilarious because they evince a meaning that the context of presence does not necessarily want revealed. Usually the humour is by association, I suspect; that is, it strikes a chord for the reader or listener that others do not share. Again, something forces its way through the smooth, botoxed exterior of presence. We can speculate that it is another entity/ set of entities that is showing itself up for our perception, perhaps even mocking presence (Mika, 2015c). The ability to laugh at presence is most likely available everywhere but depends on the entity disclosing itself within presence. Some examples occur here, and these are simply my reactions to particular entities. *Thus, however, indeed and certainly* are all authoritarian, seeking to have the final say in response to something but cannot really contain the fullness of the world. *Thus* has recently become complicit with *thusly*, which, at a solely instinctive level, I cannot take seriously. *Like* is used in rational contexts to signal the similarity of one thing to another – and it therefore has aspects of finality and conclusiveness to it – but its overuse as a filler ("like, I don't know") dilutes its decisive nature, even though they are used in different contexts. These examples, whilst seemingly flippant or at least peripheral, are important because they show the greater-than-intended nature of language for indigenous approaches to worldedness. They are instructive for further thinking; they dispel "the illusion of the individual substantial self and the true nature of reality" (Morreall, 1989, p.261) because they exist outside of the control of both presence and the self.

Summary

Neither presence nor worldedness (in its holistic sense) have limits, and the issues they raise call to be further speculated on. What I have attempted to cover is just an aspect of it from an indigenous/Maori perspective – a perspective that thinks of education from a particular (worlded) perspective and considers it in the light of that most classic of metaphysics, presence. I sought to conjoin presence and worldedness, my own term, within speculative thought. There are various ways of addressing presence and worldedness, with poetry and art probably the most effective way of these, but my focus has been on those of us who have academic convention and learning as our primary means of representation. The full extent of presence and worldedness, and their necessary co-constitution, is probably impossible to describe. The final word on the messiness of the exchange between presence and worldedness for indigenous peoples is best expressed in the following quote of Deloria's:

> *Who can walk into an unknown woods and head directly for the other side?*
> (Deloria & Wilkins, 2012)

Bibliography

Adorno, T. (2001) *Metaphysics: Concept and Problems*. Stanford, CA: Stanford University Press.
Bakhtin, M. (1981) 'Discourse in the Novel', pp. 259–422 in M. Holquist (ed) *The Dialogic Imagination*. Austin, TX: University of Texas Press.

Beattie, J. (1778) *Essays: On Poetry and Music, as They Affect the Mind; on Laughter, and Ludicrous Composition; on the Utility of Classical Learning*. Edinburgh, Scotland: William Creech.

Beiser, F. (2003) *The Romantic Imperative: The Concept of Early German Romanticism*. Cambridge, UK: Harvard University Press.

Calderon, D. (2008) *Indigenous Metaphysics: Challenging Western Knowledge Organization in Social Studies Curriculum*. Doctoral dissertation, The University of California, Los Angeles.

Cassirer, E. (1953) *The Philosophy of Symbolic Forms*. New Haven: Yale University Press.

Connaway, L. and Powell, R. (2010) *Basic Research Methods for Librarians*, 5th edn. Oxford, UK: Libraries Unlimited.

Deloria Jnr, V. (2001) 'Power and Place Equal Personality', pp. 21–8 in V. Deloria Jnr and D. Wildcat (eds) *Power and Place: Indian Education in America*. Golden, CO: Fulcrum Resources.

Deloria Jnr, V. and Wilkins, D. (2012) *The Metaphysics of Modern Existence*. Golden, CO: Fulcrum Publishing.

Driskill, Q., Finley, C., Gilley, B., et al. (2011) 'Introduction', pp. 1–28 in Q. Driskill, C. Finley, B. Gilley, et al. (eds) *Queer Indigenous Studies: Critical Interventions in Theory, Politics, and Literature*. Tucson, AZ: The University of Arizona Press.

Freire, P. (1970) *Pedagogy of the Oppressed*. London: Penguin.

Friedman, M. (2011) 'Ernst Cassirer', in E. Zalta (ed) *The Stanford Encyclopedia of Philosophy*.

Heidegger, M. (1962) *Being and Time*. Oxford, UK: Blackwell.

Heidegger, M. (1966) *Discourse on Thinking*. Pfullingen, Germany: Verlag Günther Nesk.

Heidegger, M. (1977) *The Question Concerning Technology and Other Essays*. New York, NY: Garland Publishing, Inc.

Lather, P. (2007) *Getting Lost: Feminist Efforts toward a Double(d) Science*. Albany, NY: State University of New York Press.

Martin, K. (2014) 'The More Things Change, the More they Stay the Same: Creativity as the Next Colonial Turn', pp. 293–6 in A. Reid, E. Hart and M. Peters (eds) *A Companion to Research in Education*. Dordrecht, The Netherlands: Springer.

Mika, C. (2013a) *Reclaiming Mystery: A Māori Philosophy of Being, in Light of Novalis' Ontology*. Unpublished PhD dissertation, University of Waikato.

Mika, C. (2013b) 'Western "Sentences that Push" as an Indigenous Method for Thinking', pp. 23–6 in A. Engels-Schwarzpaul and M. Peters (eds) *Of Other Thoughts: Non-Traditional Ways to the Doctorate. A Guidebook for Candidates and Supervisors*. Rotterdam, The Netherlands: Sense.

Mika, C. (2014) 'Maori Thinking with a Dead White Male: Philosophizing in the Realm of Novalis', *Knowledge Cultures* 2(1): 23–39.

Mika, C. (2015a) 'Counter-Colonial and Philosophical Claims: An Indigenous Observation of Western Philosophy', *Educational Philosophy and Theory*: 1–7.

Mika, C. (2015b) 'Thereness: Implications for Heidegger's "Presence" for Māori', *AlterNative* 11(1): 3–13.

Mika, C. (2015c) 'The Thing's Revelation: Māori Philosophical Research', *Waikato Journal of Education* 20(2): 61–68.

Mika, C. (2016a) 'The Ontological and Active Possibilities of Papatūānuku: To Nurture or Enframe?', *Knowledge Cultures* 4(3): 58–71.

Mika, C. (2016b) 'Some Thinking from, and Away from, Heidegger', *Educational Philosophy and Theory*.

Mika, C. and Southey, K. (2016) 'Exploring Whakaaro: A Way of Responsive Thinking in Maori Research', *Educational Philosophy and Theory*.

Mika, C. and Stewart, G. (2015) 'Maori in the Kingdom of the Gaze: Subjects or Critics?', *Educational Philosophy and Theory*: 1–13.

Mika, C. and Tiakiwai, S. (2016) 'Tawhiao's Unstated Heteroglossia: Conversations with Bakhtin', *Educational Philosophy and Theory*.

Morreall, J. (1983) *Taking Laughter Seriously*. Albany, NY: State University of New York.

Morreall, J. (1989) 'The Rejection of Humor in Western Thought', *Philosophy East and West* 39(3): 243–65.

Pere, R. (1982) *Ako: Concepts and Learning in the Māori Tradition*. Hamilton, New Zealand: University of Waikato.

Royal, T. A. (2008) *Te Ngākau*. Te Whanganui-a-Tara, New Zealand: Mauriora Ki Te Ao Living Universe Ltd.

Smith, L. (1999) *Decolonizing Methodologies: Research and Indigenous Peoples*. London, UK: Zed Books.

Smith, L., Maxwell, T., Puke, H., et al. (2016) 'Indigenous Knowledge, Methodology and Mayhem: What Is the Role of Methodology in Producing Indigenous Insights? A Discussion from Mātauranga Māori', *Knowledge Cultures* 4(3): 131–56.

Tau, T. (2001) 'The Death of Knowledge: Ghosts on the Plains', *New Zealand Journal of History* 35(2): 131–52.

Wood, D. (2007) *Novalis: Notes for a Romantic Encyclopaedia*. Albany, NY: State University of New York Press.

Index